INTO THE IMAGE

Into the Image is concerned with the significance of screen and image in contemporary society, and with the nature of our imaginary and psychic investments in visual culture. It considers modern image technologies as means to monitor and survey the world, whilst at the same time maintaining distance and detachment from it. In the coverage of contemporary war, we see most clearly how the world is screened and yet its reality screened out. *Into the Image* also reflects on the contemporary desire to create an alternative world by means of new image technologies. It asks what is behind the fantasies of migrating into an alternative, virtual reality.

Critical of the dominant technoculture, this book seeks to develop an alternative approach to visual culture based in the realities of the contemporary social order. In its exploration of culture and politics in the field of vision, *Into the Image* acknowledges the continuing significance of the 'old' technologies of photography, cinema and television alongside that of the new digital developments. The crucial issues, it argues, concern the relation of image and screen culture to experience in the modern world.

Kevin Robins is Professor of Cultural Geography at the University of Newcastle.

INTO THE IMAGE

Culture and politics in the
field of vision

Kevin Robins

London and New York

First published 1996
by Routledge
11 New Fetter Lane, London EC4P 4EE

Simultaneously published in the USA and Canada
by Routledge
29 West 35th Street, New York, NY 10001

Typeset in Garamond by
Ponting–Green Publishing Services, Chesham, Bucks
Printed and bound in Great Britain by
Biddles Ltd, Guildford and King's Lynn

British Library Cataloguing in Publication Data
A catalogue record for this book is available from the
British Library

Library of Congress Cataloguing in Publication Data
Robins, Kevin.
Into the image: culture and politics in the field of vision /
Kevin Robins
p.   cm.
Includes bibliographical references and index.
1. Visual sociology.   2. Visual communication.
3. Cybernetics.   4. Image processing—Digital techniques.
I. Title.
HM73.R54   1996
306.4'6—dc20   95–52813
CIP

ISBN 0–415–14576–7 (hbk)
ISBN 0–415–14577–5 (pbk)

Werk des Gesichts ist getan
tut nun Herz-Werk
an den Bildern in dir, jenen gefangenen; denn du
überwältigtest sie: aber nun kennst du sie nicht.

(Work of the eyes is done, now
go and do heart-work
on all the images imprisoned within you; for you
overpowered them: but even now you don't know them.)
(Rainer Maria Rilke, 'Wendung')

Die Träne, halb,
die schärfste Linse, beweglich
holt dir die Bilder.

(The tear, half,
the sharper lens, movable,
brings the images home to you.)
(Paul Celan, 'Ein Auge, Offen')

For my mother and father,
Dorothy and Eric Robins

CONTENTS

ACKNOWLEDGEMENTS

This book does not claim to be a systematic account of contemporary image technologies and of the new visual culture. Its chapters should be read as essays, intended to move against the grain of the dominant technoculture agenda, and to open up other ways of looking at culture and politics in the field of vision. In many cases, they have been written in reaction to events in the world which have brought home to us the power of the image in contemporary culture. And, of course, in all cases, they embody my own particular vision, with all its blindnesses and also, I hope, some insights.

In some cases, also, chapters, or versions of chapters, have been written in response to the requests of others. Here I should like to thank those who have encouraged and, in some cases, driven me to produce them: Paul Wombell, Roberta McGrath, Martin Lister, Mike Featherstone, Tim Druckrey, Jon Dovey, Stephanie Donald, James Donald and John Corner.

I would also like to thank my immediate colleagues at the Centre for Urban and Regional Development Studies – Andrew Gillespie, James Cornford, Ranald Richardson – for putting up with me, and for making it a very congenial place to work. I owe a particular debt of gratitude to John Goddard for opening up a space for me in the Centre. Thank you also to Charon Downie for typing this text.

Finally, I would like to express my appreciation to Frank Webster, David Morley, Paul Marris, Les Levidow and Asu Aksoy for their close support.

Some of the chapters have appeared elsewhere, in most cases in a shortened form. Chapter 2 appeared, under a different title, in Paul Wombell (ed.), *Photovideo: Photography in the Age of the Computer* (Rivers Oram Press, 1991). Part of Chapter 3 appeared in *Media, Culture and Society*, 15 (2), 1993; and part in Gretchen Bender and Timothy Druckrey (eds), *Culture on the Brink: Ideologies of Technology* (Bay Press, 1994). Chapter 4 appeared in *Body and Society*, 1 (3–4), 1995. Chapter 5 appeared in *Media, Culture and Society*, 16 (3), 1994. Chapter 7 appeared in Martin Lister (ed.), *The Photographic Image in Digital Culture* (Routledge, 1995).

INTRODUCTION
Image technologies and visual culture

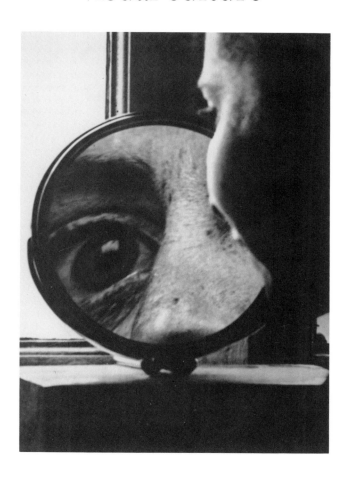

INTRODUCTION
Image technologies and visual culture

> N'est-ce pas triste que nos yeux se ferment?
> On voudrait avoir les yeux toujours ouverts,
> pour avoir vu, avant le terme,
> tout ce que l'on perd.
>
> (Isn't it sad that our eyes close?
> We'd want our eyes always open,
> to have seen, before the end,
> all that we lose.)
> (Rainer Maria Rilke, 'Verger')

> Only by mastering itself through the recognition of the nullity of images does
> subjectivity partake in the hope that images can only, vainly, promise.
> (Max Horkheimer and Theodor W. Adorno,
> *Dialectic of Enlightenment*)

There is a great interest at the present time in new vision and image technologies. Unsurprisingly, extravagant claims are being made about their radical implications for social and cultural transformation. It is said that we are undergoing an 'image revolution' on an unprecedented scale, and this supposed revolution is then associated with the historical transition to a postmodern era. The proliferation of screen culture is now routinely associated with projections about the coming into being of a new order of simulated reality. We are enthusiastically appraised of the pleasures of the interface and the possibilities of techno-sociality. Mundane realities and experiences seem to pale in comparison to dreams of virtual life and cyberculture. Have faith in these technologies of the future, the new techno-visionaries exhort us, embrace the emancipatory potential of the new technoculture. Invest your trust and optimism in this brave new vision. What we have in this idealisation of image technologies is the basis of a new utopianism (in what seem otherwise to be post-utopian times).

This idealistic vision assures us that the new images – the next images – are immeasurably superior to the ones that have come before. It embodies the modern teleological narrative of development and progress towards a

technological perfection to come. As with all previous technological innovations, there is the absolute certainty and conviction that this time – this time,
at last – the new technology will enable us to transcend our flawed human
condition, to release our true creative powers, and to found an ideal new
world. And, as always before, commitment to the next technology is
associated with bitter disappointment about what come to be classified as old
technologies. Within the teleological perspective, new image technologies
seem to contain boundless possibilities, while those that are now, consequently, defined and disdained as past and finished can only be seen in terms
of their inadequacies and limitations (there is an innocent forgetfulness about
the idealistic expectations that were invested in those old technologies when
they were once the new ones). What exactly are these new horizons that seem
to be opened up by developments in image technologies? Progress is
essentially measured as a factor of the expanding power of rationality in the
field of vision; it is to be understood in terms of the continuing elaboration
of the (Cartesian) logic of disembodied and transcendental vision. New image
technologies are valorised, then, in so far as they provide greater resources
for the visual appropriation, manipulation and control of the world. The new
images are judged superior within the context of a social and human project
driven by the logic of transcendence through order and rationalisation.

My own approach to transformations in contemporary image culture is
opposed to this perspective. The present book constitutes, in one respect, a
critique of the prevailing (technocratic, progressivist, rationalistic) idealism
surrounding the new technologies.[1] In the chapters that follow, I seek to
distance myself from the new technoculture – which has now become the
prevailing orthodoxy – for what I consider to be its narrowness and
conformity of vision. I am against its obsessive and exclusive concern with
technological innovation, and against the uncritical esteem and reverence it
shows towards mere technological novelty. That which presents itself in
revolutionary or utopian terms actually turns out to be the conservative
contrary, I argue. What we have is the recycling of old fantasies of technological mastery and transcendence, serving to inhibit and occlude alternative
agendas for meaningful social and cultural transformation. I am distancing
myself from technological progressivism (and often triumphalism), then, not
in order to deny the value of change, but precisely to consider what would
really be significant and meaningful forms of change in our visual culture
now. How, that is to say, against the closed and deterministic logic of the
dominant techno-imaginary, might we endeavour to change the terms by
which vision is validated in our culture? On what other basis might we seek
to renew the force of images and revitalise our ways of seeing? This is to ask
how, other than in terms of mastery and transcendence, images figure in our
cultural lives, and how, otherwise, we might consider our investments in
visual culture and experience.

Beyond just critique, then, this book is concerned, in its more substantive content, to develop some alternative perspectives and agendas. In the following chapters I seek to explore different ways in which we might relate to our contemporary image culture, to consider different values and priorities around which to make judgements on what is happening in the field of vision. In considering these issues, I find myself involved with the meaning and significance of vision in our culture now – with the experience of seeing, looking and watching. I am wanting to connect the discussion of technological image culture to the wider debate that has been undertaken recently concerning vision and modernity.[2] Whereas this debate has been preoccupied with the privileging of vision over the other senses (ocularcentrism), my own interests are generally somewhat different, being concerned with the nature of the investments we make in vision, and particularly in mediated vision. What are we doing with our images? How are we using them and misusing them? I am posing these questions, not in theoretical or philosophical terms, but sociologically and psychologically and in a way that is culturally grounded and situated. I do not seek to identify transformations in the 'regime of vision' or the emergence of a new (postmodern?) 'scopic regime', but, rather, to explore the ordinary and diverse uses of images in our actual culture now. Contrary to the prevailing teleological perspective, I also suggest that we think in terms of the contemporaneity and simultaneity of different image forms. Against the dominant technoculture, which tends to dismiss them as simply historical, and thus obsolete, I regard 'old' images (those of photography, cinema, television) as still significant and engaging visual media. What is important, I suggest, is the common actuality and the interplay of different order of images within a specific social space.[3] The point is that there are not just new technologies, but a whole range of available image forms – and consequently of ways of seeing, looking, watching – all of which are actually being mobilised and made use of, and in ways that are diverse and complex.

When it comes to the uses of images, my concerns extend considerably beyond those of the technoculture. This book seeks to explore how images and image technologies are involved in the ways we know, experience, feel about, and respond to, the world. It must necessarily be concerned, then, with the psychic investments we make in vision and image. What impresses me is the extent to which, whatever the course of visual rationalisation, images connect with pre-rational forces – with desires and fantasies, and even more fundamentally, I shall argue, with our basic anxieties and fears. We must take into account the relation of vision to the unconscious processes – J.-B. Pontalis describes it in terms of the 'osmosis between the unconscious and the visual'.[4] What is it, beyond what we consciously understand and declare, that we are seeking in the visual world? Margaret Iversen suggests that what may be at stake in the encounter with the photographic image, for example, is 'the encounter with the Real [in the Lacanian sense] which is ultimately an encounter with the persistently denied fact of one's own mortality'[5] (she is pursuing the analysis developed by Roland Barthes in his book *Camera Lucida*; for further discussion of this, see Chapter 7, below). In this psychic context, we might also think of images in terms of mechanisms of denial or disavowal. Referring to Freud's interpretation of the Medusa myth, Peter Benson suggests the protective power of images. 'The image serves', he says, 'to divide and protect pleasure from horror, in the same way that Michelangelo separates a noble Moses from the vengeful figure in the Bible.'[6] I am interested, then, in how images can be used to know and understand the world, but, at the same time, I want to emphasise that they can also be used to avoid, deny or disavow the reality of the world's events. There is the question of what is screened, and, even more importantly, there is the question of what is screened out.

The concerns of this book also extend, beyond the sights of the technoculture, to the social and political world we are living in now. The tension between engagement and disengagement is also important in terms of how images are implicated in human and cultural encounters. Through our screens we are witnessing the emergence of a new world order. It is most commonly through their screen images that we encounter the others in this globalising culture. But what kind of witnesses are we? What is the nature of the close encounters we have with those who are far away? In discussing the Bhopal disaster, Shiv Visvanathan argues that two parties should stand accused. The first is the party of those whose negligence directly caused the explosion. 'The other accused is ourselves,' he continues. 'As a spectacle, Bhopal has left behind a psychically numbed audience. Television may have created an electronic village, but no one rushed to help his neighbour.'[7] And then, of course, there was the Gulf War, when we should have learned a great deal more about the nature of the screen, and about the numbed condition of its viewers:

> Instead of shots of the sublunary world and blissful visions, the screen replicates images of devastation and ruin, a traffic jam of blazing vehicles, lethal fumigations from planes skimming the ground, carbonised bodies, helicopters vomiting flames, scenes of panic, ants scattering frantically, human torches, the gasping faces of women and children, deprived of oxygen, fire, more fire, apocalypse, horror, one vast collective cremation.
>
> (Voice-over: 'Say hello to Allah!')[8]

And then came Bosnia. . . . Our contemporary image culture has not evolved in some abstract realm (the imagined pure realm of scientific and technological reason), but in the disorder of the real world. This has fostered an omnipotent identification with the new technologies as a means to keep its perceived threats and dangers at bay. It involves us in a paranoid-defensive position of simultaneous engagement and disengagement with the others we encounter in the space of the screen.[9]

The technoculture celebrates the new image technologies unconditionally; it believes that they are, all of them, inherently liberating. I argue against this wishful idealisation, but in so doing I do not simply intend to be the voice of iconoclastic negation. Like Richard Kearney, I am arguing that we must learn 'to discriminate between a liberating and incarcerating use of images, between those that dis-close and those that close off our relation to the other, those that democratise culture and those that mystify it, those that communicate and those that manipulate'.[10] The crucial thing is to make distinctions and judgements in thinking about new images (as we should about old ones too). In order to do so, I think that we must remove the discussion of contemporary image culture away from the narrow preoccupations of the technoculture, and that we must re-locate it in the broader perspective of contemporary social and political transformation. The technoculture tells us that 'community has come increasingly unglued from geography', and that we are now in the process of 'planning and designing truly world-wide communities'.[11] But anybody who is even half awake to the world can surely see that 'geography' is far from being abolished, and that localised and territorial investments and conflicts will remain a fundamental issue in the new world order. The technoculture believes that virtual community can and will provide a solution to the world's problems. I am arguing that any progress in this respect must remain a question of political encounter and compromise, and that the new technologies remain a secondary issue. Let us indeed consider how they affect our relations with others – and, of course, we should acknowledge that they can function to impede as well as to facilitate engagement – but let us not identify with the fantasy of technological resolution. Those who have read too many cyborg manifestos should be reminded that their virtual culture is only a small bit of a big world.

This book is critical of much of what is now being written about new images and new image technologies. My intention is to put forward some contrary perspectives to those of the dominant technoculture, in the hope of making possible a wider and more open-ended discussion of what is happening in the transformation of our contemporary image and vision culture. Perhaps you will be tempted to identify my arguments as simply negative and oppositional (to put me in the position of techno-pessimism, in polarised confrontation with the positivity of the techno-optimists). So let me try to forestall you, and suggest that my stance is, in fact, one of ambivalence. Bernard Sharratt reminds us of the essential ambivalence of images, which exist in the 'dual sense of both representation and misrepresentation, both reliable appearance of a real and mere chimera, both reflection and fiction'.[12] It seems to me inevitable, then, and also appropriate, that we should experience an ambivalence in our relation to images (we may be seduced by them, and we may, equally, be distrustful of them). We should recognise and articulate both responses – and both responses in relation to *all* image media. Through our equivocation we may come to understand both the limits and the possibilities of image forms, for both are inherent.

Chapter 1

THE TOUCH OF THE UNKNOWN

1

THE TOUCH OF THE UNKNOWN

There is nothing that man fears more than the touch of the unknown.
(Elias Canetti, *Crowds and Power*)

Through the sense of touch we risk feeling something or someone as alien. Our technologies permit us to avoid that risk.
(Richard Sennett, *Flesh and Stone*)

What is at stake in the development and proliferation of new images in our culture (from global media, through surveillance systems, to virtual environments)? According to the prevailing scenario, we are presently undergoing a 'revolutionary' transformation in image culture. Great expectations are being sustained: that the new image culture may enhance our knowledge and awareness of the world; that it can extend our range of experiences, pleasures, fantasies; that it could create new forms of sociality and bind together new kinds of community; that it will afford us increased security and protection from the dangers of the world. According to the scenario that prevails, we are on the threshold of an unprecedented new techno-order and what is at stake is a new order of freedom and empowerment, for the individual and for society. As if the technological future would be another world, a utopian world, a world more in conformity with our desires and our ideals. As if the present world and all its frustrations and limitations – all its reality, that is to say – could be denied and superseded.

Whatever the promises of a new cultural, and even existential, order to come, there is really nothing that we should find surprising or unexpected in this techno-rhetoric. What is presented to us in revolutionary guise should, in fact, be recognised and understood in terms of restitution and restoration. For aren't we all now familiar enough with the illusion of technology, that distinctively modern illusion of transcendence? An ordinary illusion (are we not all susceptible to its magical promises?), a compulsive illusion (it is sustained whatever its disappointments; there is always another technology, a next and therefore better technology, to believe in) – do we not recognise how fitted it has been to survive in modern times? It is the force of this technological illusion – now being revitalised through the new wave of

11

utopian projections around digital image technologies – that will concern me in the discussion that follows. What I want to consider is how technologies are mobilised in the cause of psychic needs and demands, which may be individual or collective.

We may think of this initially in terms of the struggle to bring order and coherence to the world. The question of technological development can be considered in terms of the modern project for human empowerment, involving the establishment of rational mastery and control over an ordered techno-space. But we must take the analysis further. For this, of course, immediately poses for us the question of the disorder and disempowerment (real or imagined) that is to be technologically obviated and overcome; it brings us necessarily to reflect on the defensive and protective motivations that promote the logic of technological rationalisation. And from there, I suggest, it must lead us to confront the fears that drive this logic. What is psychically compelling about the technologies I am considering here, I shall argue, is their capacity to provide a certain security and protection against the frightful world and against the fear that inhabits our bodies. They provide the means to distance and detach ourselves from what is fear-provoking in the world and in ourselves.

It is this question of fear (and the occlusion of fear) that is crucial to understanding the hold of the technological illusion, and its significance will be central to the following argument. Such a concern continues that articu-lated by Horkheimer and Adorno, who understood the logic of rational-isation as being 'aimed at liberating men from fear and establishing their sovereignty'. 'Man imagines himself free from fear when there is no longer anything unknown,' they observed, 'Nothing at all may remain outside, because the mere idea of outsideness is the very source of fear.'[1] It also extends the concern of Elias Canetti, for whom, too, culture was about organising and containing elemental fear. 'All the distances which men create round themselves', Canetti maintained, 'are dictated by this fear.'[2] Fear of the unknown, fear of being touched by the unknown, this is the fear that never goes away. It is with this fear that we must come properly to terms.

In considering the technological response to fear, I shall be focusing specifically on image technologies and on technological ordering in the field of vision. Vision has always provided a particularly important means of defending against what is unknown, outside and beyond (most cultures have attributed special and protective powers to images). It was the achievement of modernity, however, through the elaboration of formal and abstract ways of seeing, to rationalise these visual mechanisms of defence. Technologically mediated vision developed as the decisively modern way to put distance around ourselves, to withdraw and insulate ourselves from the frightening immediacy of the world of contact. What are now at issue are the con-sequences (usually referred to as 'postmodern') of this historical process of rationalisation in the field of vision. For those who have access to them, new

12

image technologies are facilitating greater detachment and disengagement from the world. Vision is becoming separated from experience, and the world is fast assuming a derealised quality. The proliferating system of new vision and image technologies is now instituting what can only be regarded as a structural and generalised condition of dissociation from the world (from its perceived threats and dangers). What is being idealised by the technoculture in terms of (visual) transcendence is, it seems to me, no more than the distinctive, modern strategy of retreat and flight from the world.

I believe that the real crisis confronting contemporary societies is a crisis of the social order, a crisis of social relationships and of forms of sociality. What is fundamentally at issue is the nature of our 'postmodern' involvement in the world – increasingly weakened by the technological means we have developed to sustain the more primitive desires we have for disinvolvement. The point now is not whether we can achieve a certain distance and detachment from the fearful principles of reality, but whether we can ever become reconnected to a world that we no longer take for real, a world whose reality has been progressively screened out. From what alternative perspective might we seek to make sense of the developments now occurring in our visual culture? How might we relate to images differently? These are questions I pose in the latter part of this discussion. In considering these difficult questions, I return to the question of fear, and to the relation of fear to outsideness. And I come back again to touch, to consider what is significant, and what is possible, in the touch of the unknown. I believe that it is through what is denied or disavowed in the dominant, rationalistic culture that we can find the basis of real cultural experience. Here are the real sources of cultural transformation and possibility, and if we are not open to these there can only be closure and stagnation. This is what must be recognised, I suggest, by whoever seeks to reaffirm the transitive dimension of visual culture and to reconnect image and experience.

THE 'OTHER' OF ANY PLACE

The new image and information culture is now associated with a renewed confidence in technological solutions to the problems of human culture and existence. The new technologies have revitalised the utopian aspirations in the modern techno-rationalist project. This progressivist and utopian spirit is articulated through ordinary, spontaneous and commonsensical accounts of what is happening: throughout the culture, there is the sense of almost limitless possibilities inherent in the 'cyber-revolution'. Indeed, such is the hold of the dominant technological imaginary, that it is almost impossible to discuss the new technoculture in any other way.

I want to indicate the force of the techno-utopian vision through two representative illustrations – one journalistic, one academic – before going on to develop a critical interpretation and perspective. Consider first a typical and conventional expression of utopian sentiments in a recent issue of *Newsweek* magazine. Here, journalist Steven Levy makes the claim that the new technologies are bringing into existence a new world and an alternative reality. This is now presenting us, he maintains, with 'an opportunity to rethink civilisation at the dawn of the new millennium'.[3] The virtual revolution is about transforming, not just ways of life, but, much more fundamentally, the nature of life itself. Through our expanding capacity to 'remake the world with the products of mind,' Levy maintains, we are on the point of 'shifting our concept of reality.'[4]

In trying to explain the basis for this ontological transformation, Levy seeks to establish a primary distinction between the world of atoms and the world of bits:

> The former are the building blocks for physical stuff, which until now has formed the basis of our economy as well as our consciousness. Bits, however, are ephemeral – they are simply ones and zeros. From that slight scaffolding, we have the bounty of the information age: all the documents, spreadsheet, audio CDs, multimedia, CD-Roms, movie special effects and virtual-reality environments. As more of our experience comes to us by way of bits, reality itself gradually changes. Literally out of nothing, a new dimension emerges: cyberspace, a place made out of bits, whose intangible nature does not prevent it from becoming a second home, or a primary workplace, for masses of infonauts.[5]

The crucial inference, of course, is the teleological one: that the palpable world of atoms is giving way to – being progressively substituted by – the ephemeral and virtual world of bits, and that this is an inevitable, even natural, process in so far as the latter is superior to the former. What is it that is superior about this 'place made out of bits'? The new reality – which is a new kind of reality – is imagined as one that is constituted by principles of mastery and empowerment. Human existence will be drawn into the space of the image, it is suggested, and rational sovereignty will be established over its virtual expanse. What is invoked is an alternative reality of an 'intangible nature' – a reality that we cannot touch, and which, by the same token, cannot touch us. This drive to order is, at the same time, an expression of the desire to escape the deficiencies and disorder of the 'physical stuff'. In the most ordinary and commonsense way (we would surely expect no less in the pages of *Newsweek*), Levy is articulating the logic of transcendence, which, I shall argue, is so problematically at the heart of the technological imaginary.

My second illustration of the techno-utopian vision – again I consider it to be typical and representative, and exemplary for that very reason – is an article by Roland Fischer that deals with virtual reality specifically in the context of the history of utopian thought. Again, what is emphasised is the logic of transcendence, and, particularly, the potential of new image and simulation technologies to 'realise' a transcendental order. 'Originally,' Fischer argues, 'utopian desires and dreams had religious, that is, transcendental, foundations and were projected into immeasurably distant spaces.' But as time went on, he continues, 'the distance of these faraway places in the "nowhere" started to shrink and the utopian imagination came closer to the real spaces in the here and now.'[6] In the next stage of its historical development, utopia transformed itself first into science fiction and then, crucially, into 'applied science fiction', aspiring to actually 'mimic a world around us as virtual reality'. 'Departing from distant, untouchable, fictitious places,' says Fischer, 'utopia at last arrived at the virtual reality of "cyberspace".'[7] And now, finally, the science fiction has been 'taken over painlessly by dynamic developments in science and technology'.[8] Virtual culture has become, precisely, a reality: 'is this not another utopian dream, but in the here and now?'[9] Fischer's teleological narrative culminates in the 'utopian realm of virtual reality'.

In one respect, we are being given a conventional narrative (metaphysics) of technical progress. With the development of these miraculous new technologies, it is being argued, we have arrived at the historical moment at which we can actualise our visionary aspirations for 'improving the human condition'. Dreams can be turned into realities. With the products of mind, we are now in a position to remake the world. Does this not give us good reason to invest our rational hopes and expectations in technological de- liverance? But, in another respect, what is being posited is a continuity in utopian desiring and dreaming (and this is clearly fundamental to the other than rational investments that are being made in virtual culture). The virtual realm is attractive precisely because it is a distant, untouchable, fictitious place. It is conceived as an alternative world – one that is more in conformity with our desires and dreams – with the potential to substitute for the limited and flawed reality of the here and now. In this virtual new world, Fischer is wanting to persuade us, we can fulfil the 'ancient dream' of transcendence – we can finally realise 'the desire to be something we are not'.[10]

In both of these representative accounts, then, what is crucial is the idea, and ideal, of a place of transcendence, a place that is 'elsewhere' ('in the "nowhere"'). It is an idea that has played a fundamental part in the modern social imaginary (we may say that each of the above accounts is representative as a consequence of its conformity to, and continuing idealisation of, this idea). Modernity's dynamic, in both its expansionist and utopian aspects, has always involved escaping from the gravity of given and immediate reality. 'Modernity is, first and foremost, a *frontier civilisation*,' observes Zygmunt Bauman; and, as such, 'it can survive only as long as some frontier is still left as a site for the promised, hoped for, beginning.'[11] Louis Marin notes the affinity between modern utopias and new frontiers ('beyond the horizon, in the imagination, appear Utopias').[12] In so far as real places elsewhere have been exhausted, it has become necessary to find new kinds of place and frontier to sustain the needs of the modern imaginary. Now the new frontier opens up onto cyberspace, the place of virtual life, and it is there that the self-proclaimed pioneers of the new technoculture (Steven Levy's 'infonauts') believe they will find another beginning. Virtual culture should be seen as continuing the modern struggle against the limitations of the actual world (the world that must always exist on this side of whatever is the next frontier), sustaining and perpetuating the idea of a different and better world, a place of possibility and transcendence (it is in this fundamental sense that we can say there is nothing surprising or unexpected in the new technoculture).

There is, it seems to me, something deeply problematical about this project of transcendence. It is apparent in the way in which the utopian destination is imagined. Utopia, as Louis Marin makes clear, involves the idea of a journey to a place that is 'absolutely different': it is a 'place without place, a moment out of time, the truth of a fiction'.[13] This pure place is one in which the conflicts and antagonisms that characterise the real world may be overcome. In this empty place, there are no longer the frustrations of intractable reality: 'Utopia develops and displays a virtual or potential spatial order: it offers the beholder-reader an ambiguous representation, the equivocal image of significations that are contrary to the concept of limit.'[14] 'Utopia is the neutral name,' says Marin, 'the name of the "neutral".'[15] Within its containing space, there are no constraints and inhibitions on what is possible. The utopian destination is imagined in terms of a place that is beyond disappointment and disillusion, and the utopian desire is to be in unity, at one, with such an environment. In this respect, we can say that it is 'the "other" of any place'.[16]

It is precisely these qualities of neutrality and transcendence that characterise the imagined 'alterity' of cyberspace – which is quite literally a virtual or potential spatial order. As Ralph Schroeder argues, the appeal of cyberculture is in the technological promise of 'new forms of human self expression . . . which will release human beings from the material constraints of their current lives'; virtual reality systems 'hold out the promise that human beings may one day be able to live within artificially generated virtual worlds limited only by their imaginations'.[17] What is crucial is the suspension of the principles that regulate human existence in the mundane and real world. Cyberculture seems to open up new horizons of creative expression and imagination. For Kiersta Fricke, everything seems possible in the new reality that is the utter antithesis of the real world:

> The potential of virtual reality technology to free us from the constraints of time and space appeals to a human longing for transcendence. We want to experience other circumstances without any real threat of danger. We want to be gods, to be able to change shape and form at will. Virtual reality assures us that we can – that we can reach the sun without melting our wings.[18]

The virtual world is a place that is absolutely different. The 'otherness' of this virtual place is now conceived as the ultimate utopian destination.

I think we must take these aspirations seriously. But not on their own terms, not because of what they might tell us about what our culture might become in the future. We should consider them, rather, because of what they can tell us about its present condition. What is this desire that constantly seeks the 'other' of any place (and which cannot be satisfied by any real place)? I have so far described it as the desire for transcendence, the desire to create an ideal new order, one of freedom, sovereignty, omnipotence. Virtual reality constitutes the most ambitious and absolute attempt to thus substitute an imaginary or utopian order for the (perceived) disorder of actual reality (to shift our concept of reality, to remake the world). But we may also consider this desire in the contrary sense: in terms of the expression of dissatisfaction with the real world. The utopian journey may be seen in terms of the flight from reality. The creation of artificial environments may be understood in terms of the drive to override and efface the difficult nature of the real social environment. From this contrary perspective, what are significant are the motivations and logic of denial, disavowal, evasion. Manifestly, it is a question of the refusal, or the inability, to come to terms with the condition of situated and placed existence: an unwillingness to confront and deal with difficulty and disappointment, a reluctance to acknowledge and accept the limits and constraints of real situations. More profoundly, it may be an expression of resentment, and even hatred, against our condition of human existence – against both nature and human nature. Transcendence may then be envisioned in its absolute sense, the negation of human reality itself.

A WORLD WITHOUT REALITY

How are we to make sense of this desire to be subsumed into the containing space of virtual reality? How might we develop a critical perspective? In most accounts – including serious, intellectual contributions – the issue is presented in terms of cultural innovation as a consequence of technological revolution. Thus, Arturo Escobar associates the new technologies with a 'fundamental transformation in the structure and meaning of modern society and culture', and he argues that this now calls for a new 'anthropology of cyberculture'.[19] Ralph Schroeder similarly emphasises what he perceives to be new in the emerging technoculture. 'Since VR technologies seemingly create a whole new horizon for human expression,' he maintains, 'and since science is no longer seen as a tool for mastery over the world but rather as the handmaiden of magic, perhaps VR is the perfect vehicle for the belief in merging human beings with information and communication machines, or that cyborgs represent a form of consciousness suited to the new age.'[20] Such accounts are declaring technological change to be the dynamic factor in promoting cultural renewal. As such, it seems to me, they are serving to perpetuate the technological illusion.

How might we disillusion ourselves? It is a question, I want to suggest at this point in my argument, of coming to terms with the nature of the psychic investments we make in technological forms. The case of simulation and virtual technologies provides an excellent focus for identifying these psychic processes – those, indeed, of 'magic' and 'merger' (which are precisely strategies of mastery). We should consider what is clearly a very real and powerful identification with the ideal of rational transcendence, I shall argue, in terms of its negative motivations, in terms, that is to say, of the disidentification with actual existence (because of what are experienced as its fearful and threatening qualities). We are concerned with defensive and protective instincts, seeking to achieve distance and detachment from worldly contact. In this context, I am particularly interested in how vision is mobilised to avoid touch. What is at work, I maintain, is a logic, not of innovation, but rather of inertia and even reversion. Technological change is embraced and accepted in order to avert psychic and cultural transformation.

To pursue this line of argument, it is necessary to establish an alternative (richer) basis for human purpose and motivation than that of progressive rationalisation and the extension of rational sovereignty. We have to inscribe reason – which is far more than instrumental rationality – within a more complex understanding of human nature and culture. Here we must incorporate a psychoanalytical perspective, and, more specifically, let me suggest, certain ideas from psychoanalytical metapsychology (in the space and context of this chapter, what I have to say must necessarily be abbreviated and indicative). For Cornelius Castoriadis, whose work is particularly valuable, human existence merges out of the Chaos, and the dilemma for human beings is that 'they cannot accept the Chaos and accept it as Chaos, they cannot stand up straight and confront the Abyss':

> What some have called the need for religion corresponds to the refusal on the part of human beings to recognise absolute alterity, the limit of all established signification, the inaccessible underside constituted for every place [endroit] to which one has access, the death dwelling within every life, the non-sense bordering on and penetrating all sense.[21]

Human beings seek to establish order and meaning so that they may 'cover over the Chaos', but that order is perpetually threatened, the Chaos 'never ceases, under one form or another, to announce itself to the individual and to be present for it.'[22] These ideas are taken up by Zygmunt Bauman. 'Human beings exist', he maintains, 'in the never ending, since never fully successful, effort to escape from Chaos. . . . Society, we might say, is a massive and continuous cover-up operation.'[23] The distinctively modern way of disavowing the Chaos, Bauman argues, has been through faith in Reason and belief in secular Progress ('Reason-about-to-rule lent meaning to the present . . .').[24] Bauman also emphasises the fearfulness that exists as a consequence of living in this condition between meaning and its dissolution: 'Society is an escape from fear; it is also the breeding ground of that fear, and on that fear it feeds and from it the grip in which it holds us draws its powers.'[25]

The work of the psychoanalyst, Wilfred Bion, is also very valuable for understanding this fundamental predicament of human existence, illuminating particularly the condition of perpetual fearfulness. What are crucial for Bion, as Michael Eigen makes clear, are the catastrophic foundations of human existence: 'The self is born, evolves and dissolves with a sense of catastrophe.' This is a basic fact of our emotional lives:

> Bion tracks a free floating sense of catastrophe which is a fundamental term of our existence. It functions as an invariant which can be filled in with a range of more specific contents (dread of birth, death, change, boundlessness, sameness, the predator, castration, disease, burning, drowning, suffocating, falling, etc.). One strains to see its face clearly in what can be seen but it grips one blindly from behind the scenes.[26]

Paul Hoggett also emphasises this aspect of Bion's analytical worldview. This nameless dread, he argues, is 'something indwelling within our subjectivity which could be likened to a basic fear'.[27] The fundamental mechanism of defence against this elemental fear is that of projection: 'the psychical process through which a fear which cannot be contained is visited upon the external world where it fuses and blends with the real violence and poison of our social environment ... the fear that was immanent within ourselves becomes the danger immanent within the Other'.[28] The fear cannot be accepted as a fear within. Human cultures project their fears onto what is outside and unknown, and then set to work to protect themselves from the threat that is imagined to be 'out there'.

This primacy of fear – presenting itself as a fear of what is beyond, though, more fundamentally, it is a fear of reality itself – is central to my arguments concerning psychic investment in technologies and technoculture. Returning now to this substantive issue, I want to consider how technologies, and specifically image and vision technologies, are mobilised in protection against the (imagined and real) fearfulness of existence in this world. In what way does the social institution of technology work to sustain (what must always be an illusory) order against the always impending threat of disorder? What is distinctive about this modern form of reality evasion?

Technologies function to mediate, to defer, even to substitute for, interaction with the world. We use them to avoid contact with the world and its reality. Through contact we risk feeling the world as alien; through the sense of touch we risk exposure to its chaotic or catastrophic nature. The aversion to touch is, as Serge Moscovici argues, primitively rooted in human culture, and is associated with the idea of contagion and contamination.[29] There is nothing we fear more than the touch of the unknown. Our technologies keep the world at a distance. They provide the means to insulate ourselves from the disturbing immediacy of the world of contact. Of particular significance in this respect has been the mobilisation of vision, the human sense most associated with detachment and separation from the world. 'Man always tends to avoid physical contact with anything strange', says Elias Canetti. 'In the dark, the fear of an unexpected touch can mount to panic . . . . He wants to *see* what is reaching towards him, and to be able to recognise or at least classify it.'[30] New technologies of vision have been continuously developed and perfected to ensure such visual sovereignty. The progressive rationalisation of vision has aimed to dispel the darkness and make visible whatever strangeness it contains. Sight against touch.

Martin Jay has observed how much modern vision, in its dominant form (what he calls 'Cartesian perspectivalism'), has been associated with the rationalist project of controlling the world from a distance, combining detachment and mastery. Rational vision was conceived as a function of the 'disincarnated absolute eye'. 'The participatory involvement of more absorptive models was diminished, if not entirely suppressed, as the gap between spectator and spectacle widened', argues Jay. 'The rational spectator existed as a disembodied subject entirely outside the world it claims to know only from afar.'[31] From this transcendental perspective, the world could be surveyed in its totality: nothing would remain invisible, nothing would remain outside the field of vision. The world thus surveyed by absolute vision was a world that could be ordered and thereby controlled – made into 'a "standing reserve" for the surveillance and manipulation of a dominating subject.'[32] What seemed possible by these means was the reconstitution of the world as the kind of world over which human beings could be sovereign, a world without disorder (this was the utopian impulse).

We should consider just what modern vision technologies have achieved in transforming the way we live in the world. First, let us acknowledge how they have changed our experience of the surrounding world. Referring to Simmel's now classic observations on the fear of contact (*Berührungsangst*) in the early twentieth-century city, Anthony Vidler emphasises how much vision figured in modernist strategies to neutralise and contain what provoked anxiety and distress. Modern planners and architects sought to erase what we might call the city of touch, and in its place to construct 'a glass city, its buildings invisible and society open'. The fundamental objective was that of 'transparency', the achievement of which would make the city a 'transcendent space' (Le Corbusier's 'radiant city').[33] Through the principle of rational vision, aspiring to the ideal of universal panopticism, it seemed possible to achieve order, and consequently mastery, in the urban space. This logic of substitution (transcendent vision for fearful touch) has remained crucial in modern strategies for dealing with encroaching reality. It has been massively facilitated by the development of a succession of new technological means, which have rendered the surrounding world ever more transparent and visible. The surveillance camera has now become the familiar and banal symbol of disincarnated vision, watching and knowing from a distance. A recent newspaper article describes the routine activity that takes place in the 'electronic eyrie' of a small English town:

> At the back of the room are 14 monitors, each of which shows four separate images – 56 continuous views of King's Lynn. On Roger's desk there are eight monitors displaying selected quadrants from the 56 in full-screen glory. If he detects anything interesting, he selects it for the full-screen treatment. He can zoom, pan and focus from where he sits. . . . While we talk, Roger displays the abstracted concentration which one sometimes sees in children intent on video games. He is with us, and yet not with us. His fingers are constantly on the go, incessantly flicking from scene to scene.[34]

What strikes me about this small illustration is not its 'Big Brother' quality, but, rather, its ordinariness (it is akin to the vigilance practised with video games). When Roger watches what reaches towards him (recognises it, classifies it), he is doing so on behalf of the collectivity. He may be seen as personifying the collective desire to see what is going on in the surrounding world without the risk of being touched by it. In our culture, surveillance is ordinary.

Increasingly, we have come to see the world by means of mediated vision, and, as we have done so, we have increasingly been able to distance and detach ourselves from contact with its reality. And, of course, it is no longer a question of seeing and monitoring the proximate world: new visual media have progressively expanded the field of vision. With the development of global television, there is, it seems, the capacity for unlimited observation of the world's events. What was possible became apparent with CNN's coverage of the Gulf War, and has been consolidated through the coverage of subsequent wars and disasters across the world. I shall not discuss this at any length here.[35] Let me just make my substantive point through a small, but highly pertinent anecdote, showing what now seems possible in the new media order. In his *Newsweek* article, Steven Levy reports a speech by Newt Gingrich, making the prediction that, in wars of the future, the military combatants will be 'tak[ing] direction from armchair warhorses on the home front'. It is a vision that is chilling for its combination of banality and obscenity:

> 'CNN will be in your living room . . .' said the Speaker [Gingrich], 'and you will be able to see the battle in real time. You'll then be able to pick up your telephone and call your son or daughter who you are watching real time in a firefight. You will chat with them about your view of how they are conducting their squad operations.'[36]

We can imperiously observe what is going on 'out there', Gingrich is suggesting, without ever being touched by it (even when our son or daughter is out there). In his extreme way, he is registering the ordinary belief in the

21

protective power of the image: through the screen, he is saying, we can see the world and, at the same time, be safeguarded against the impact and consequences of what we are seeing.

Through mediated vision, then, we can keep a distance from the real-world environment. But vision technologies contain a further, and more radical, possibility for transforming the way we live in the world. For it is through the capabilities of visual simulation techniques that it becomes possible to imagine shifting one's existence to an alternative environment, one that has been cleansed of the real world's undesirable qualities. This has, of course, been a long-standing ambition. The panorama mania of the mid-nineteenth century was driven by this same desire to be immersed in a substitutive visual environment: people used panorama scenes as 'vehicles of personal and social fantasy – as a kind of escape from the spatial, temporal and social limitations of their lives'.[37] With developments in cinema – from early side-show entertainments (like Hale's Tours, which created 'a remarkably convincing illusion of railway travel'[38]) through to contemporary Imax systems – wrap-around images were, with increasing degrees of sophistication, put into motion. New technological developments continue to respond to this desire to enter into the space of the image. Now, with digital image technologies, it seems possible make a complete escape from the limitations of real life by entering into the ultimate illusion, that of virtual life in a virtual reality.

Perhaps the virtual city will substitute for the real city, its order compensating for the latter's disorder? Already we have the digital 'other' of Amsterdam. Visitors to this city find that it is all they imagined it to be: 'the red light of a sex shop beckons from a dark alley, Rick's music place promises to take you to Paradise, brown cafés hum with conversation and on the corner a drug-dealer peddles his wares.' But here, 'sex is strictly safe – as are all the other slightly louche attractions'.[39] This is a city that has already celebrated its first virtual marriage, complete with virtual guests and virtual champagne. 'The happy couple', we are told, 'has never met in the flesh; nor do they particularly want to.'[40] And we are now encouraged to fantasise about such possibilities on an even greater scale. Imagine a global network of digital cities, imagine the simulation of the entire world. 'Within five years', *Time* magazine predicts, 'virtual reality "tours" of the Himalayas or Venice will be widespread.'[41] Imagine a whole world of possibilities for virtual encounter and interaction (and maybe marriage). And all of it safe and free from fear.

If surveillance technologies seem to offer protection against the unknown that is feared to be out there in the beyond, the attraction of simulation technologies is in their promise to transcend the more basic fear of reality itself. The world of simulation is a world without bodies (the very means of touch have been suspended or annulled). It is a world without chaos and catastrophe (there is nothing which exceeds or escapes the order of the technological system). It is a world without reality. And it is its very distance from the real world (from what seems so undesirable about the real world) that makes it seem to be a space of potentiality. We are told that, once we are freed from the burden and fear of real-world existence, new horizons can be opened up for self-expression and creativity. In a world without limits, it is said, new dimensions of experience will become possible.

TECHNOLOGY AND EXPERIENCE

> Our love of order is a consequence of our terror of chaos, of the definitive collapse of every edifice, an outcome that provokes so much dread that what is formless, that which does not submit to a defined form, frightens us.
>
> Our beliefs, the ones we are hooked on like addicts to their substance, are our way of alleviating the failure of mental order.
>
> (J.-B. Pontalis, 'Le souffle de la vie',
> *Nouvelle Revue de Psychanalyse*)

The prevailing debate on technology and culture is narrow, insular and evasive of social and human realities: that has been the burden of my argument to this point. So, we must ask, are there other possible contexts for thinking about contemporary transformations in vision technologies? Are there alternative perspectives from which we might make better sense of the uses (and misuses) of visual experience? I believe that there are. Beyond the limits of the technoculture, I want to suggest, there are vital issues and concerns that might have relevance for our discussion (and we should be disturbed that the technological agenda, with its single-minded commitment to technological transcendence, has remained so closed to them). I now want to admit some of these into the consideration of contemporary image culture. In seeking new contexts and perspectives, I suggest, we may have the possibility to re-view (and re-describe) what is at stake in the development of images. We might achieve a different awareness of the relationship between the world of screen and image and that of sensation, sensibility and sense-making.

Where the technoculture argues that what we now need is a new anthropology of cyberspace and cyberculture, I am saying that it is a question, rather, of dealing with old and sustained forms of investment in techno-order. Where the technoculture invokes the ideal and measure of progress to claim that the new technologies are bringing about an expansion and enrichment of experience, I am suggesting, to the contrary, that we consider the development of these technologies in terms of a logic of regression, where the technological system is understood to have been evolved as a socially instituted means of reality evasion. I am saying that, beyond the manifest and declared objective of technological rationalisation, which is to extend the scope of visual experience, we should be concerned with other, obscure and deep-seated drives, which have sought to neutralise the visual relation to the world and escape the consequences of visual encounter. I want to consider the nature and significance of our investment in technological developments in terms of the possibilities that are inhibited and foreclosed. My concern is with what has been repudiated in the development of technological culture, and this, I shall argue, must be fundamentally a concern with the repudiation of experience.

What is at stake, then, is the question of experience: we are contemplating the denial and disavowal of experience in modern culture, and the implication of vision technologies in this attenuation of modern experience (and then we shall have to consider the conditions of possibility for the revalidation of experience). Of course, I recognise that it is by no means unproblematical to discuss these technological developments in terms of experience. On what basis can I argue that the new visual media are an obstacle to experience? How could I seriously make the claim that they do not enhance our awareness of the world? In *Newsweek* magazine, I read of a young man who 'is bored with being human' and is 'ready to mutate', now prepared to become a 'posthuman android':[42] can I deny that this cyborg aspiration represents a new and innovative kind of experience? How could one kind of experience not be just as valid as any other? Why should it not be counted as equally significant and meaningful? You may even feel that the very idea of experience is now problematical. In the context of the technoculture, this may seem a residual phenomenon, a conceptual relic from the days before post-humanity seemed the most desirable state of being. It might appear, then, that nothing is to be gained from using such a problematical concept. But I believe that we have to persist with it: we must hold on to the significance and value of experience precisely because it is what is disowned and demeaned by the technoculture. The category of experience is important because it identifies and stands for qualities of existence that have been repressed and disavowed in modern technological societies. Rather than 'progress', then, I am suggesting that we use 'experience' as the ideal and measure by which to assess the achievement of technological culture.

In developing such an alternative perspective, it is vital that we move out beyond the circumscribed imagination of the technoculture (it is a general problem for our intellectual culture that it is divided into restricted, and often parochial, domains of interest and concern: in the particular case of the technoculture, we have an especially clear example of intellectual insulation and insularity). We should be seeking now to re-locate the technology debate in relation to wider cultural and political agendas, bringing into consideration broader issues and concerns of contemporary society. The technoculture has elaborated its own distinctive social vision (seeking to persuade us of the utopian qualities of mediated communication, electronic community and virtual (post-)selfhood). Elsewhere in the intellectual and cultural field, there are alternative – and I think far more radical – ways of imagining and thinking about how the world could become. There are other points of intellectual departure, and there are other values and ideals according to which we might consider how the world could be a better place. Elsewhere (in current debates in philosophy, psychoanalysis and political theory), I believe that there are intellectual resources which could be highly productive for the way we think about technology and culture. For the purposes of the present discussion and its particular concerns, I am especially interested in those possibilities that can help us to understand new technologies from the point of view of experience. I want to consider technological culture in the context of what it means for the way we relate to the world and its events (existentially, morally, politically, aesthetically). In seeking to develop some aspects of this broader context, I intend to suggest alternative vantage points from which we might see the technological culture in a different light, and with reference to which we might make more complex judgements about its social and human significance.

Experience has been an important theme in recent psychoanalytical thinking, particularly in the writings of Wilfred Bion and those influenced by his work. We might draw on this psychoanalytical understanding to resist or oppose the dominant, rationalist and instrumental conception of technological development. From this perspective, we may better compre-hend the ambiguous nature of the investments made in technology, and we may also acknowledge the limits and constraints that we accept (though generally we do not do so knowingly) by subjecting ourselves to the technological system. In the terms of psychoanalysis, what is at issue is, fundamentally, the ambivalence of our relation to experience. Bion's work is concerned with experience and knowledge of the world, but it is at the same time about the retreat from experience and the difficulty of learning from experience.[43] As Hans Thorner puts it, 'side by side with the desire for knowledge, there is a resistance to knowledge. Getting to know inevitably brings the individual into contact with objects that arouse displeasure. Hence tolerance to pain and displeasure is a precondition for the ability to think.'[44] Whilst there is the possibility of incorporating the unknown and of modifying the frustrations associated with it, there is commonly the desire to evade difficult and disturbing experiences, and, consequently, the tendency to oppose the discovery of new truths. That the retreat from experience is not generally recognised as such can then be explained in terms of what Thomas Ogden refers to as the creation of 'substitute formations, which involve turning the condition of non-exper-ience into the illusion of experiencing and knowing, thereby filling the potential space in which feeling states and transformational processes might occur'.[45] What Bion crucially recognised was that these tendencies are not only present in individual behaviour, but are also integral to the functioning of collective institutions.[46] While the group may ideally embody the collective wisdom and provide a vehicle for collective action, it is also the case that 'the group, organised as a community or institution, resists the very opportunities for transformation which its own resourcefulness provides', developing its own characteristic 'ways of resisting or *escaping* from the meeting with the unknown'.[47] As if it were faced with the stark choice between, on the once hand, cohesion and coherence, and, on the other, fragmentation and dissolution, the group works to maintain its integrity and conserve its known identity (evolving its own collective substitute formations). The collective institution tends all the more readily towards inertia and closure, and it is all the more difficult to open it up to the unknown and to the demands this makes for accommodation and transformation.

For it is transformation that is crucial in Bion's account. The imperative is to overcome our own spontaneous tendencies towards the closure of experience and the inhibition of knowledge. Experience must involve us in a dynamic link with the world, always and continually impelling us to introduce new elements of disorder into the static and consolidated ordering of past experiences. What this requires is that we relinquish our postures of omnipotence and recognise the potential inherent in the complexity and indeterminacy of a world that is beyond our subjective powers. And the precondition for this is the capacity to tolerate the experience of not knowing – which is both to acknowledge the reality of that which remains unknown (Other) to us, and to realise the creative possibilities that may emerge from the uncertainty and discomfort of not knowing.[48] 'If an idea, an experience, a thought, a feeling belongs to *us* or to *me*, then we or I may feel it is at least under our or my control,' observes David Armstrong. 'But suppose it belongs neither to us nor to me. We or I do not know what it will do, what it will lead to, whether it will burgeon into a saviour or a monster, whether it will give us new life or kill us.'[49] Learning from experience involves the ability to contain and modify these painful and fearful emotions occasioned by the encounter with the unknown.

What is necessary for experience to occur is the capacity to admit the catastrophic or chaotic foundations of our human existence. There must be the awareness that what is the cause of fearful and dreadful feelings (as I have made clear above) is at the same time the source of innovation and transformation. Bion describes the appropriate response to catastrophe, in somewhat mystical terms, as the attitude of faith: 'faith saves catastrophe and grants this term of our origin, growth and end its due. It recognises catastrophe as a basic condition of our being. To blunt our awareness of catastrophe is to lose or never gain our sensitivity to ourselves.'[50] Faith implies an open and receptive sensibility, and one that is capable of living the experience of fragmentation and the dissolution of certainties ('whirls of bits and pieces of meaning and meaninglessness'). It is an attitude that 'undercuts and transcends our controlling needs and enables us to experience the impact of emotional reality in a way that allows the latter genuinely to evolve'.[51] In similarly emphasising how important it is that we should tolerate the sense of catastrophe, Christopher Bollas urges us to recognise 'inner senses of generative chaos'.[52]

He is identifying this turbulent flux and disorder as the very basis of innovation and creativity in human culture.

This psychoanalytical perspective coincides very much with that of Cornelius Castoriadis (which is developed in the context of a broader political and philosophical framework). Again it is a question of how the fundamental Chaos that first makes everything seem precarious and fearful is also the basis for instituting new significations. The Chaos is constantly invading the given and the familiar, and it is out of this absolute alterity – 'the death dwelling in every life, the non-sense bordering on and penetrating all sense' – that new experiences, feelings and understanding can emerge:

> This invasion is manifested both through the emergence of the irreducibly new, of radical alterity, without which what is would be only the Identical, absolutely undifferentiated – that is to say, nothing – and through destruction, nihilation, death. Death is the death of forms, of figures, of essences – not simply of their concrete exemplars – without which, once again, what is would be only repetition, indefinitely prolonged or merely cyclical, eternal return.[53]

Castoriadis considers this interaction of destructive and innovative forces to be vital to both democratic creation and aesthetic creativity – 'For what art presents is not the Ideas of reason, but the Chaos, the Abyss, the Groundless, to which it gives form. And through that presentation, it is the window onto Chaos, abolishing the docile and stupid assurance of our daily lives, and reminding us that we always live on the edge of the Abyss'[54] – and the fundamental question concerns our capacity to tolerate the drive to continuous alteration and self-alteration.

These concerns may be directly related – if I may suggest one further intellectual agenda that is of relevance to the present discussion – to contemporary debates around the meaning and significance of the Stranger or the Other. For the figure of the Stranger also stands for that which catastrophically challenges our sense of order and stability, and yet, at the same time, through its very otherness or negativity, represents the possibility of social and cultural replenishment and revitalisation (it is an otherness that is both beyond and within ourselves). Consideration of the Stranger has developed in a number of intellectual contexts,[55] but perhaps the most significant, for the present argument at least, has been the analysis elaborated by Emmanuel Levinas and those who have been influenced by his writings. Levinas in fact traces a correlation between the human confrontation of death and confrontation with the Other. Death is unknowable, it is what marks 'the limit of the subject's virility', it is where 'the subject loses its very mastery as a subject'. 'This end of mastery', according to Levinas, 'indicates that we have assumed existing in such a way that an *event* can happen to us that we no longer assume, not even in the way we assume events – because we are always immersed in the empirical world – through vision.'[56] Death exists and exerts its force over our lives as an imperative, and it is through the Other that we experience that imperative force (mortality lies in the Other). As Alphonso Lingis puts it, 'the imperative, death, and the other reveal one another':

> It is in our mortality that we know the force of the imperative; in the exteriority of the imperative the absolute exteriority of death summons us. The figure of our fellow human whose face is somehow more exterior to us than the surfaces of the exterior world, exterior as death, turns to us as the concrete phenomenon of the imperative.[57]

For Levinas, it is this encounter – in which we are exposed to, and afflicted by, the vulnerability and mortality of the Other – that is the basis of our moral and ethical relations:

> [I]n its expression, in its mortality, the face before me summons me, calls for me, begs for me, as if the invisible death that must be faced by the Other . . . were my business. It as if that invisible death, ignored by the Other, whom already it concerns by the nakedness of its face, were already 'regarding' me prior to confronting me, and becoming the death that stares me in the face. The other man's death calls me into question, as if, by my possible future indifference, I had become the accomplice of the death to which the other, who cannot see it, is exposed; and as if, even before vowing myself to him, I had to answer for this death of the other, and accompany the Other in his mortal solitude.[58]

The moral imperative is conveyed in the move by which the Other *faces* me: I am called to respond to the Other who *faces*.

What I am raising is the fundamental question of how we experience and relate to the world. First, I have assumed that we shall do our best to evade and defend ourselves against experience. Then I have invoked experience as an ideal, valued in terms of its creative and transformational possibilities. This is the context in which I choose to make sense of the new technologies – that are so powerfully affecting the way we see and relate to the world. In considering what we are doing with these technologies – and what they are at the same time doing to us – I find the conventional rationalist and progressivist accounts both ingenuous and improbable. I am saying that what motivates our psychic and emotional investments is, in fact, the difficulty we have in tolerating our own emotional capacity. We believe in the technological order because it provides the means to neutralise experience – and this belief is, indeed, our modern addiction. Experience should be the measure by which we judge the narcotic potency of the developing technological system.

VISION AND TOUCH

Sur nos écrans, les corps s'éloignent.
(Vincent Amiel, 'Le corps en images (de Buster Keaton
à John Cassavetes)', *Terminal*)

In this final part of my discussion, I shall bring vision into encounter with touch (my interest is not in these two senses as such, but, rather, in the cultural – and psychic – meanings and values that have been invested in them in the modern period). I want to suggest the connection, in our modern techno-logical culture, between the dominance of the visual sense, the drive to disembodiment, and the retreat from experience. Then I shall consider the relation between the sense of touch, the acceptance of embodied existence, and the possibility of experience (meaning the possibility of being touched by the unknown). What is at issue is the way in which modern sensory – and consequently cultural and intellectual – experience has become so powerfully associated with vision (the detached sense), while at the same time, the significance of touch (the intimate sense) has been repressed and devalued. In one respect, this must involve us in confronting what is problematical in the visual hegemony of modern culture and, in another, it should provoke us into reconsideration and re-estimation of what is distinctive in the sense of touch. But it cannot simply be a question of reversing the polarity (where we would end up with the denigration of vision and the compensatory idealisation of the immediacy of touch). The fundamental problem lies with the division and separation of sensory experience in modern culture – this is what makes such polarisation possible. To work against this, it is necessary to think in terms of the relation – the association, the affinity, the complementarity – between senses. In the context of this particular discussion, it is a question of bringing touch to bear on vision, and doing this because it might help us to really enhance – in more than just a technological sense – our powers of vision.

All the elements of modern techno-vision are clearly present in William J. Mitchell's utopian manifesto, *City of Bits*. His cyber-paradise is a supremely visual domain: Mitchell refers to the Internet as a 'world-wide, time-zone spanning optic nerve with electronic eyeballs at its endpoints'.[59] Consider this scenario (it betrays a great deal about cyber-evangelism):

> Fancy hotel room, Riyadh. A one-way electronic window opens onto the CNN newsroom in Atlanta. An arrow on the bedside table points the prayerful to Mecca, but the satellite dish on the roof turns news junkies and insomniacs toward Georgia. An amplified muezzin, calling from somewhere outside, marks the moment for morning devotions; beyond the electronic window, the news anchor greets the top of the hour with a fast-paced rundown on the day's top stories. Right now, the same window is open in thousands and thousands of similar hotel rooms spread around the world.[60]

We – 'we video cyborgs' – are joined in a community of global surveillance of the world's events (who would listen to the muezzin when they could

29

watch Ted Turner's channel?).[61] In this visual–virtual domain, the dangers and the challenges of the real world are neutralised (there are no muezzins or ayatollahs; and, furthermore, 'as networks and information appliances deliver expanding ranges of services, there will be fewer occasions to go out'[62]). We shall also lose our vulnerability as we shed the body that experiences fear and threat. Our destiny, we are told, is that we shall come to live in and through 'the incorporeal world of the Net'; and we shall live there as 'disembodied and fragmented subjects who exist as collections of aliases and agents'.[63] Touch is not entirely foreign to this utopian scene, but it is not touch in any meaningful, or resonant, sense. Mitchell is interested in prosthetic devices that will 'both sense gestures and serve as touch output devices by exerting controlled forces and pressures'. With cyborg touch, he predicts, 'you will be able to initiate a business conversation by shaking hands at a distance or say goodnight to a child by transmitting a kiss across continents'.[64] This is a world in which we can only be reached by what is already known and familiar. Here we will only come across cyborgs like us – with, it seems, the same western, suburban, middle-class cyborg occupations and aspirations.[65]

The cyber-world is utopian because it is a world of order, and it is an ordered world because it is pre-eminently a visual world. Here, as Julian Stallabrass argues, 'the world seems to make transparent sense': 'The transparency of meaning in cyberspace, the absolute match between concept and appearance, is a utopian feature which stands in marked contrast to the real world, of meaningless detail.'[66] We are sovereign masters in the spectacular world we have created in order to be free of actual and corporeal existence. Here we transcend the chaotic and catastrophic condition of our primitive reality. Perhaps there may be some truth in the belief that, in this world of disembodied subjects, 'delight will have unimagined new dimensions'.[67] But this delight will have its real costs. The pleasures of interacting with other virtual aliases and agents must be set against what is lost to our spiritual and moral life. John Berger has expressed concern about the separation of appearances from existence in the modern world. In the lightness of spectacular culture, he argues, the conditions and the burden of embodied existence and encounter are lifted: 'No body, no suffering, and no Necessity – for Necessity is the condition of existence; it is what makes reality real.' And with the conditions, the possibilities – 'there is no longer any imparting of experience.'[68] No learning through experience, no transformation through experience. Our unreal predicament is that we can see but cannot be touched by the other. The significance of the other – as 'the locus where vulnerability, susceptibility, mortality are materialised, exposed to me and afflict me with the obsessive urgency of an imperative'[69] – is effaced. In our hyper-visual culture, we live without face (counting only on the pleasures of the interface).

The techno-visionaries believe that they are involved in the instauration of a new, utopian order. 'We have reinvented the human habitat,' proclaims William Mitchell.[70] This utopia is presented to us in terms of the positive achievements of new vision and image technologies, but I am suggesting that we should consider it negatively, in terms of flight from the living realm of contact and touch. And what is portrayed in terms of social and cultural innovation should rather be understood as simply continuing the long historical project to escape the conditions and imperatives of embodied existence. Richard Sennett has described the desire and the logic that have shaped the formation of techno-environments throughout the modern period. Remarking on the continuity between the space of the screen and the space of urban life, he observes in both cases the modern sense of disconnection from space. The objective in the construction of modern environments is 'freedom from resistance'. 'This desire to free the body from resistance is', says Sennett, 'coupled with the fear of touching .... Today, order means lack of contact.'[71] Modern technological culture has had the effect of 'weakening the sense of tactile reality and pacifying the body'.[72] 'Sensate realities and bodily activity have eroded to such an extent that modern society seems a unique historical phenomenon,' and this, Sennett argues, has '[brought] to the fore deep-seated problems in Western civilisation in imagining spaces for the human body which might make human bodies more aware of one another.'[73] This is the appropriate and the necessary context in which we should be situating the ideal of virtual community – Mitchell's 'soft city' with its 'virtual gathering places, exchanges and entertainment spots for its plugged-in pop-ulace'.[74] The cyberspace environment sustains the modern desire to construct, not an alternative society, but what is, rather, an alternative to society. And it is such an alternative because it is a place in which there is no longer embodied existence and encounter – or it is a place in which it becomes possible to relate to others as if they had no bodies.

Sennett puts forward the argument that the predicament of the modern city will only be resolved when modern bodies are brought back into contact with one another. He makes the case that urban life has everything to do with bodies – with the coexistence, cooperation and confrontation of bodies. How bodies come together is a measure of urban culture and experience. 'What then', asks Sennett, 'will bring the body to moral, sensate life? What will make modern people more aware of each other, more physically responsive?'[75] When we come to consider the 'soft city' – where bodies are no longer just passive, but are now imagined as non-existent – Sennett's questions assume even greater force and poignancy. The technoculture encourages us to fantasise about the pleasures of release from the human body. William Mitchell talks of 'we multiply augmented cyborgs' – post-humans with 'electronically augmented, reconfigurable, virtual bodies that can sense and act at a distance' – who can now look back nostalgically on 'the cultures of those long, pre-silicon centuries in which our ancestors had to do it all with protoplasm'.[76] In so far as we have gone along with this cyber-rhetoric, we have thought about the gains of omnipotence, and we have failed to take account of what is lost and lacking in such a culture. We have come to the point of inhumanising and dehumanising ourselves when we no longer recognise and acknowledge the significance of embodied involvement in the world. If we experience the world, it is because we are bodily present in it: experience is inherently embodied. It is as embodied beings that we come upon others: 'To recognise another is not to identify a sensible essence or even a style in a succession of significant dealings with the other; it is to be touched by a body.'[77] And as embodied beings, we come across others in their difference, others who extend our awareness and experience, but others who also frustrate our expectations or put demands on us. We have to recognise our separation from others – as Ian Craib puts it, 'we are isolated in a body'[78] – and therefore our dependency on them. This has been the basis of our sociality and this is what we are disavowing in the drive to disembodiment.

In thinking about embodied existence and encounter, I bring the discussion back again, finally, to the sense of touch. I began with touch in relation to the fear of the unknown – with Canetti's invocation of 'the whole knot of shifting and intensely sensitive reactions to an alien touch'.[79] Now I am drawing the argument of this chapter to a close by considering touch in terms of the experiential and transformational possibilities inherent in the unknown. Touch is the primary and elemental faculty. As Elizabeth Grosz puts it (she is articulating the important arguments of Luce Irigaray), it is 'the tangible [that] provides the preconditions and the grounds of the visible': 'The tangible is the invisible, unseeable milieu of the visible, the source of visibility; it precedes the distinction between active and passive, subject and object: "I see only through the touching of the light".'[80] Of course, we are concerned not just with the act of physical contact, but with touch also in its metaphorical and, let us say, philosophical aspects – just as our language of vision (seeing, perceiving, reflection, taking a view, adopting a perspective) also extends well beyond simple ocular activity. Indeed, we are concerned with touch in so far as we want to move beyond the limits of the visual imagination (to escape the Cartesian dualism between vision/mind and touch/body). 'While it is clear', says Elizabeth Grosz, 'that in the case of touch, the toucher is always touched, in traditional philosophical models of vision, the seer sees at a distance, and is unimplicated in what is seen.'[81] These are quite different ways of being in the world.

In touch, we are immersed in the surrounding world. In touch, there is not the possibility to be alone or to be above it. We are involved and implicated in the reciprocity of contact. And in this we cannot be the sole initiators – we cannot escape from being touched by the Other. We are also exposed to being touched by the Other in our emotional and moral senses. Emmanuel Levinas describes such openness and receptivity to the Other in terms of 'caress':

> The caress is a mode of the subject's being, where the subject who is in contact with another goes beyond this contact. Contact as sensation is part of the world of light. But what is caressed is not touched, properly speaking. It is not the softness or warmth of the hand given in contact

that the caress seeks. The seeking of the caress constitutes its essence by the fact that the caress does not know what it seeks. This 'not knowing', this fundamental disorder, is the essential.[82]

The caress precedes the visual: 'what the caress seeks is not situated in a perspective and in the light of the graspable'.[83] It is in terms of this precedent world, this world that is prior to vision, that we may think of what it means to be touched by the Other and by the Other's catastrophic possibilities. Then we may consider whether we can bring this to bear on the field of vision. The question is whether our eyes can ever be made to touch the Other again. 'The eyes *touch* the imperative and vocative force that faces', says Lingis, 'when the gaze finds its intentions troubled, its self-assurance decomposed, its agility held in the gaze of another.'[84]

LEARNING TO SEE

Have I said it before? I am learning to see. Yes, I am beginning. It's still going badly. But I intend to make the most of my time.
(Rainer Maria Rilke, *The Notebooks of Malte Laurids Brigge*)

In 'Eye and mind', Merleau-Ponty wrote of the limits of scientific thinking – then it was the ideology of cybernetics – in relation to vision:

Scientific thinking, a thinking which looks on from above, and thinks of the object-in-general, must return to the 'there is' which underlies it; to the site, the soil of the sensible and opened world such as it is in our life and for our body – not that possible body which we may legitimately think of as an information machine but that actual body I call mine, this sentinel standing quietly at the command of my words and acts.[85]

We should think of ourselves as embodied beings, he argues. We are bodies that envision the world, and we are also bodies that move as visible presences in the world, for we move among other bodies ('the others who haunt me and whom I haunt'). Merleau-Ponty wants to think of vision as being on a continuum with touch, to imagine the world as visibly palpable. In his essay on Cézanne, he describes the artist as seeking 'to make *visible* how the world touches'.[86] To see thus is to be involved in the field of vision in a way that is quite other to that abstract and transcendental act posited in the rational-scientific tradition. To see is to be in the world, to be 'caught in the fabric of the world', and to be open to the world.

With the development of image and vision technologies, of course, this orientation to the world becomes more difficult and problematical. Our relationship to the mediated world cannot so readily be one of engagement and reciprocity. As we have 'perfected' our image media, perhaps we have been putting ourselves at a greater and greater distance from the palpable reality of the world. Vincent Amiel argues that in the case of cinematic images, there was still a sensory and tactile quality, a feeling of bodily encounter, but that, with the emergence of electronic images, this has been dissipated.[87] There is a growing distance between the space of the image and the world of objects. And absorption into the former no longer has any clear or necessary relation to our being in the latter. With the prospect of virtual environments – of moving into the image space – we may come to feel that we no longer have any need of the real world (and, from there, to believe that that kind of reality no longer means anything). When the disincarnation of reality reaches this absolute point, all that can be seen are our own projections – vision is autistic.

For the technoculture, this is no bad thing. The phantasmatic and pleasurable world of cyberspace is a more than acceptable alternative to the frustration and pain of the object world. (Paul Virilo is surely right when, putting the development of cyberculture alongside the global narcotics business, he argues that this 'electronic narco-capitalism' is as much about the subjection of populations as the narco-capitalism of hard drugs.[88]) I am arguing, to the contrary, that the imperative is to re-locate ourselves in the world. In my view, it will be deeply problematical if we cannot do this. I am thinking of embodiment and immersion in the philosophical sense of Merleau-Ponty, of the need to be open to the experience of the world. But this is clearly not a world in the abstract. It is a historical and a political world. So I am also thinking of our involvement and implication in this world of turmoil that is the so-called new world order. For 'ultimately,' as Julia Kristeva asks, 'where do the world's events take place? On the television screen? Or in the pneumatic spaces of our bodies, of our sensations, of our imaginaries which, in the final analysis, confer *sense on everything that comes to be*?'[89] It is most probable that we shall carry on denying the reality and the truth of this observation – that we shall continue to use technologies as a means of distancing and detaching ourselves from the world's events, and that we shall prefer to immerse ourselves in an alternative world of virtual events. But we should at least recognise that there is an alternative possibility: that we might choose to resist the logic of the technological system; that we might decide to recognise our embodiment and immersion in the disorder of the real world; that we might try to find ways to see and be touched by the world's events. Let us at least believe that we have a choice. Will we take the cyborg option, or shall we be able to find our humanity?

Chapter 2

THE SPACE OF
THE SCREEN

2

THE SPACE OF THE SCREEN

The hermit turns his back on the world and will have no truck with it. But one can do more than that; one can try to re-create the world, to build up in its stead another world in which its most unbearable features are eliminated and replaced by others that are in conformity with one's own wishes.

(Sigmund Freud, *Civilisation and its Discontents*)

'It's the end of chemical photography', David Hockney says:

We had this belief in photography, but that is about to disappear because of the computer. It can re-create something that *looks like* the photographs we've known. But it's unreal. What's that going to do to all photographs? Eh? It's going to make people say: that's just another invention. And I can see there's a side of it that's disturbing for us all. It's like the ground being pulled from underneath us.[1]

For 150 years chemical photography held a special position as a representation of reality, and now, it would seem, that standing is being called into question. New vision technologies have made it possible to expand the range of photographic seeing – 'beyond vision' – through the remote sensing of micro-wave, infra-red, ultra-violet and short-wave radar imagery. As John Darius suggests, 'the result in all cases is an image; at what point it ceases to be a photograph is a matter of semantics'.[2] If there have been notable developments in the ways of seeing, there has also been a significant breakthrough in the recording and handling of images. New image technologies, based on digital electronics, have also challenged what we mean by photography. We can say that these new vision and image technologies are post-photographic.

'The computer's done this', as Hockney says. We are seeing the convergence of still and moving images, and with it the emergence of a generalised image technology and culture. But what has made this possible is the more fundamental convergence of image and computer technologies. Images have become subsumed within an overarching information system. To talk of images now is to talk of computers. The image-information product, in the form of digital electronic signals, is then opened up to almost unlimited possibilities of processing, manipulation, storage and transmission. And, once it becomes possible to record photographs and other visual images in the form of digital information, then it also becomes feasible to reverse this process and to generate information that will produce or simulate an image *ex nihilo*, as it were. This capacity to generate a 'realistic' image on the basis of mathematical applications that model reality is the most dramatic and significant development of the new post-photography. It has become the major focus for research and development. Thus, at MIT's Media Lab, more sophisticated and futuristic developments of these technological principles are centred around the creation of computer-generated holograms and even the virtual reality of an artificial computer universe. Here, we are told, the convergence of artificial intelligence, robotics and animation technologies is about 'reinventing the world from scratch', about moving on from the old realities to a brave new virtual world.[3]

The capacities of these new image technologies are certainly impressive. But just *how* significant are these developments? And, indeed, *what* is the real nature of their significance? These are the questions that I want to pursue through the course of this chapter. To do so, it is necessary to move beyond the technological, and often technocratic, framework within which most discussions of post-photography have so far been conducted. We should be suspicious about talk of a technological revolution or of an emergent information age. The question of technology, as I shall argue, is not at all a technological question. What seem to me of the utmost importance are the social and cultural forces that are stimulating the development of automatic and cybernetic vision. The new image technologies have been shaped by, and are informed by, particular values of western culture: they have been shaped by a logic of rationality and control; and they are informed by a culture that has been both militaristic and imperialistic in its ambitions. In this light, we may be less impressed with the techno-revolutionary claims being made about the transition from chemical photography to electronic imaging. In refusing to fetishise the technologies, we are less likely to experience the disturbing sense of future shock that David Hockney invokes, and more able to recognise and acknowledge the continuities and transformations of particular dynamics in western culture.

BEYOND THE REALITY PRINCIPLE?

I want to begin by looking at what I would call the techno-fetishistic approach to new image technologies. What is immediately striking about it is the feeling of euphoria and the sense of omnipotence that these new technologies can arouse. There is an exultant sense of unbounded possibilities being opened up:

Photographers will be freed from our perpetual constraint, that of having, by definition, to record the reality of things, that which is really occurring. . . . Freed at last from being mere recorders of reality, our creativity will be given free rein.[4]

The introduction to a recent conference programme is more flamboyant still. Here we are told that 'the increasing progress in digital images and the perfecting of display and multisensorial interaction systems, henceforth, make it possible to immerse oneself physically in totally constructed symbolic, visual, sonorous and tactile spaces'. The new computer images, it continues,

these beings which achieve such a singular hybridisation of the intelligible and the visible, give us access to a new world, a tabula rasa, where the most gestural metaphors and the most formal logic, the most spontaneous movements and the most tortuous models, are inextricably intertwined.

How are we to answer the Cassandras of derealisation? We have long dwelt in the land of images, and we know full well that illusion ceases where enjoyment begins.

We are offered experiences that shatter all certitude; experiences that 'ostensibly pose the problem of the nature of reality, and that of our relationship to its representations'.[5] Suddenly released from the mundane reality we have always had to come to terms with, we have the freedom now to enter new worlds, 'the worlds we wish to know'. For those who 'conspire in electronic visualisation', there can no longer be any meaningful return to some 'authentic reality'. According to Gene Youngblood,

The fear of 'losing touch with reality', of living in an artificial domain that is somehow 'unnatural', is for us simply not an issue, and we have long since elected to live accordingly. What matters is the technical ability to generate simulations and the political power to control the context of their presentation. Moralistic critics of the simulacrum accuse us of living in a dream world. We respond with Montaigne that to abandon life for a dream is to price it exactly at its worth. And anyway, when life is a dream there's no need for sleeping.[6]

One is forcibly struck by the idealisation of the new technologies and by the quasi-mystical feelings that they arouse.

These are powerful expressions of fantasy and desire. What is significant, however, is that they are articulated through the discourse of science and rationality. The discussion of image futures quickly translates into one about computers and their logic. The computer is the symbol of omnipotent reason. For Youngblood, the computer is the ultimate metamedium, the medium that can simulate, and thereby contain or become, all other media (and image generation is just one part of its multimedia domain). Indeed, it may well be 'the most profound development in the history of symbolic discourse'; it is possible 'to view the entire career not only of the visual arts but of human communication in general as leading to this Promethean instrument of representation', this 'universal machine'.[7] The universal machine is (western) scientific rationality brought to its culmination. Finally reason has been harnessed to overcome worldly limitations and to make all things possible.

In this ideal domain, the mundane laws of reality are suspended and transcended, and all phenomena exist virtually, that is to say they exist in effect, 'for all practical purposes', though not in actual fact. Thus, 'if photography is making marks with light, then computer imaging is a kind of photography, but one in which the "camera" is only a point in virtual space and the "lens" is not a physical object but a mathematical algorithm that describes the geometry of the image it creates'.[8] Computer images may 'exist informally in an intuitive space with other visual objects, but they derive from a formal space in the computer's memory'.[9] What is created, it is argued, is a new kind of data space – a virtual logical space – and the image exists essentially in this space 'as a kind of Platonic ideal':

> We gaze in fascination upon these digital simulacra: they possess an 'aura' precisely because they are simulacra, vivid chimera of a new kind of eidetic vision. They refer to nothing outside themselves except the pure, 'ideal' laws of nature they embody. They have that 'quality of distance' no matter how many degrees of manipulative freedom we have over them, because they exist in the dematerialised territory of virtual space.[10]

Through the creation of this simulated and surrogate reality, it is suggested, our sense of, and allegiance to, older realities may be fundamentally transformed.

At one level, it is a discourse on pure reason and on the purity of reason. But it is more than this. What is desired in this worldview is the revitalisation and re-enrichment of reason. Contemporary society is experienced in terms of a crisis of imagination and creativity. For Youngblood, it is about trying to change impoverished attitudes and values, about 'trying to rethink ourselves, realign ourselves, trying to live up to our troubled and inarticulate sense of new realities'. This process of re-socialisation, he suggests,

> presupposes an ability to hold continuously before ourselves alternative models of possible realities, so that we might visualise and conceptualise other ways of being in the world. It implies not merely 'consciousness raising' but the redefinition and reconstruction of consciousness. It is comparable to religious conversion, psychotherapy, or other life-changing experiences in which an individual literally 'switches worlds'

through a radical transformation of subjective identity. This requires continuous access to alternative social worlds ... that serve as laboratories of transformation. Only in such autonomous 'reality-communities' could we surround ourselves with counter-definitions of reality and learn how to desire another way of life.[11]

The new technologies are seized upon as possible means to construct an alternative culture, and maybe even a new age. In this age, this new renaissance, it is projected, reason may once again be united with imagination, and science and art may be harmoniously re-united.

Another way of life sounds desirable, but it is difficult to imagine that it can be served up courtesy of these new image-information technologies. This idea of new 'reality communities' is more a fantasy projection than a serious proposal for social change. Nonetheless, if we cannot believe in the radical programme of 'switching worlds', we can agree that the new technologies do raise important philosophical questions about actually existing reality. One agenda concerns how we know and apprehend the world – questions of epistemology, representation and truth. It is this question of veracity that David Hockney finds disturbing about post-photography. Digital technologies put into question the nature and function of the photograph/image as representation. The essence of digital information is that it is inherently malleable and plastic: 'The unique computer tools available to the artist, such as those of image processing, visualisation, simulation and network communication are tools for changing, moving and transforming, not for fixing, digital information.'[12] Through techniques of electronic montage and manipulation, what we once trusted as 'pictures of reality' can now be seamlessly, and undetectably, edited and altered.[13] The status of the photographic document as evidence is thereby called into doubt.

Whole new vistas are then opened up for the manufacture of fakes, fabrications and misinformation. The relation between the photographic image and the 'real world' is subverted, 'leaving the entire problematic concept of representation pulverised ... and destabilising the bond the image has with time, memory or history'. What this represents can, indeed, be justifiably described as 'a fundamental transformation in the epistemological structure of our visual culture.'[14] This is all the more so when the images are computer-generated rather than simply computer-manipulated. If the computer image appears 'realistic' – if it 'positively enshrines photographic realism as the standard, unquestioned model of vision' – it is the case that the referent is not, in fact, 'in the real world', but is itself an image, a mathematical-informational representation.[15] Reality is no longer represented, but is simultaneously modelled and mimicked. Through this process of simulation, the whole question of accuracy and of authenticity becomes not simply problematical, but apparently, at least, anachronistic and redundant.

This brings us to a second philosophical agenda occasioned by the proliferation of these imaging technologies. The crisis of the relation between image and reality raises questions concerning the status of the image realm. The techno-futurists emphasise particularly the ontological question of decidability between the real and the unreal. As Gene Youngblood puts it:

> a digitally processed photograph, for example, can no longer be regarded as evidence of anything external to itself. Digital scene simulation has deprived photography of its representational authority just as photography disqualified painting in the nineteenth century; but this time the question of representation has been transcended altogether.[16]

The dislocation of image from referent reinforces its perception as a domain in its own right. Through the problematisation of any indexical or referential relation to reality, the image-space, or data-space, assumes for itself an increasing autonomy. In the factitious space, the formal and logical space, of the computer, it has become possible to simulate a surrogate reality, a kind of alter-reality, which is difficult to differentiate from our conventional reality, and which, it is claimed, even threatens to eclipse it. It might seem as if what we have got used to calling the real world had been both displaced and replicated by a ghostly double. But maybe it was actually that the old reality was only ever an imperfect precursor or prefiguration of the emergent virtual world anyway. Maybe that old reality was only a kind of pre-technological simulation:

> We habitually think of the world we see as 'out there', but what we are seeing is really a mental model, a perceptual simulation that exists only in our brains. That simulation capability is where human minds and digital computers share a potential for synergy. Give the hyper-realistic simulator in our heads a handle on computerised hyper-realistic simulators, and something very big is bound to happen.[17]

The belief is that when we finally come to be immersed in this 'cyberspace' we shall be able to realise our true and full potential.

There is a new frontier, it would seem, and there are those who see themselves as the new settlers. The new image and simulation technologies are supposed to provide the doorway to new and other worlds: 'when you're interacting with a computer, you are not conversing with another person. You are exploring another world.'[18] This new world is an ideal world, a world beyond gravity and friction. In this world, human consciousness and intelligence are amplified. Cyberspace is imagined as 'an amusement park where anything that can be imagined and programmed can be experienced. The richness of the experiences that will be available in cyberspace can barely be imagined today.'[19] This, at its most hyperbolic, is 'where the interpersonal, interactive consciousness of the world mind is emerging ... where minds of tomorrow will mirror themselves, meet each other, enter the universe of information and knowledge'.[20] Metaphors turn mystical.

This is what they call 'imagining the future'. Computer images mark the shift to a new visual paradigm, to a new age when we shall see things differently:

> Visually-oriented computer interfaces, film, photography, and before them, painting and drawing, all changed the way people see the world. People ran screaming out of movie houses at the sight of the first extreme close-ups of giant faces on the screen. The Renaissance was influenced as much by the introduction of perspective as by the rediscovery of Greek philosophy. It is part of a cultural evolutionary process: every time a widely seen visual paradigm breaks into a new dimension, reality shifts a little. In the case of the cyberspace transformation (because of the nature of the digital computer), it looks like reality is going to change a lot.[21]

Of course, it is true that images have always served to disrupt our taken-for-granted and habitual sense of reality. And photography has had disturbing implications for what we have understood to be the real world, exposing us to the unreal dimensions of that reality and even encouraging us to believe that the captured image is somehow more real. But now we are asked to seriously consider the idea that images can, literally, displace and replace reality. We are asked to believe that we could inhabit this other-world of simulation.

What does it actually mean, though, to 'dwell in the land of images' and to 'abandon life for a dream'? If we aren't moved by this scenario, we might be tempted just to dismiss it as vacuous fantasy. Perhaps, however, we should take it seriously, in so far as it is a symptomatic reflection of the kind of world we are living in. We should take seriously the cultural, psychic, and also political, roots that nourish this desire and this vision. And we should consider it, not only in terms of its positive aspirations (to imagine and visualise other ways of being in the world), but also in terms of the negative motivations (discontentment with the perceived inadequacy of the existing world). In Freud's terms, this 'reality shift' might be seen in terms of strategies aimed at the 'avoidance of unpleasure'; it is about coping with frustration from the external world. To this end the new technologies can be mobilised, either to 'loosen the connection' with reality, or, alternatively, to 'remold' it.[22] Hasn't this instinctual need always been a driving force in technological innovation? We can follow Susan Sontag's insight that photography is both 'a defence against anxiety and a tool of power'.[23] In the light of a felt sense of insecurity, images are mobilised to achieve symbolic or imaginary possession over space: they are about containment and control.

43

VIRTUAL REALITY: INTO THE MICROWORLD

Everywhere the transparency of interfaces ends in internal refraction.

(Jean Baudrillard)

The idea that we are living in a simulation culture has by now become almost a cliché. We are already more than familiar with Jean Baudrillard's descriptions of simulacra and simulations, of a deterritorialised hyperreality, of images or models of a real without origin or reality. The idea has slipped almost effortlessly into the discourse of postmodernism, and we have actually come to feel rather comfortable with our new condition of derealisation. There is, of course, an important truth in this analysis. We do live in a world where images proliferate independently from meaning and referents in the real world. Our modern existence is increasingly one of interaction and negotiation with images and simulations which no longer serve to mediate reality. As Scott Lash has argued, postmodernism is centred around the problematisation of reality.[24] We now articulate our identity through coming to terms with the image rather than the reality. The system of images, apparently self-contained and auto-referential, comes to assume its own autonomy and authority.

But if there is a kind of truth in this analysis, what is its significance? What kind of truth is it? The spectacular culmination of this tendency to replace the world around us with an alternative space of images and simulations is the creation of so-called virtual reality environments. In this new computer-image technology, we can identify some fundamental aspects of the social and psychic investment in simulation culture. The terms 'virtual' or 'artificial' reality 'refer to the computer generation of realistic three-dimensional visual worlds in which an appropriately equipped human operator can explore and interact with graphical (virtual) objects in much the same way as one might in the real world'.[25] Through the use of a range of input devices (a helmet-mounted display panel, data-gloves, data-suit), it becomes possible to generate the simulation of a three-dimensional world in which the operator is an active and involved participant. It is as if he or she were inside the image, immersed in the new symbolic environment, with the 'means of interacting with that virtual world – of literally reaching in and touching the virtual objects, picking them up, interacting with virtual control panels, etc'.[26] The virtual environment is one in which cybernetic feedback and control systems mimic interaction with real objects, such that the environment appears to be real and can be used as if it were real.

Virtual reality technologies have emerged out of space and military programmes (an absolutely fundamental point, to which I shall return). The original developments involved techniques of telepresence and telerobotics, with the objective of controlling, or potentially controlling, operations at distant or hazardous sites (space and deep-sea exploration, battlefield situations, nuclear and toxic environments). If the means was to create the illusion of presence at such a site, the clear objective was to manage or transform real situations. In the projected US space station, for example, it is envisaged that the astronauts will be able to control a robot outside the station with 'the robot's camera system providing stereo images to the operator's head-mounted display while precisely miming his head movements, and the robot's dexterous end-effectors would be controlled by dataglove gestures'.[27] If the initial aim was to control reality through illusion, it became apparent that it was also possible to use the illusion in its own right. Such 'free-standing' applications could be used for a range of practical and commercial purposes: aircraft cockpit simulation to analyse the decision-making procedures of pilots under controlled conditions; architectural simulation to model buildings cheaply in virtual space before physical construction; surgical simulations for training medical students. It is this exploitation of 'pure' simulation that characterises virtual-reality systems proper.

And it is this dimension that has become the basis of subsequent educational and entertainment applications. There are already numerous companies in Britain (W Industries, Division), the United States (VPL, Autodesk) and Japan (Sharp, Mitsubishi, Sanyo) vying for what seems to be a burgeoning new market. It has already been announced that the world's first virtual-reality theme park will open in the Japanese city of Osaka. Already, and predictably – the key index, perhaps, of popular (read male) acceptance – the idea of cybersex and virtual pornography is on the cultural agenda. As yet, we should be clear, such virtual-reality applications are much less than perfect, and many technical problems still have to be resolved.[28] Nonetheless, there is a strong and growing belief in the potential of 'cyberspace entertainment'. Already it has become a matter of interest and speculation in the non-specialist press. What is so attractive about (the idea of) artificial worlds? What is it about the current dissatisfaction with 'real' reality that makes liberation through simulation – 'switching worlds' – seem so desirable?

As the idea of virtual-reality entertainment comes to public awareness, what is clear is that the imaginative mould has already been set: there is already a wholehearted agreement about its 'revolutionary' significance and a deafening consensus about its 'challenging' potential. The discourse turns out to be extremely predictable, and invariably quite pedestrian. The visionary cyberspace rhetoric embodies the all too familiar *imaginaire* of high-tech futurism. There is a clichéd feel. In all the material on virtual reality the same reference points are invoked over and over again. There is the almost obligatory mention of MIT's Media Lab, particularly as it has been mythologised by Stewart Brand. There are invariably quotations from the post-LSD Timothy Leary. Then we generally have a scattering of aphorisms from Jaron Lanier, described as 'the inventor of the EyePhone and DataGlove', who has become the techno-spiritual guru of the new movement: 'Information is alienated experience'; 'the computer is the map that you can inhabit'; 'a sharing of many imaginations'; 'the first medium to come along that doesn't narrow the human spirit' (and there's plenty more of this unsparkling visionary wisdom). And, of course, there is the almost religious reference to cyberpunk fiction writers like Bruce Sterling and, particularly, William Gibson. Gibson is the seer of seers. It was he who invented the very idea of cyberspace ('A consensual hallucination . . . A graphic representation of data abstracted from the banks of every computer in the human system. Unthinkable complexity . . . clusters and constellations of data',[29] and so on). Cyborg movies from *Tron* and *Blade Runner* to *Terminator 2* and *The Lawnmower Man* are also key points of reference. And, on top of all this science-fiction stuff, there is finally the inevitable reference to Baudrillard's writings on simulation and hyperreality.

This, when it's all shaken together, becomes the founding dogma through which all mortal beings might learn to find their way to the other world. These are the canonical texts, and seldom are they departed from. What it represents is the convergence of cybernetics, science fiction, postmodernism and New Age philosophy into a synthetic new utopianism. This convergence reflects the belief that we are at the threshold of a fundamental cultural and psychic transformation. We are told that virtual reality 'can be explored as a new mode, an instrument which questions how we have defined reality, where we draw lines, if the lines are necessary'. Virtual reality, it is said, opens up a 'universe of questions' and 'challenges us to the roots of how we define reality, presence, point of view, even identity'.[30] But who is being challenged? The new reality seems strangely more reassuring than disturbing; it can be readily and easily accommodated within prevailing cultural and philosophical agendas. It is a kind of fantasy-game icing on an old technological cake:

> There seems to be a flavour of longing here which I associate with the desire to converse with aliens or dolphins or the discarnate. For a long time now technology has been about the business of making the metaphorical literal. Let's reverse the process and start to reinfect ordinary reality with luminous magic. Or maybe this is just another expression of what may be the third oldest human urge, the desire to have visions.[31]

This is a discourse that is at once romantic and technocratic.

Theodore Roszak describes the emergence, in the 1960s and 1970s, of a counter-cultural movement in the United States of what he calls 'reversionary technophiles'. These 'guerrilla hackers' were entirely committed to computer electronics and global telecommunications, but sought to contain the new technology within an organic and communitarian context; what they sought was 'a synthesis of rustic savvy and advanced technology'.[32] It is difficult not to see the virtual-reality gurus as their latter-day successors. There is a direct lineage from Timothy Leary then to Timothy Leary now, and from Timothy Leary then to Jaron Lanier now. If the Californian counter-culture has been a crucial institutional base for this kind of techno-romanticism, there have also been variations and transformations in other social and geographical contexts. In Britain it has been New Age philosophy that has sustained the same, or similar, cultural objectives. Here we can see the interest in virtual reality developing in the context of a broader holistic metaphilosophy (*avant-garde* arts, chaos theory, 'soft' business philosophies, artificial intelligence, mysticism and ecology).

It is on the basis of these cultural-institutional interest groups that the discourse has subsequently diffused into mainstream and popular expectations about the promise of virtual-reality environments. It is not difficult to see why it is so appealing. If, in the past, technologies have created a sense of alienation, what these new technologies promise is nothing less than the 're-enchantment' of our mundane existence. 'You can go to distant planets and sit on the rings of Saturn', says Jaron Lanier. 'Enter the prehistoric world of the Tyrannosaurus or fly across cities.'[33] The discourse appeals because it is all about imagination and creativity. 'I know', writes another cyber-pioneer, 'that I have become a traveller in a realm that will be ultimately bounded only by the human imagination, a world without any of the usual limits of geography, growth, carrying capacity, density or ownership.'[34] And all this is so very acceptable because it never once challenges conventional (that is, Romantic) beliefs about the relationship between imagination and technology, art and science. The idea of such creative empowerment has always been central to the dominant technological *imaginaire*. But if the new technologies of the past always let us down, this time, finally, through this revolutionary new technology, there is a conviction that the ambition will be realised. In the world of virtual reality, at last, the ideal can be made real. In this (probably adolescent male) aspiration to creative omnipotence, the promise of a technological utopia is kept alive and kicking.

To understand this great belief in virtual-reality technologies, we need to understand what is so engaging about them and how they implicate their believer-users. What of themselves are these users investing in the virtual reality? What is the particular combination of rational and pre-rational pleasures that the technologies speak to? Discussions of these technologies have tended to place greatest emphasis on the seductive realism of the virtual-reality image. So realistic is it that it seems to be an alternative, and better, world of its own. But, if the fascination of the reality-effect is important, perhaps more so is the question of *interactivity*, and it is through this dimension, I think, that we can gain a better insight into the involvement of both conscious and unconscious energies in the new technologies. Virtual-reality environments, we are told, depend on the 'ability to interact with an alter ego':

> Interfaces form bridges between the real and the virtual and back again. We cross them to inhabit a strange place that is both concrete and abstract. A human hand grasping a real sensor holds, at the same time, a virtual paint brush or the controls of a virtual space vehicle.[35]

Interactivity is fundamental to simulation. What is exciting about the virtual-reality experience is that it involves 'interaction not with machines but with people mediated through machines: it's interaction with intelligence, with mind'. With this high level of interactivity, 'the environment changes as a result of the user's interaction with it, so that possibilities are generated that the author didn't think of'.[36] The objective (still a long way from being realised) is to make the interface as direct and immediate as possible: 'with a little imagination, one can envision human–machine interaction beyond a keyboard and mouse to the natural and kinesthetic way we encounter the real world. Input devices for our hands, arms, head, eyes, body, and feet can sense positions, gesture, touch, movement, and balance.'[37] The challenge is to create a direct connection between the technology and the human nervous system. The dream of eliminating the interface – 'the mind–machine information barrier' – reflects the desire to create a perfect symbiosis between the technology and its user.

What is this concern with the continuity of our relation to the computer? What is significant about the fantasy of union? There is a radical possibility. To provoke these questions could be to undermine our belief in human distinctiveness and to challenge our commonsense assumptions about self and identity. What kind of people are we becoming? Where, now, is the line between the natural and the artificial? These are questions raised, not only by virtual reality, but by artificial intelligence and cybernetic technologies more generally. They are not new questions, but they remain important ones.[38] It is this relation between technology and identity that has been developed in popular cultural explorations of cyborg culture – the fiction of William Gibson, for example, and also films like *Robocop* and *Blade Runner*.[39] What is significant about these kinds of cultural discourse, at their best, is that they have staged the encounter of the human and the technological in terms of radical confrontation; they have explored the risks and anxieties presented to our immediate sense of reality by new technologies.

What is notable about the champions of virtual reality, however, is their refusal of this radical confrontation. Their fantasy is structured round the evacuation of the real world, as it were, and the redefinition of self and identity in terms of the virtual and private microworld. Theirs is a regressive strategy. The microworld is a container: in it 'reality' is made tractable and composable. The virtual world 'fosters a fetishised relationship with the simulation as a new reality all its own based on the capacity to control, within the domain of the simulation, what had once eluded control beyond it'.[40] The real world that was once beyond is now effaced: there is no longer any need to negotiate that messy and intractable reality. The user is now reconceived as an aspect of, and operates entirely in terms of, the logical universe of the simulation. That is to say, the virtual-reality environment is 'user-friendly':

A 'user-friendly' machine, method, or mode of social organisation is one in which the user detects no difference between the environment and his idea of it. 'User-friendly' technology thus has to do with efficiency, and pure efficiency is an isomorphic state – a system in which all parts are in such coordination as to relieve all tension.[41]

Real experience is denied; everything is simulation. Desire and lack are disavowed. The tensions and frustrations and anxieties of existence are allayed: 'The expenditure of forces is restricted to mere maintenance and control. There is novelty, but nothing – strictly speaking – that is new.'[42]

The microworld is an artificially constructed domain which is self-contained and independent of the complexities of the real world 'outside'. The concept, developed originally in the context of educational computing by Seymour Papert, is that through exploring the particular properties of a microworld, it is possible to affirm 'the power of ideas and the power of the mind', and to do so without being disturbed by 'extraneous questions'.[43] The microworld is a safe and predictable environment. Like other kinds of micro-environment (board games or card games, for example), it is structured by a set of rules, a set of assumptions and constraints, and within the terms of these rules everything is possible, though nothing can be arbitrary or contingent. In the case of the virtual microworld, however, what is significant is that the user is removed from the fullness of 'real' human existence. As with video games, the machine 'takes the player out of this world'; it encourages 'disembodied activity'.[44] It is possible to become immersed, even drowned, in the simulated reality: 'Like Narcissus and his reflection, people who work with computers can easily fall in love with the worlds they have constructed or with their performances in the worlds created for them by others.'[45] In those who have gone 'into' the image you see the solipsism of what Baudrillard calls 'narcissistic refraction'.[46]

Virtual reality is a 'mind space'. It is projected as a domain of cognition and rationality, 'where minds of tomorrow will mirror themselves, meet each other, enter the universe of information and knowledge'.[47] In this sense, to enter the microworld is apparently to enter a world of order and reason. But it is more than this. The microworld is also responding to deeper needs and drives than those of reason. This image space is also a container and a scene for unconscious and pre-rational dramas: getting 'into' the image is also about acting out certain primitive desires and fantasies or about coming to terms with fears and anxieties. Philippe Dubois has argued that two mythological figures – Narcissus and Medusa – can symbolise our psychic investment in, and our neurotic ambivalence about, the image. The one reflects our (infant-ile) desire to take the image for real, to embrace it, and to become submerged in and joined with it. The other stands for the anxieties we experience in the face of the images we have created, for the conflicting feelings of attraction and repulsion, desire and fear, that are aroused by their power.[48]

In the image world of virtual reality, I would argue, the same psychic dramas are at stake. Thus, in Christopher Lasch's terms, the aspiration towards perfect symbiosis with the microworld may be rooted in the narcissistic longing for fusion. Such narcissistic regression, he suggests, seeks freedom from 'the prison of the body'; it is driven by an infantile 'longing for the complete cessation of tension'. Narcissism is a state in which the organism forms a closed unit in relation to its surroundings. It seeks to recover the lost, infantile, paradise:

> Narcissus drowns in his own reflection never understanding that it is a reflection. He mistakes his own image for someone else and seeks to embrace it without regard to his safety. The point of the story is not that Narcissus falls in love with himself, but, since he fails to recognise his own reflection, that he lacks any conception of the difference between himself and his surroundings.[49]

Narcissus was captivated by, and sought union with, his own image. The users of virtual reality, as I have been suggesting, may similarly be driven by the desire to embrace – to become one with, to form a closed unit with – the simulated image.

Alternatively, the possibility of virtual reality may arouse profound anxieties, and interaction with image simulations may be about the struggle to master those anxieties. Gillian Skirrow's observation about video games is insightful. She argues that there is, in our culture, a deep fear of technological power, and, consequently, there are 'anxieties about exploitation and manipulation, about inability to separate oneself from it':

> To this fear video games are in many ways the predictable male response: the video screen makes the fear visible, but obliquely, for like the Medusa, it must not be directly confronted; the visibility of the fear allows it to be expressed but remains unspoken; the quest for the performer's destiny occupies the fantasy space in which infantile battles were fought in the mother's body and won; the male references in the intertextuality of the content of the games gives the male player a sense of familiarity which helps him over the strangeness of the new technology; the domestic image and setting of the home computer constantly remind the performer of his mastery and his power to switch the machine off, even if it does beat him at his own game. And as his own game seems to be the rehearsing of his own death, to lose is only to affirm his own resurrection.[50]

In virtual-reality technologies, these kinds of anxiety and ambivalence promise to be raised to new levels. How to face this Medusa? The power of these new technologies stirs up turbulent feelings of desire and fear. The fantasies associated with entering 'into' this image space can reactivate infantile feelings of regression and omnipotence illusions. What will happen 'inside' this fantasy space? What will happen if the 'outside' world loses its reality?

HOSTILE VISION: SIMULATION, SURVEILLANCE – AND STRIKE

> On the evidence of the games the preferred male solution seems to be to bury themselves in the mother's body with their phantasy weapons and forget about the very real dangers in the world outside until these dangers manifest themselves as disputes about boundaries, as in the Falklands 'crisis', in which case they can be understood and dealt with by playing the war game, again.
> (Gillian Skirrow, 'Hellivision: an analysis of video grames', *Screen*)

In all the outpourings about the humane and creative potential of virtual-reality technologies, there are occasional references to the pioneering role of NASA and the US military. Little is made, however, of the significance of military research and development. Simulation technologies are simply and straightforwardly welcomed as a spectacular and beneficial 'spin-off' from the military project. What is not acknowledged is the scale of military involvement in this technological domain; it has been estimated that the US military alone accounts for about two-thirds of the global simulation and training market.[51] There has been little recognition of how extensive the role of simulation technologies has become in military activities, from training, through battlefield modelling, to combat management. What, then, is the nature and significance of the military development of vision technologies? In looking first at simulation technologies and then at surveillance systems, I want to suggest how fundamental they have become to contemporary military strategies. The Gulf War provided the showcase. What I also want to consider are the broader social implications of this militarisation of vision. What are the cultural, the ethical and the psychological consequences of the military-cybernetic project?[52]

A US army colonel argues that the conditions of modern warfare require advanced modelling capabilities. One such technique he describes as 'virtual prototyping', that is to say the creation of 'an engagement simulation of a battlefield, complete with friendly and threat systems'. This would allow developers to

> hypothesise a notional system and assign it certain technical parameters. The characteristics of that notional system can then be placed into a simulation and fought in a variety of scenarios. The operator of the notional system would be trained just as if that system were real.[53]

The virtual prototype is a kind of simulation game, a kind of war game. Like other kinds of game, this too is a closed world with its own internal logic and formalised rules. Like other computer games it too is a microworld. And the point about microworlds is that, whilst they are internally consistent, they are 'simpler than the open universe of which they are a partial model'; and this simplicity means that they 'cannot recognise or address entities or processes beyond those that are given or taught to them'.[54] The key question, then, concerns the significance of this ontological closure.

What becomes clear with military simulation is that the relation to the wider universe (what we should still call the real world) remains fundamental. In certain applications it might seem as if the simulation were 'pure', that is to say self-contained. The virtual prototype appears to be simply a hypothetical model. But it is increasingly the case that the simulation itself has become a strategic element in real-world confrontations. In the case of possible nuclear war, for example, the real consequences of engagement are terrifying:

> Thus the technological preparations and logistical analyses assume the atmosphere of a game, whose object is for each side to try to produce and maintain a winning scenario, a showing that victory is theoretically possible, a psychological and political effect. It is not so much a true standoff or 'deterrence' as a simulation of a standoff, an entirely abstract war of position. Like a video game, the object is not to win but simply to continue the race as long as possible, at ever-increasing speeds.[55]

A good example is the simulation testbed that was developed for the Strategic Defence Initiative (SDI). If it was not feasible to test SDI 'in a full deployment mode', what was possible was the simulation of 'sensor and battle management algorithms', with this simulation itself then functioning as a gaming strategy.[56]

At the same time that simulation becomes a weapon of 'real-world' military strategies, what we also see is the tendency for real wars, when they are waged, to assume the appearance of a simulation. There is a *derealisation* effect, which makes it *seem* as if the war is being conducted in cyberspace. The scale and speed of contemporary war are associated with an intensification of what Paul Virilio calls the 'logistics of perception'. 'The bunkered commander of total war suffers', he argues, 'a loss of real time, a sudden cutting-off of any involvement in the ordinary world'.[57] Simulation then becomes the form in which military activities are represented, and, for the commander, involvement in those activities is a question of interaction with this simulated image. Even for the unbunkered fighter pilot, the experience of combat becomes derealised: the US Air Force is reported to be currently developing a virtual-reality helmet 'that projects a cartoonlike image of the battlefield for the pilot, with flashing symbols for enemy planes, and a yellow-brick road leading right to the target'.[58] It is as if the simulation had effaced the reality it modelled; as if commander and fighter were engaged in mastering a game logic, rather than involved in impassioned, bloody and destructive combat. It is as if this were the case, but, of course, the truth is that it is not: mastery is an illusion, and reality always threatens to break through the simulation. The case of the USS *Vincennes*, which shot down an Iranian Airbus in 1988 is graphic. For nine months before it went to the Persian Gulf, the crew trained with simulated battlefield situations. The overflight of civilian airliners, however, was not included in the simulation, and with the reality – the very unsimulated reality – of the Airbus on 3 July the *Vincennes* could not cope:

> nine months of simulated battles displaced, overrode, *absorbed* the reality of the Airbus and electronic information of the moment. The Airbus disappeared before the missile struck: it faded from an airliner full of civilians to an electronic representation on a radar screen to a simulated target. The simulation overpowered a reality which did not conform to it.[59]

When it intruded into the military microworld, when its reality transgressed into the simulation, the implications for the airliner were fatally real.

The power of the simulation should not deceive us into believing that war is now a virtual occurrence. If military simulation reminds us of a video game, we should recognise that its objectives go far beyond symbolic mastery of the screen. We should remember that the simulation is a model of the real world, and that the ultimate objective is to use that model to intervene in that world. It is precisely the functions of telepresence and teleoperation that are crucial in this context. The computer-simulation technology is part of a cybernetic system, which includes sensors and weapon systems, to remotely monitor, and then to remotely control, real-world situations and events. If one agenda concerns the so-called man–machine interface (questions of ergonomics and interactivity), another concerns the interface between the simulation technologies and the real world. It is here that the technologies of surveillance become crucial.

Surveillance has, it is well known, been integral to the evolution of photography. Through being photographed, things become part of a system of information, which then opens up enormous possibilities of control. And new technologies have always been sought to enhance this capacity to monitor and record, to make it more extensive, more intrusive, more systematic, more furtive. The fundamental development in this trajectory of photographic surveillance was, undoubtedly, the externalisation of vision through aerial reconnaissance and intelligence.[60] What began in the nineteenth century with camera-carrying balloons has now culminated in the orbiting vision of surveillance satellites. And, of course, it is the military, above all, that has sustained this surveillance culture. 'From the original watch-tower through the anchored balloon to the reconnaissance aircraft and remote-sensing satellites,' Paul Virilio emphasises, 'one and the same function has been indefinitely repeated, the eye's function being the function of a weapon.'[61] It is to the information needs of the military that we can attribute the new generation of ultra-high-resolution cameras and other remote-sensing technologies; to its intelligence needs that we can ultimately attribute the new digital technologies of image processing and manipulation. The development of space reconnaissance has been associated with the increasing militarisation of vision.

Satellite surveillance technologies, euphemistically described as 'national technical means' (NTM), have been one of the most fundamental military developments in the twentieth century. The origins of the programme were in the 1960s when, in the context of the Cold War, there was a 'need to know' what was going on in the 'evil empire' behind the Iron Curtain. The programme was driven by the dream of 'being able to look down on events happening perhaps halfway around the world and watch them from right up close, virtually as they happened, the way an angel would'.[62] For a long time this panoptic ambition was frustrated by the low resolution of the images produced and by the indirectness and inconvenience of having to parachute film pods back to earth.

The real breakthrough came in the mid-1970s with the launching of the KH–11 series of satellites which use charge-coupled devices to transmit digital signals back to a receiving station at Fort Belvoir in Virginia, and thence to the CIA's National Photographic Interpretation Center in Washington DC. The KH–11 is like a television camera in space, and is able to combine near real-time monitoring capability with high resolution images (probably six inches across). Subsequently this keyhole series of satellites has been enhanced by a new generation of technologies that allow them to 'see' at night and to 'penetrate' through cloud cover. The so-called Lacrosse satellite, launched at the end of 1988, uses radar imaging to provide all-weather day and night coverage. The enhanced KH–11 (sometimes called the KH–12) was launched in 1989 and has infra-red imaging capabilities for night-time surveillance. It is believed that currently the United States uses two KH–11s, two Advanced KH–11s and one Lacrosse (though the relationship between the Advanced KH–11 and the Lacrosse remains unclear).[63]

In addition to the $5 billion that the United States invests in space reconnaissance each year, there is now a growing commercial involvement, particularly with the development of the French SPOT programme. There is a constituency which sees this development as beneficial, opening the way for independent arms-control verification and also for crisis monitoring (Chernobyl, oil slicks, and so on).[64] It appears, however, that the line between commercial and pacific applications, on the one hand, and military applications, on the other, has become extremely thin. SPOT advertisements have promoted military applications, promising to provide the technical means for 'a new way to win' to those who buy its intelligence. It is also the case that military agencies are turning to commercial satellites to supplement their own intelligence activities. In the face of proliferating military agendas – early warning, target location, damage assessment, anti-terrorist applications – it would seem that international peacekeeping and monitoring functions will only come a poor second. Transparency from space is more likely to sustain the military information society than to undermine it.

The details of space reconnaissance and surveillance technologies are arcane and are shrouded in secrecy. The point, however, is to be clear about the scale and the implications of military vision. As to the scale, it is estimated that the United States can now monitor 42,000 separate targets across the globe. This surveillance is also increasingly a matter of continuous vision, constantly 'revisiting' targets in order to monitor significant change, watching through all weathers, round the clock. The earth is thereby 'becoming encapsulated by whole networks of orbital devices whose eyes, ears, and silicon brains gather information in endless streams and then route it to supercomputers for instantaneous processing and analysis – for a kind of portrait of what is happening on planet Earth painted electronically in real time'.[65] That is the manic ambition for these 'national technical means'.

If the very scale of military intelligence activities is itself alarming, there are broader implications to these developments. What I want to emphasise is the way in which optical technologies have come to function within total weapon systems. Surveillance and simulation technologies feed off each other. And surveillance and simulation technologies together feed into the control of a new generation of 'smart', vision-guided strike weapons. Thus, the most advanced surveillance satellites are involved, not only in active reconnaissance, but also in digital terrain mapping. The US Defence Mapping Aerospace Agency is currently involved in producing digital data bases of the earth's surface, and these are then used for such applications as mission training and rehearsal simulation, plotting low-altitude flight routes, missile navigation, and precision weapon-targeting. Perhaps the ultimate achievement to date has been the Tomahawk cruise missile. For most of its lethal journey, the Tomahawk navigates through a radar altimeter which compares the topography of its flight path against detailed computer maps stored in its memory. As it reaches its 'terminal end point', a new guidance system takes over, with a small digital camera comparing the view from the nose cone against a library of stored images prepared from earlier satellite photography of specified targets.[66] The space-defence systems that are currently being developed are simply the ultimate extrapolation of this systemic approach to weapons technologies. The Strategic Defence Initiative has been described in terms of the cohesion of Surveillance, Acquisition, Tracking and Kill Assessment (SATKA).[67] It was about the total coordination of surveillance, simulation and strike technologies to ensure military omniscience and omnipotence. With the end of the Cold War, this particular programme may be suspended, but the overall project continues, with the aim of policing the new world order.

What I want to emphasise are the ontological implications, and then the ethical consequences, of this military-cybernetic project. The new systems of surveillance, simulation and strike technologies operate across, and through, two different levels of reality, the virtual and the material. It is the split between these two realities, I would argue, that underpins the contemporary experience of existential dislocation and moral disengagement. It is right to observe that there has been a kind of derealisation of military engagement: postmodern warfare is, indeed, increasingly a mediated affair, characterised by simulation, telepresence and remote control. But this insubstantial and synthetic reality has an interface with another reality that we are still right to call our real world. This world is defined as the world of targets; new satellite images can turn entire countries into targeting information (into 'target-rich environments').

When these targets are 'taken out', however, they scream; and when they are 'neutralised', they bleed. The commander and the fighter are beings in the world. They have bodily existences, and they should understand the realities of pain and suffering. They live in a universe of moral obligation, and they should be aware of their ethical responsibilities and obligations. But they also live and exist otherwise. They also function as components in the virtual domain of the military technological system. And within that system, they have a disembodied existence: they operate at a purely cognitive level, and their engagement with the real world becomes indirect, mediated through the images on video screens. Within the system of that microworld, existential and moral questions are meaningless: 'Though individuals inside a military system do make decisions and set goals, as links in the chain of command they are allowed no choices regarding the ultimate purposes and values of the system.'[68] The logic of the system prevails over individual and social morality.

The video game player is 'apparently a double or a split subject since the game is simultaneously in the first person (you in the real world pressing keys) and the third person (a character on the screen, such as a knight, who represents you in the world of fiction)'.[69] The military game player is, similarly, a double or a split subject, a first person pushing buttons and a third person involved in the combat on the screen. But with the military commander and fighter there is a more disturbing dimension to this splitting process. James Grotstein describes psychotic behaviour, in which the psychotic 'may projectively identify a split-off, disembodied twin self who is free to move about at will, leaving the body self abandoned'. This, he argues, 'is a defence mechanism which, at its most benign, postpones confrontation with some experience that cannot be tolerated, but which, at its worst, can negate, destroy, and literally obliterate the sense of reality'.[70] This, it seems to me, is highly suggestive. The psychoanalyst, Hanna Segal, also observes this psychotic tendency. In contemporary military activity, she comments, 'there is a kind of prevailing depersonalisation and de-realisation. Pushing a button to annihilate parts of the world we have never seen is a mechanised split off activity.' 'This obliteration of boundaries between reality and fantasy', she believes, 'characterises psychosis.'[71]

TO BE SERGEANT ABLE F. COOPER

Humankind lingers unregenerately in Plato's cave, still revelling, its age-old habit, in mere images of the truth.

(Susan Sontag, *On Photography*)

What I want to address, in conclusion, is the relationship between image technologies and vision cultures. More specifically, I am concerned with what the developments I have been looking at in this chapter tell us about the western culture that has spawned them.

Images have a particular resonance in this culture and they have been used in particular ways, for particular objectives. Two broad agendas can be said to have shaped and defined western self-identity. The first has been the principle of scientific and technological rationality: 'Modern western culture is, in short, the rational, self-rationalising and rationality-conscious culture par excellence.' The second has been 'a uniquely intensive confrontation with other cultures', that is to say the imperial and post-imperial encounter with non-western societies.[72] In this encounter, the west has always resisted the recognition of its own difference and particularity in favour of justifying its successful domination on the basis of the superior, that is to say universal, truth of its values and its project. What Georges Corm calls the 'narcissistic history of its modernity', is rooted in the passionate belief that, whilst non-western cultures are eternally frozen in the Dark Ages, 'the flowering of its own civilisation was the founding moment of universal modernity'.[73] And that modernity was precisely about the harnessing of science and technology to human progress. Technological rationality has been fundamental to the justification and legitimation of western hegemony over other cultures.

This presumed reciprocity of technological superiority and cultural supremacy is quite clear in the discourses surrounding the new image technologies. There is a tendency, as I have argued, to consider the end of chemical photography and its replacement by digital-image technologies as straightforwardly a matter of scientific and technological progress. There is the common sentiment that, like other technological innovations, these new electronic techniques will enhance human possibilities and potential – in this case, that they will create new kinds of vision, other ways of seeing, alternative worlds of experience. This progress is associated with processes of *universalisation*: the computer is the *universal machine* and the images it generates are a *universal medium*. According to Pierre Lévy, the universal machine subsumes all earlier and all other cultures. If, he argues, 'we take into account the appearance of a new temporality; the leap in storage and processing capacity; the redefinition of knowledge and know-how; the change in behaviour, sensibility and intelligence; and also the universal scope of the information culture, then comparison with the shift from pre-history to history does not seem absurd'. The universal machine, in which all cultural forms are translated into the same digital language, brings us to the moment of 'post-history'.[74] Insofar as it provides the logical structure for culture in general, and for each art form in particular, it represents the supreme vindication and fulfilment of western culture. With the development of new information and cybernetic technologies, all cultures and cultural forms converge, and are harmonised within the universal discourse of western rationality.

What are we to think of this post-history? Are we persuaded by these claims to universalism? In the nineteenth century, chemical photography was hailed as the first universal language. We can see more clearly now how those old photographic technologies reflected the vision and the values of western culture.[75] In the name of universalism they were mobilised against, and intruded into, other cultures. It is difficult to believe that it could be otherwise with the new digital electronic technologies. When we look at this new so-called universal medium, we can see that it, too, reflects, and reinforces, a *particular* vision culture. Like nineteenth-century photography, it, too, is western-eyed. Through the course of empire, the image has monitored and documented 'alien' populations. From nineteenth-century anthropological records through to contemporary photo-reconnaissance in the new world order, observation and control have always been closely related. The other is diminished by the look, and, at the same time, the west's superiority seems to be confirmed.

For western culture – the culture of Enlightenment – knowledge is associated primarily with vision (illumination). Vision is the most detached (perhaps we might say the most deaf) of the senses, underpinning the ideal of objective and scientific (value-free) knowing. It is the eye that penetrates to the essence and truth of things. On this basis, it then becomes possible to believe that superiority in vision, that is to say in vision technologies, is itself a reflection of the inherent supremacy of western civilisation. A small example from the Gulf War reveals this claim to universal reason, and also the orientalist attitude concealed in the discourse of vision. Saddam Hussein was accused of keeping his equipment 'under wraps'. This implication was that he was deceitfully avoiding the scrutiny of vision and the light of truth:

Saddam Hussein's armies last week seemed to be enacting a travesty of the Arab motif of veiling and concealment. In the Arab world, women often veil themselves not because they are punished or shamed but because women, who produce life, must be protected, as a plant in the desert might be. Houses turn inward, the living quarters hidden. The true treasures are concealed. Saddam similarly appeared – or wished to appear – to be masking his strength, hiding it in bunkers in the sand.

In contrast, the report emphasises that 'Generals and Presidents need a clear eye for the truth'.[76] No doubt the spy satellites out in the 'deep black' helped to make that eye more clear.

When we talk about an imperialism of the image now, however, we may mean something different: we may also be referring to the hyper-real proliferation of images in these times. We are then expressing our feeling that images have become an autonomous force, a power in their own right; and we are articulating a belief that older realities, and senses of reality, might become eclipsed by this power of the image. The image, it seems, has itself become the substance of a new world, a virtual world. An awareness of this uncharted land stirs an atavistic western reflex: the desire for discovery, exploration and colonisation. Techno-explorers now gaze upon this factitious landscape as Cook must once have surveyed the *tabula rasa* of Botany Bay. Or, as one techno-enthusiast distastefully puts it (invoking a different forbear), 'Columbus was probably the last person to behold so much usable and unclaimed real estate (or unreal estate) as those cybernauts have discovered.'[77] In this technologically unreal estate everything seems possible. It is like the Torec in Primo Levi's story 'Retirement Fund':

> You understand: whatever sensation one might wish to obtain, one only has to pick a tape. Do you want to go on a cruise to the Antilles? Or climb Mount Cervino? Or circle the earth for an hour, in the absence of gravity? Or be Sergeant Able F. Cooper, and wipe out a band of Vietcong? Well, you lock yourself up on your room, slip on the helmet, relax and leave it to him, to the Torec.[78]

This is, indeed, a brave new world.

Only it is not a new world. Everything is strangely familiar and very unsurprising. For this is no more than a virtual extension to our habitual western civilisation. This is a world of omnipotence fantasy where to be or to do something it is only necessary to wish it. It is a world outside of morality where we can all be Sergeant Able F. Coopers without facing the consequences. In this timeless world we can play out our most unreasonable fantasies. There is nothing culturally innovative in this. But this is the image world that our western narcissism recognises and is drawn, in fascination, to embrace. As with the Torec, 'while the tape lasts, it is indistinguishable from reality'. We can try, our age-old habit, to linger inside the image. But when the tape stops, that other reality is still there waiting, with all its discontents.

Chapter 3
SIGHTS OF WAR

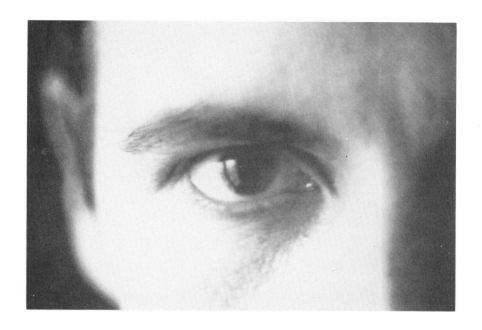

3

SIGHTS OF WAR

Augen weltblind,
Augen im Sterbegeklüft,
Augen Augen:

(Eyes world-blind,
eyes in the fissure of dying,
eyes eyes)
    (Paul Celan, 'Zuversicht')

O so much has vanished
in smoking fiery skies.
The closing century's shadow is
cast across all our eyes.
        (Tony Harrison,
'The gaze of the gorgon')

THE WATCHERS AND THE WATCHED

The trend in military technology is clear: 'new global networks of sensors keeping track in real time of most targets ... and long-range, non-nuclear, very accurate weapon delivery systems embedded in that network – all tied together with digital computers'.[1] This became quite apparent in the war against Iraq, and the role of vision technologies in these systems was even more clear.[2] Military strategy has always been about seeing and not being seen; about combining vision with stealth. It is the increasing automation and systemation of this principle, however, that makes the new generation of weapons 'smart' and even 'brilliant'.

From the earliest days we were told of the American spy satellites orbiting across the Middle East. Iraq was being 'surveyed from space and pinned down for precise military surgery'.[3] In this war, it became ever more apparent that the weapons of destruction had electronic eyes too. Aircraft like the American F–15E and the British Tornado were equipped with an imaging system which illuminates objects with infra-red beams, allowing low-altitude flying and the location of targets in the desert night. In the nose of Apache helicopters was a forward-looking infra-red navigation and targeting system that projected information onto screens in the visors of the crews' helmets. We also learned

63

about how the Tomahawk cruise missile had a 'mind of its own'; fired, and then forgotten, it could 'see' its deadly way to the target. Through its vision guidance system, the missile was able to achieve the 'precision' penetration of a 'surgical strike' – 'down the air vent' and 'through the front door'. Then, after the strike had been launched, photo-reconnaissance aircraft would sweep across the skies of Kuwait and Iraq to undertake 'battle-damage assessment', feeding their photo-information back into the central intelligence computers. The war was, quite literally, a showcase for western image technologies. It was a war between the watchers and the watched.

These high-tech weapon systems dominated our perception of the war, creating a sense of technological euphoria. We saw what they did to enemy targets (though the sanitised images we saw did not reveal what to 'cleanse' or 'neutralise' really meant). But, as Robert J. Lifton has argued, we are less clear about what they were doing to the watchers. What they brought about, he suggests, was a process of psychic numbing: 'the splitting or inner division of parts of the individual mind, in this case a separation of knowledge from feeling. We know that our weapons are murderous, but we cannot afford to feel the pain of death at the other side of them.'[4] In this war, soldiers and spectators alike were drawn in to a new kind of 'tele-topology': no longer 'tele-vision', but now the immediacy of 'tele-action'.[5] And, as they entered into the image, both soldiers and spectators, they became detached from reality and its painful principle.

For the soldier to be able to launch his precision weapons, it is necessary for him to achieve some kind of moral dissociation. As Zygmunt Bauman argues, the victims must be psychologically invisible. Killing must be done 'at a distance', through technological mediation, without the shock of direct confrontation and violence; it is necessary to break the causal link between the firing button and the deaths that follow. This kind of psychological insulation is likely to be enhanced if the victims are 'optically separate' from their killers.[6] What the Gulf War made clear, however, was that moral invisibility was not necessarily undermined by optical visibility, at least by certain kinds of mediated and remote visibility.

In the war, we saw that the vision of the long camera shot could sustain the same kind of moral dissociation. The silent movie filmed from the bomb bay or from the nose of the missile could have the same numbing sense of distance. What became more clear in this war, however, was how far this rationalisation of vision could be pushed. Here we had an apparently greater visual proximity between the killer and his victim. Indeed, the missile-nose view of the target simulated a super-real closeness that human beings could never attain. Yet this remote–intimate kind of watching could sustain the moral detachment of earlier military technologies. The visible was separated from the sound and feeling of pain, from the smell and taste of burning and death. We could zoom in on the action, but the enemy remained a faceless alien. For us, the voyeurs, the reality of their deaths became de-realised.

The Gulf War was a screen-gazing war. Through the cameras in their guided weapons, the western military forces were able to replay their destruction of enemy targets to analyse the pinpointedness of their accuracy. Through the replays, they could re-activate the *frisson* of excitement: 'I am now going to show you the luckiest man in Iraq on this particular day', General Schwarzkopf bantered to the world's media as he showed them footage of an Iraqi vehicle passing through the cross-hairs of a bomb sight shortly before the bomb 'took out' the bridge it had been travelling across.[7] It was perhaps the most costly tracking shot ever. But to watch it, to linger over its slow-motion precision, was to know what technological supremacy was all about.

Meanwhile, back in the west, other screen-gazers could tele-consume these same images (or some of them, at least) in their homes. The new weapons proved their worth telegenically. We could even listen to American generals giving voice-over commentary on the video bombing. The high-tech strikes were played over and over on the western networks, watched and then re-watched. Yes, it *was* the Nintendo war. That phrase has become probably the biggest cliché of the war, but it remains a telling observation and judgement. It *was* like a video-game war. However, if the war was on our screens, its truth was screened out. Remote images obscured distant realities. Through the evidential force of the image, we knew about the war, but it was a kind of derealised warfare we were knowing. It was at once a way of seeing and a way of not seeing. If was possible to be a voyeur before an image, and yet to be deaf to its reality.[8]

But the reality was always there. And there was always the danger that the images might eventually give access to that reality. Certain videos were only for private screening. General Schwarzkopf did not want the world to see what the camera saw on the driver's face as it was propelled into the cab of another Iraqi lorry. And what of the night-vision shots from an Apache helicopter (some of which eventually leaked out)? 'Even hardened soldiers', it was reported, 'hold their breath as Iraqi soldiers, as big as football players on the television screen, run with nowhere to hide. These are not bridges or aeroplane hangers. These are men.' The Iraqi soldiers looked 'like ghostly sheep flushed from a pen – bewildered and terrified, jarred from sleep and fleeing their bunkers under a hellish fire. One by one they were cut down by attackers they could not see.'[9] These images had to be censored. They were too eloquent records of the west's technological supremacy (or of the deadly expertise it calls supremacy, at least).

But not all 'disturbing' images could be screened out. As the war developed, the repressed reality had to break through. The watched had to implicate the watcher. On 13 February 1991, at Baghdad's Amiriya air-raid shelter, we saw the first real pictures of burning, mutilation and death. For the first time we saw the faces and heard the voices of the victims. Television news felt that it was necessary to 'edit' these images, because of their 'disturbing nature'. No doubt they would disturb our unreal sense of a sanitised war without bloodshed, and show how deadly precise precision weapons can be. And again, 'apocalyptically', on the road from Basra, reality threatened to spill over the images. The carnage made a mockery of surgical strikes and Nintendo wars. 'Far from the smart bomb videos and "target-rich environment" jargon', wrote one correspondent, 'the grim reality of war is a horror to behold.' An American intelligence officer, he reports, 'lifted his camera to snap a photo of a cluster of blackened bodies. Then he let the camera drop.'[10] The reality principle was, for a moment at least, reasserting itself.

From this final 'turkey-shoot', we have an image, a charred mask of ash, that was once an Iraqi soldier's face. Already it has been hailed as a classic war photograph; it has come to symbolise the 'reality of war'. It was, says, Harold Evans, 'a necessary shock': 'It was a solitary individual in the transfixation of a hideous death. Before this, it had been possible to enjoy the lethal felicity of designer bombs as some kind of video game.' Here we are confronted with the consequences of our belief in this 'just war'. And here too, through this image, we could experience 'an elemental human sympathy'. 'The disputed photograph', Evans writes, 'did something to redress the elusive euphoria of a high-tech war.'[11] But did it? Could it? The reality, of course, was that this was, precisely, the outcome of the video-game war fantasy. What could the still silence of this corpse tell us about post-heroic warfare? Of course, those who have seen this image 'will never forget it'. But, what will they remember?

The war showed us something about the role of images in our society; something about our culture of viewing and ourselves as viewers. It gave us some insights, particularly into the relationship between vision and morality in our western culture. Through the new vision technologies it became possible to obscure the reality that there were real people, living others, somewhere on the other side of the electronic image. 'Four or five times a day', John Berger writes, 'the public received a TV lesson about how to become deaf to the voice of their memory, of their conscience or of their imagination.'[12] We could see, but we were deaf to what we saw. We were de-linked from the real world, from the reality of listening and feeling and responding to the war. Drawn too far into the image, we were morally knocked out and neutralised.

* * * * *

THE WAR, THE SCREEN, THE CRAZY DOG AND POOR MANKIND

We are faced with a paradox; we are struggling both to retain such civilised capacity as we are capable of and at the same time to make evident the primitive and dangerous nature of the situation.

(Wilfred Bion, *Bion in New York and São Paulo*)

What happened in the television coverage of the Gulf War? What happened to us, its viewers?

There is a basic assumption that the role of the media is all about providing information for the rational and reasoning citizen so that he or she may consequently make informed judgements about the world's events. In times of war, however, it is clear that the ideal may not be sustainable. Informing the public 'at home' has to be balanced against other criteria, such as military security; the risks to morale that might result from showing real war (the Vietnam syndrome); or the strategic value of exploiting the media for disinformation and propaganda purposes. The issue, then, is to what extent, under these adverse conditions, it is possible still to hold on to the ideals of democratic media.

This is the major preoccupation for both David Morrison and Philip Taylor. In *Television and the Gulf War*, Morrison reassures us that, together, the coalition forces and the coalition media got it about right. And the coalition audience appreciated how right they had got it. Morrison's audience surveys revealed that a massive 86 per cent were 'satisfied' with the coverage of the war. On the question of reliability and accuracy, 'it was obvious that a great deal of trust existed towards television news on the part of the viewer'. On the question of secrecy, it is clear to Morrison that 'the viewer had a very good understanding of the strictures placed on the flow of news – far more so than was the case during the Gulf conflict'. And then there was the simple matter of taste and decency. Television has 'a responsibility not to present surprise shocks. . . . Very few people really wish for the full horror of war to be shown on their screens.' Television was discreet, and it showed 'fairness'.[13] And that's about it as far as Morrison is concerned. This 86 per cent kind of media sociology doesn't see it as its business to look beyond or behind 'satisfied'.

Philip Taylor is more engaging in his *War and the Media*, though he too is caught up in the same old familiar 'public opinion' agenda as Morrison. What concerns him are the consequences of increasingly efficient propaganda techniques for democratic media. In this latest war, the coalition established a 'controlled information environment' such that 'it became virtually impossible to distinguish between what was simply information and what was in fact propaganda'. The ideal is that television should be a 'window on the world'; the reality was that 'the window becomes a mirror for the images generated by those controlling the information'. Like a good many other commentators, Taylor concludes that 'there were essentially two wars going on: the war itself, fought by the coalition's combined military forces against the regime of Saddam Hussein, and the war as portrayed by the media'.[14]

The logic of Taylor's argument pushes towards the conclusion that the principles of rational knowledge and opinion formation were overwhelmed in this media war. He points to the CNN phenomenon, whereby 'television war addicts were in a sense mesmerised by the live coverage, reducing their capacity to stand back from the images objectively or critically'. More than this even: 'As for the role of journalists as custodians of the public's right to know, the Gulf War has presented a new challenge: the public's apparent desire *not* to know beyond the sketchiest details what is going on while it is going on.'[15] The very idea of a rational and reasoning public seems to have exploded. But war is an exceptional state, and maybe propaganda is only information by other means. 'So long as the truth comes out in the end,' Taylor suggests, 'the democratic publics of Britain and the United States do indeed seem prepared to suspend their right to know, provided they believe the war to be just and the anticipated gains worth the price of a certain number of professional soldiers.'[16] Even as it is apparently overwhelmed, the ideal of the fourth estate can be salvaged as the fundamental reference point. In the end, being mesmerised is treated as, probably, only a temporary aberration of the basically rational, knowledge-seeking model citizen.

Christopher Norris's *Uncritical Theory* is also concerned with reason and its vicissitudes. He is more profoundly concerned, however. Like other commentators, Norris accepts that the Gulf War can be described as a 'postmodern' war, 'an exercise in mass-manipulative rhetoric and "hyper-real" suasive techniques'. He points to the 'extraordinary inverse relationship between extent of coverage and level of informed public grasp' and to the 'mood of collective indifference to issues of factual or documentary truth that enable such a mass of false information to circulate largely unchallenged from day to day', concluding that there was 'a wholesale collapse of the "public sphere" of informed debate'.[17] Norris inscribes his discussion of the war within a broader debate and polemic directed against the philosophers of postmodernism who, he believes, are actively promoting and encouraging irrationalist and counter-Enlightenment values. His point of both departure and termination is Baudrillard's much-maligned essays on the Gulf War. It is Baudrillard's absurd belief, says Norris, that 'truth has gone the way of enlightened reason and suchlike obsolete ideas', and it is his mad contention that 'we had better make peace with this so-called "postmodern condition", rather than cling to an outworn paradigm whose truth claims no longer possess the least degree of operative (i.e. suasive or rhetorical) force'.[18] Against the 'intellectual fad' of postmodernism, Norris wants to vindicate, and to re-ground, what he calls 'enlightenment truth-seeking discourse'. It is 'the issues of real-world truth and falsehood that provide the only basis for reasoned opposition on the part of conscientious objectors'.[19] Postmodernism is presented as a kind of propaganda and misinformation campaign within the intellectual world. It is as if the perversion of communication and the confusion of Reason could be laid at the door of this thing called postmodernism. And Baudrillard is the Great Satan.

In their different ways, at different levels of abstraction, and with differing degrees of success, Morrison, Taylor and Norris are all concerned with what happened to the informational public sphere and to reasoned debate during the Gulf War. How we hold on to critical and ethical Reason has become a fundamental issue in the aftermath of the war, and quite rightly so. What I want to draw attention to here, however, are the limits to the way in which this issue is posed. The limits, that is, to an exclusively rationalist approach to Reason. What interests me are the conditions of possibility of reason, which must necessarily take into account what lies before or beyond Reason; and then, more than that, the uses to which reasoning is put. The psychoanalyst Wilfred Bion once suggested that academic theories, just as much as commonsense theories, might represent 'a way of blocking the gap of our ignorance about ourselves. . . . We can produce a fine structure of theory in the hope that it will block up the hole for ever so that we shall never need to learn anything more about ourselves either as people or organisations.'[20] To imagine the public sphere in terms of rationality alone does, I would suggest, 'block up the hole', inhibiting any real understanding of what happened to us as spectators of the war (and also any sense of how it might have happened differently).

Such an approach reproduces in academic discourse our spontaneous desire to see ourselves as rational animals. In watching Gulf War television, however good or bad it was, we think of ourselves as having made reasoned judgements about the rights and wrongs of the conflict. But did we? Ernest Larsen puts forward an alternative possibility: 'The numbing effect of hours of television-watching is obviously inimical to ordinary rationality. Isn't it possible that for many in the television audience, it is more desirable to be numb than to be informed?'[21] We might argue that the condition of viewing was not conducive to the condition of reasoning. But we might go further and suggest that there are also other desires at work than the desire to reason. Like the desire to be numb, to not know, to not reason.

It is here that Baudrillard's *La Guerre du Golfe n'a pas eu Lieu* is important: important because it directly confronts our rational pretensions. The scandal of Baudrillard is to distance himself from the cause of Reason. In the war, Baudrillard argues, Reason was transformed into Enlightenment fundamentalism, 'as fierce as that of any tribal religion or primitive society'.[22] Was it not some kind of archaic thinking, he asks, that denounced the Other as 'absolute Evil'? What Baudrillard sees as the driving force behind coalition behaviour is not Reason but, rather, fear. There was a fear, he says, of the real: a fear of the powers of death and destruction. It was because we – soldiers and on-lookers both – were haunted by the real that we sought refuge behind video screens. We preferred 'the exile of the virtual, of which television is the universal mirror, to the catastrophe of the real'.[23]

Fear was more compelling than reason. Writing from a psychoanalytic perspective, Paul Hoggett describes how all human beings carry a primordial fear, a persistent dread, a sense of imminent catastrophe, within themselves:

So what is this fear, what is this catastrophe that stalks us like a crazy dog? We cannot say because we cannot name it. But it is there, right in our guts, and as soon as we find the means to do so we seek to represent it, despite the fact that it cannot be represented. We construct an endless series of misrepresentations all of which share one essential quality, the quality of otherness, of being not-me.[24]

Whatever the political realities, the Gulf War offered itself as an occasion, a rich opportunity, to rid ourselves, for a while at least, of this crazy dog, through the projection of our fears outwards. This time the not-me we used to embody the sense of catastrophic danger was Saddam, vilified as child-molester, rapist, murderer, monster.[25] His scuddish evil, George Bush assured the western world, confirmed us as the guardians of enlightened and civilised values. In so far as Saddam symbolised the forces of irrationality, it became possible for us to imagine ourselves as all Reason. To protect our new-found peace of mind, it seemed both reasonable and inevitable that we should attack the 'new Hitler', hold him at bay. Now that the crazy dog had a name we would 'cut it off' and 'kill it'. 'Our fear comes first,' says Hoggett, 'our violence and hatred comes after.'[26]

What is, of course, significant about a world-historical event like the Gulf War is how individual fantasies are drawn into a collective strategy of psychic defence. The collective expulsion of fear becomes the basis for reaffirming group solidarity. Membership of a social group, of a society, is never an easy or an uncomplicated matter: belonging to it is associated with feelings of discomfort, from indifference to resentment and anxiety. At particular historical moments, however, such tensions are eased as the collectivity reasserts itself through what, following Didier Anzieu, we might call the working of the 'group illusion'.[27] The group discovers its common identity at the same time as its individual members are able to avow that they are all identical in their fears, and then that they are consensual in the defensive violence and hatred they direct against the threat that is not-us. It is a moment in which the individual can fuse with the group: for a time, at least, the defence of individual identity can be displaced onto the group. And for as long as danger and threat can be projected from its midst, the group experiences a sense of exultation through its new-found wholeness and integrity. It was this exultation that infused the *esprit de corps* of the coalition nations. What it reflected was the pleasure of experiencing harmonious community and in joining in righteous struggle (the just crusade). It was, however, like so many times before, predicated on a consensual misrepresentation: on the illusory belief that the dangers and threats were all simply 'out there' and that the crazy dog really was Saddam.

So, how does television fit into all this? In the above discussion I have drawn attention to the group processes at work, rather than invoking the more conventional focus of the public sphere, because I am, for the moment, more concerned with the emotional and libidinal, rather than the rational, dimensions of collective behaviour. In most discussions of Gulf War TV, there has been a tendency to privilege the informational role of television and to overlook the significance of the screen and the screening process for the psyche-at-war. As the conflict developed, however, the television screen played a crucial role, first in projecting our fears outwards and creating the image of external threat, and then in mobilising defensive violence against that threat. It was in the form of the television audience (the audience-as-group) that the group illusion, functioning as a defensive mechanism against persecutory anxieties, manifested itself most powerfully. The screen mediated between the dangers we imagined out there and the fear, anger and aggression we were feeling inside.

The nature and functioning of the screen are crucial. The screen has allowed us to witness the world's events while, at the same time, protecting us – keeping us separate and insulated – from the reality of the events we are seeing. It has exposed audiences to the violence and catastrophe of war while they have still remained safe in their living rooms. Remember Vietnam. But on what terms is this kind of watching imaginable? To survive what we might see requires a numbing of our sensibilities; it is only possible if the moral constraints regulating our relation to the other can be neutralised. This is what screening does – does to us. As John Berger has argued, screen voyeurism has permitted an unprecedented kind of ruthlessness and indifference to life: 'The screen replaces reality. And the replacement is a double one. For reality is born of the encounter of consciousness and events. To deny reality is not simply to deny what is objective. It is also to deny an essential part of the subjective.'[28] The force of the screen works to make moral response more difficult.

Difficult, but never impossible, because the force of evidence of screen images has always carried the potential to arouse feelings of shame, pity or outrage. Remember Vietnam. The screen has distanced reality, but it has never actually, literally, succeeded in replacing it. But what if it did? What would happen then? These are questions we must now consider in the aftermath of the Gulf War. Forget Vietnam. This was a different kind of television war. It was a war which was censored into invisibility, void of images of real violence and suffering (we never saw, nor will we ever see, the slaughter on the Basra road). What we had instead was something new, a surrogate experience, which has been described as the 'Nintendo war': the images resembled those of video games and computer simulations. In Baudrillard's terms, the phenomenon of 'realist war' had given way to that of 'virtual war'. The screen had finally displaced reality. And with this a new era of war-screening was inaugurated.

Whilst realist television had been an invaluable asset in mobilising public opinion and emotion in times of war, there was always the awareness that it was ultimately unpredictable and unreliable. The remoteness of the television image could encourage callousness and indifference towards the fate of the

71

enemy, but its documentary nature always threatened the possibility that indifference could turn to sympathy. The evidential quality of the image could always make an appeal to moral reason. The video-game treatment of war does away with this possibility. In dispensing with the image as document, it is able to work more effectively on the unconscious processes associated with the screening phenomenon. The screen becomes more directly a function of our internal impulses: 'The ego lives there by attacking the other in fantasy, but in this continual and imaginary aggressive game it loses its own positive real forces, its positive representation of itself, and lives as if it were always threatened by the other.'[29] Video games activate infantile terrors and defences, creating a 'paranoiac environment' in which players are continually and repeatedly struggling to save themselves from being over-whelmed or annihilated by alien, destructive forces. The video-game images during the Gulf War worked in the same way 'to involve us as vicarious participants in destroying perceived threats to our bodily integrity, our physical existence and our social order'.[30] When it is severed of reference to events in the real world, the screen answers more readily to our basic fears than to our moral selves.

So, what does all this mean for the idea of the public sphere and the rational citizen (and viewer)? Does it add up to some kind of postmodern farewell to Reason? What I am arguing is that Reason must take seriously those forces in us that can work against the possibility of reasoned debate and informed opinion; it must take into account those forces which may actually prefer to not think, not know, not reason. Wilfred Bion's great insight was to show how thought develops as a way of coping with primitive sensations and feelings (fear, anxiety, distress, pain, longing), as a means of 'ridding the psyche of stimuli'. The capacity to think only develops subsequently as a method or apparatus for dealing with these thoughts. Thoughts can be dealt with, says Bion, either by evasion or modification: 'The problem is solved by evacuation if the personality is dominated by the impulse to evade frustration and by thinking the objects if the personality is dominated by the impulse to modify the frustration.'[31] The 'non-thinking' way of handling thoughts and feelings is through evacuation, expulsion or projection of the unbearable material. In contrast, the 'thinking' way is able to 'contain' the unconscious impulses sufficiently to transform them into understanding and awareness and to learn from emotional experience. Thinking, reasoning, is always a possibility, then, but it is only one possibility. Evasion may be a more appealing alternative. 'Thinking is a development which is very unwelcome,' writes Bion, 'it is difficult to know what to do with the capacity to think.'[32] Thinking involves change, and change is something we resent and resist, individually and socially.

If Reason is to be civilised, then it must accommodate our primitive and basic fears. It cannot be based on the repression, the evasion or the expulsion of these unconscious materials. As Cornelius Castoriadis emphasises, it can never be a question of eliminating one psychical level in favour of another. The point, rather, is to alter the relation between levels, and that becomes possible when the conscious level is capable of 'taking in the contents of the unconscious, reflecting on them and becoming able to choose lucidly the impulses and ideas it will try to enact'.[33] There must be recognition of the unconscious contents and reflection on them. Reason is not a given endowment or attribute of the human animal. It is, rather, something that we must aspire to, something that we must struggle to achieve. Nor, finally, is it just by being reasonable or rational alone that we should count ourselves as human. What makes us human, all too human, is the flux of impulses, fears and desires at the centre of our being. What makes us human and civilised too is the endeavour to transform that flux (with the help of our powers of reason) for moral, creative and imaginative ends.

What was called for during the war, writes John Berger, was that we should 'give expression' to the human suffering we knew was happening. That we should 'declare the tragic tragic'. What is fundamental for Berger is the sense of compassion: whether we are able to 'recognise loss when it is not, in the first instance, our own'.[34] So, too, for Tony Harrison in his poem, 'Initial illumination':

> let them remember, all those who celebrate,
> that their good news is someone else's bad
> or the light will never dawn on poor Mankind.[35]

We all have the potential for compassionate behaviour. What the Gulf War showed us is how effectively that potential can be neutralised.

Tragedy? Compassion? Am I going soft? All this has taken us a million miles from media sociology. Media sociology says it was just another television war, more bad news, 86 per cent satisfied. What is all this guff about poor Mankind?

✴ ✴ ✴ ✴ ✴

THE HAUNTED SCREEN

There were 300 Americans killed in the Gulf War. During the same time, 300 Americans were murdered. What kind of country is this?
(Jean-Luc Godard, interview in *Newsweek*)

What if we ran the tape back and re-played the Gulf War after *American psycho*? What could this tell us about violence in western culture? What would it say about how we use the screen in our culture of violence? In the following discussion, I am concerned with the interaction of technology, violence and fantasy.

Not so long ago – though it now seems an age – we were watching the Gulf War being played out on our screens. We were spooked by devilish images of Saddam Hussein, the 'new Hitler'. It was an epic media event where the Good, armed with their high-tech weapons, went in to 'take apart' the Evil Empire. We did not see it, but we came to know that more than 150,000 Iraqi soldiers and civilians were slaughtered in that bloody kill. Then, just a few months later, we were gripped by another kind of slaughter: the media turned to the phenomenon of serial killing in American cities. It is said that there are between thirty and forty mass murderers at large in American cities, and their potential victims were flocking into movie houses to be shocked and haunted by knowing it. The monstrous image of *The Silence of the Lambs'* Hannibal Lecter was staring out at them.

We can use the serial-killing phenomenon to re-frame the symbolic value of the war. From the 'deep black' of outer space the penetrating look of American spy satellites maintained a constant surveillance over the Iraqi nation, continually identifying strategic targets. Stealth fighters 'lurked' in the Gulf skies, invisibly and undetectably lethal. And then death came suddenly, out of the blue, through the 'surgical strike' of a cruise missile. These 'smart' or 'brilliant' weapons allowed the allied forces to 'remove' chosen targets with precision and at will. And death came out of the black too. It came out of the night, from killers who could see through darkness. One report described how Apache helicopters, hovering fifty feet above the sand, 'took out' a group of Iraqi soldiers: they were cut down by attackers they could not see as they ran with nowhere to hide and 'did not know what the hell hit them.'[36]

Disturbingly, something like this reality then seemed to come home to overshadow the populations of American cities. In the serial-killer genre, it was the American citizen who came under surveillance, watched by the psychotic killer lurking stealthily in the urban night. The deadly penetrating stare of Hannibal Lecter has become the motif of the genre. Lecter is characterised by his 'brilliance', his 'extraordinary brain-power': like the 'smart' or 'brilliant' weapon, he (serial killers are for the most part men) too is programmed to strike precisely and at will. We cannot hide from the serial killer. He is in our midst, and he metes out death with apparent randomness: the victim is simply the wrong person in the wrong place at a particular time. We too have now become a 'bounty of targets'.

Of course, there is a certain fortuitousness in this shift in agendas. The search for novelty and spectacle in the media is in one sense a random process. But, then again, perhaps there is more to it: in their juxtaposition, these two media phenomena reflect something important about violence in our culture, and, particularly, about the screening (in both senses of that term) of violence. There is compelling affinity: the sinister connotations of terms like 'surgical strike' and 'target-rich environment' are exacerbated in the context of urban mass murder in the United States. Phrases like 'the silence of the lambs' and 'American psycho' cast a retrospective shadow over President Bush's 'black versus white, good versus evil' war in the Middle East. I think we should not de-link the two media spectacles; together they tell us much about what film director Jonathan Demme has described as the condition of 'moral disenfranchisement' that characterised 'Bush's soulless America'.

In an unusual essay on the Gulf War, Lloyd deMause, an American psychohistorian, describes this cultural condition as a 'shared emotional disorder'.[37] The war can then be seen as a kind of collective working through of that disorder. America was experiencing feelings of guilt, depression and sinfulness in the face of its own sense of chaos and impending dissolution; there was a need for expiation. In his efforts to illuminate the 'inner life of America', deMause makes the apparently strange observation that it was child abuse that provided the 'symbolic focus' for the crisis. Indeed, for some time before the conflict, he points out, the drama between the Terrifying Parent and the Hurt Child had been haunting the American psyche.

With the advent of war, the Terrifying Parent could be projected outward. It was Saddam Hussein who took on the role of child molester. Western audiences were 'sickened' by propaganda images of Saddam with his child hostages. Bush himself invoked the plight of the 'innocent children'. There were reports (which were subsequently shown to be propaganda fictions) that over three hundred Kuwaiti babies had died when Iraqi soldiers removed them from their incubators. This was child abuse on a terrifying scale: Saddam was a violent monster and a merciless beast, the violator of every 'civilised principle'.

America identified with the Hurt Child, and Bush sought to take on the role of the Good Parent. This, as he made clear, was a war between good and evil, a war to protect and defend the 'moral order' of the world. Saddam was seen as a contaminating and polluting force. As *Newsweek* magazine put it, 'the chain had to be pulled, to flush Saddam away'. In contrast, Bush's punitive violence could be seen as a cleansing and purifying force. What the war offered was the possibility of renewal and revitalisation: America could rediscover its moral purpose and emotional wholeness.

Of course, there is a simplification in this account of the Gulf War as a kind of morality play; but there is also a persuasive truth in it. For a moment, a brief moment, this epic spectacle sustained a sense of national integrity and moral regeneration. The subsequent media event, the screening of serial killers, immediately seemed to question that self-confidence. These murderous films reintroduced an element of anxiety and dislocation into the national (and the western) psyche: they brought the sense of 'moral disenfranchisement' into the midst of the daily lives of Americans. They can be seen as retrospectively and insidiously poisoning the heroic image of the just war. Now, when we re-wind the tape, the war looks different.

The Gulf War was to purify America by exorcising an evil that was projected as being outside, 'in a desolate Middle Eastern desert'. What became clear in the horror genre was the fear and anxiety that evil was really within. And, strangely, yet not strangely, it was again the drama of the Terrifying Parent and the Hurt Child that was the symbolic focus of this anxiety. In

Twin Peaks, Leland Palmer was the demonic murderer and rapist of his own daughter. In *The Silence of the Lambs*, the cannibalistic Lecter, himself a victim of child abuse, symbolically became the bad father of the detective, Clarice Starling. In John McNaughton's *Henry: Portrait of a Serial Killer*, the psychopathic Henry murdered the prostitute mother who abused him in childhood. If the American myth has the child as the symbol of innocence, there is something in that innocence that seems to arouse aggressive desires and drives in the parents who have charge of them. In America there was a wave of accusations about satanic practices, orgies, voyeurism, child rape and murder sweeping the country.[38] Terrifying Parent and Hurt Child seemed to be caught in a vicious cycle of mutual destruction. But this time the destructive force could not be projected outwards.

Creating a sense of impending dissolution and moral disintegration, it provoked feelings between anxiety and paranoia, between vigilance and panic. The films told us that this soulless America was Bush's moral order. The serial killer was the monstrous result of this moral world – and he could be anyone, the man next door, the next Henry or Jack or Norman that you had the misfortune to come across. He need have no reason or motive to kill you. Hannibal Lecter kills because that is his life, in a mockery of the idea of human motivation. The man who seems in control could suddenly explode into violent slaughter. The fictional Henry is driven by combined feelings of euphoria and dissociation: he kills because it makes him feel better. We saw this in the Gulf War, too: it was the monstrous result of this moral world. This time it was the Iraqis who had the misfortune to come across Henry, Jack or Norman. Think of the Apache pilot returning from his mission: 'When we got back, I sat there on the wing, and I was laughing . . . . I lay there in bed and said "OK, I'm tired, I've got to get to sleep." And then I'd think about sneaking up there and blowing this up, blowing that up.'[39]

Perhaps we should consider what the difference is between this man, who was capable of turning his hellish fire on men who were fleeing 'like ghostly sheep', and a killer like Hannibal Lecter who devours his victims. On the one hand, Iraq was a 'turkey shoot'; on the other, it is a question of cannibalism. The difference is that being Hannibal Lecter in Iraq was alright; being Hannibal Lecter in America is not. Whereas the Gulf War was projected as a simple confrontation between 'us = good' and 'them = evil', in the serial-killer genre this simple moral fiction is disturbed and confounded. In this genre we recognise that both the Hurt Child and the Terrifying Parent are aspects of ourselves. We get to know what it feels like to be a victim. But it also brings home to us how precarious is the line between us as victims and us as potential aggressors. We too, under certain conditions, are capable of unleashing a storm of violence. This genre forces us to confront moral complexity and ambivalence. 'Can you stand to say I'm evil?' asks Hannibal Lecter. Lecter's question is a challenge to our moral condition. It exposes our emotional disorder.

But, how do we learn to live with this violence? To ask this question is to consider the mechanisms through which we manage to screen ourselves from evil. In both of the examples I have been discussing, our exposure to violence has been mediated through the screen. Both were media events. The screen is a powerful metaphor for our times: it symbolises how we now exist in the world, our contradictory condition of engagement and disengagement. Increasingly we confront moral issues through the screen, and the screen confronts us with increasing numbers of moral dilemmas. At the same time, however, it screens us from those dilemmas: it is through the screen that we disavow or deny our human implication in moral realities.

I do not mean to say that this is intrinsically or necessarily the case. Of course, we have all looked at images of suffering (in Vietnam, South Africa, Ethiopia, Lebanon, Bosnia, Somalia, Chechnya – the list could be frighteningly without end), and we have felt moral outrage. What I am saying is that images present particular difficulties for our moral being. 'To suffer is one thing,' writes Susan Sontag, 'another thing is living with the photographed images of suffering, which does not necessarily strengthen conscience and the ability to be compassionate.'[40] Yet through the distancing force of images, frozen registrations of remote calamities, we have learned to manage our relationship with suffering. The photographic image at once exposes us to, and insulates us from, actual suffering; it does not, and cannot, in and of itself implicate us in the real and reciprocal relations necessary to sustain moral and compassionate existence. With video screens and electronic images, this moral chasm has been made wider. As we have become exposed to, and assaulted by, images of violence on a scale never before known, the affluent have also become more insulated from the realities of violence. It may no longer be a question of whether this strengthens conscience and compassion, but of whether it is actually undermining and eroding them.

If we are to come to terms with this moral condition, we must consider the nature of our engagement with screen culture. To do this, I want to focus on two episodes, one from each of the media events I have been discussing. The first is the report from the Gulf War, which I have already referred to, of Apache helicopter pilots video-recording their slaughter through cameras equipped with night-vision sights. After the carnage, the pilots returned to base to watch the footage: 'War hardened soldiers hold their breath as Iraqi soldiers, as big as football players on the television screen, run with nowhere to hide.' According to the report, the images showed one man who dropped, writhed on the ground, then struggled to his feet, until another burst of fire tore him apart. 'A guy came up to me', says one participant, 'and we were slapping each other on the back … and he said "By God, I thought we had shot into a damn farm. It looked like somebody opened the sheep pen."'

The second episode I want to focus on is from *Henry: Portrait of a Serial Killer*. In this film, Henry and his friend Otis have stolen a video camera, and this is then used to video-record themselves torturing and slaughtering a suburban family. Afterwards, they sit back to watch a re-play of their murderous and sadistic acts. 'I want to see it again', says Otis, who likes the video so much that he eventually falls asleep in front of it.

The similarity of the two episodes is disturbing. What they dramatically emphasise is how peculiar the relationship is between the act of killing and the act of watching people being slaughtered. In both examples, the killers are, at the same time, the video-makers. Acts of sadism are instantaneously transformed into acts of voyeurism. But what both of these episodes also show is that this dramatic transformation from sadism to voyeurism does not give rise to further moral dilemmas. As sadism turns into voyeurism it somehow neutralises itself; in each case, it screens out the actual reality of the killing, and it distances the killers from moral engagement. How is this possible?

In the case of Henry and Otis, we know that this is because their behaviour is psychotic: they are unable to differentiate between reality and fantasy. In their case, the reality and the image are simply substitutable. The question of moral responsibility is least problematical here, and we are concerned with how their voyeurism reflects the criminal pathology of the serial killer. But what of the Apache pilots? Surely they were not psychotic? At this point perhaps we should give up on the comparison and draw attention to the differences between the two episodes. There are, of course, clear and important differences, but I still want to push the similarities a little further. I think we can benefit from the opportunity that has fortuitously juxtaposed 'normal' pilots and psychopathic killers. We can use it, perhaps, to consider the institutionalised and normalised defiance of reality that increasingly characterises the military information society.[41]

If the pilots were not psychopaths – and, for the most part, they surely weren't – we must consider how it was possible for them to screen out the reality of violence they had unleashed. How were they able to watch the videotapes and apparently dissociate themselves from the moral implications of their actions? And what is it that still allows us to call their behaviour normal? It is clearly the case that the pilots could find ways and means to achieve moral distance from the brutal and brutalising activities in which they were engaged: they could see themselves as there to 'punish evil'. And through the defensive mechanisms of denial, disavowal and repression, they could preserve and protect a certain sanity within an insanely violent environment.

One of the most powerful defensive strategies is the mechanism of *splitting*, which involves the division of the self and even the splitting off and disowning of a *part* of the self. In their book *The Genocidal Mentality*, Robert Jay Lifton and Eric Markusen describe how this mechanism worked in a profoundly violent environment, the Auschwitz death camp. Lifton and Markusen use the term 'doubling' to describe how an element of the self can come to function autonomously and antithetically to the prior self: the individual involved in violence 'perceived that the institution wanted him to bring forth a self that could adapt to killing without feeling himself a murderer. In that sense, doubling became not just an individual enterprise but a shared psychological process.'[42] It is through this mechanism of splitting, the fragmenting of the self, that individuals can manage to coexist as both killers and as apparently normal people.

This process of splitting may be particularly important for understanding our implication in screen violence. We can describe the Apache pilots in terms of a splitting process that differentiates a spectator-self from an actor-self: in the context of the war, it became possible for them to feel that the spectator-self was more 'real' than the self that was acting devastatingly in and on the real world. This was partly because the array of communications, control and surveillance technologies in which they were immersed produced a kind of video-game scenario: it was a push-button, remote-control, screen-gazing war. The effect of these distancing technologies was to create a numbed experience of derealised and disembodied combat.

There was a sense of omnipotence and euphoria as the boundaries between reality and fantasy became disturbed. And, through this involvement in the screened war, the moral engagement of the actor-self in the reality of combat could be distanced and disavowed, for the more 'real' spectator-self, subsequently replaying the video pictures of horror, served as yet another distancing device. The screen was the only contact point, the only channel for moral engagement with the enemy Other. At the same time, though, it amplified and legitimated the sense of omnipotence and power over that enemy. The screen was the only contact point, but what we must recognise is that in reality it was no contact point at all for moral engagement.

So, what of us? What of the rest of us screen-gazers, watchers, viewers and voyeurs? Where are we in all of this? At this point, you may balk; you may feel that the comparisons are being overstated. Of course, I would have to agree in part: the behaviour of television and movie audiences is different from that of the Apache pilots and of Henry and Otis. The individuals who make up these audiences are only spectators, not actors. It seems appropriate to describe their behaviour as 'normal', and it would seem strange to describe them as sadistic. The elements of difference are fairly clear. And yet, I would argue, the pathological still casts its shadow over the normal: the 'ordinary' spectator of violence and suffering is not far removed from the extreme, the fantastic, aberrant and frightening. In this respect, the screen has the potential to extend and amplify human awareness and sensibility. Of course, this can be liberating, but it can also be very problematical. The screen encourages a morbid voyeurism, a kind of bloodlust. Ignacio Ramonet has gone so far as to condemn the 'necrophiliac perversion of television', the way that television takes nourishment from blood, violence and death.[43]

The screen affords access to experiences beyond the ordinary. But experience and awareness for what, we might ask. What does it mean to be 'fascinated' by a missile-eye perspective on death? What does it mean to

79

become quickly 'bored' by pictures of slaughter and suffering? What does it mean then to turn to horror movies to satisfy a need to be terrified? The spectator-self roves almost at random from one visual sensation to the next, a cruising voyeur.

The screen exposes the ordinary viewer to harsh realities, but it screens out the harshness of those realities. It has a certain moral weightlessness: it grants sensation without demanding responsibility, and it involves us in a spectacle without engaging us in the complexity of its reality. This clearly satisfies certain needs or desires. Through its capacity to project frightening and threatening experiences, we can say that the screen provides a space in which to master anxiety. It allows us to rehearse our fantasies of omnipotence to overcome this anxiety.

In the serial-killer genre, this rehearsal may be about containing fears about our own destructiveness or about the impending dissolution of our civilised values. In the case of the Gulf War, the threat was (projected as being) from outside, and the screen was mobilised to construct a collective sense of omnipotence over an alien 'monster'. In their different ways, both of these media events of 1991 were about imagined threats to civilised norms and values, then about the imaginary exorcism of those threats. Screen omnipotence is about the drama of anxiety and containment. In the domain of the screen, it is possible to contain anxieties that cannot be confronted in their reality.

Moral identity and responsibility can only come from our recognition of, and engagement with, the refractoriness of the real world. It must necessarily involve us in processes of dialogue and negotiation, processes in which self and other are mutually transforming and transformed. The kind of screen event I have been describing is not characterised by such reciprocity: the screen bypasses the intractable nature of reality, and it seems to put us in control of the world. This is not to say that those who watch screens are not guided by moral concerns; rather, that the act of screen-gazing may make their moral behaviour more difficult. The point is that the screen displaces (rather than supplements) reality: the very presence of the screen image testifies to the absence or remoteness of the screened reality. The screen is fundamentally inert; it does not involve us in the processes of dialogue and negotiation.

There are those who like to tell us that the screen has now eclipsed reality, that we are now living in a world of image, simulation and spectacle. There is, indeed, something suggestive in this observation. But before we become too seduced by this postmodernist scenario, we should remember the 150,000 *real* men and women who were *really* slaughtered beyond the screening of the Gulf War. We should consider the implications of the fact that there is a symbiotic relationship between fictional serial killers and *real* ones, who *really* slaughter.

It is not that we now live in the realm of the image; it is, rather, that there is, in our culture now, a kind of collective, social mechanism of splitting. The spectator-self is morally disengaged, floating about in an ocean of violent images. The actor-self is caught up in a reality whose violence is often morally overwhelming. How can we come to terms with this situation wherein the spectator and the actor seem to be going their separate ways?

Chapter 4

CYBERSPACE
AND THE WORLD
WE LIVE IN

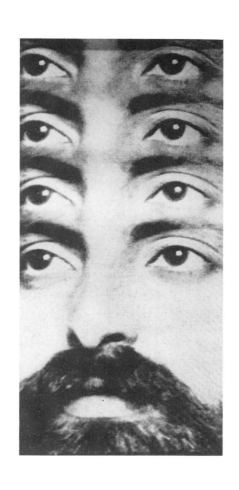

4

CYBERSPACE AND THE WORLD WE LIVE IN

The idea of an Earthly Paradise was composed of all the elements incompatible with History, with the space in which the negative states flourish.

(E.M. Cioran, *A Short History of Decay*)

And what Freud calls all the time reality, and the problem of reality, is always social reality. It is the problem of the other or the others, and it is never, never, never physical reality . . . The problem is always the difficulty or the imposs-ibility of coping with or recognizing social reality, that is, human reality, the reality of other humans, the reality, of course, of institutions, laws, values, norms, etc.

(Cornelius Castoriadis, interview in *Free Associations*)

Cyberspace is, according to the guruesque William Gibson, a 'consensual hallucination'. The contemporary debate on cyberspace and virtual reality is something of a consensual hallucination, too. There is a common vision of a future that will be different from the present, of a space or a reality that is more desirable than the mundane one that presently surrounds and contains us. It is a tunnel vision. It has turned a blind eye on the world we live in.

You might think of cyberspace as a utopian vision for postmodern times. Utopia is nowhere (*outopia*) and, at the same time, it is also somewhere good (*eutopia*). Cyberspace is projected as the same kind of 'nowhere–somewhere'. Nicole Stenger tells us that 'cyberspace is like Oz – it is, we get there, but it has no location'; it 'opens up a space for collective restoration, and for peace . . . our future can only take on a luminous dimension!'[1] In their account of virtual reality, Barrie Sherman and Phil Judkins describe it as 'truly the technology of miracles and dreams'. Virtual reality allows us 'to play God':

> We can make water solid, and solids fluid; we can imbue inanimate objects (chairs, lamps, engines) with an intelligent life of their own. We can invent animals, singing textures, clever colours or fairies.

With charmless wit (or perhaps banal gravity, I cannot tell which), they suggest that 'some of us may be tempted to hide in VR; after all, we cannot make of our real world whatever we wish to make of it. Virtual Reality may turn out to be a great deal more comfortable than our own imperfect reality.'[2]

All this is driven by a feverish belief in transcendence; a faith that, this time round, a new technology will finally and truly deliver us from the limitations and the frustrations of this imperfect world. Sherman and Judkins are intoxicated by it all. Virtual reality, they say, 'is the hope for the next century. It may indeed afford glimpses of heaven.'[3] When I read this, I can hardly believe my eyes. We must consider what these spectacular flights of fantasy are all about.

But utopia is surely about more than a new pleasure domain? Krishan Kumar reminds us that it is also 'a story of what it is to encounter and experience the good society'.[4] In this respect, too, the self-proclaiming visionaries tell us they have good news and great expectations. The utopian space – the Net, the Matrix – will be a nowhere–somewhere in which we shall be able to recover the meaning and the experience of community. Recognising 'the need for rebuilding community in the face of America's loss of a sense of a social commons', wishful Howard Rheingold believes that we have 'access to a tool that could bring conviviality and understanding into our lives and might help revitalise the public sphere'.[5] We shall be able to rebuild the neighbourhood community and the small-town public sphere and, in a world in which every citizen is networked to every other citizen, we can expand this ideal (or myth) to the scale of the global village. 'Virtual communities', says Rheingold, 'are social aggregations that emerge from the Net when enough people carry on [electronically mediated] public discussions long enough, with sufficient human feeling, to form webs of personal relationships in cyberspace.'[6] Communication translates directly into communion and community. It is a familiar dogma, and there is good reason to be sceptical about its technological realisation. But we should also consider the worth of this vision of electronic community as the 'good society'.

In the following discussion, I shall be concerned with these utopian aspirations and sentiments. But I shall not accept them on their own terms: my interest is in their discursive status and significance in the world we presently inhabit. The propagandists of the virtual-technological revolution tend to speak as if there really were a new and alternative reality; they would have us believe that we could actually leave behind our present world and migrate to this better domain. It is as if we could simply transcend the frustrating and disappointing imperfection of the here and now. This is the utopian temptation:

> Men can, in short, become gods (if not God). What need then for 'politics', understood as the power struggles of a materially straitened and socially divided world? The frequently noted contempt for politics in utopian theory is the logical complement of its belief in perfectibility.[7]

I think we should urgently set about dis-illusioning ourselves. There is no alternative and more perfect future world of cyberspace and virtual reality.

We are living in a real world, and we must recognise that it is indeed the case that we cannot make of it whatever we wish. The institutions developing and promoting the new technologies exist solidly in this world. We should make sense of them in terms of its social and political realities, and it is in this context that we must assess their significance. Because it is a materially straitened and socially divided world, we should remember how much we remain in need of politics.

The prophets of cyberspace and virtual reality are immersed in the technological imaginary. What concern them are the big questions of onto-logy and metaphysics:

> What does it mean to be *human* in today's world? What has stayed the same and what has changed? How has technology changed the answers we supply to such questions? And what does all this suggest about the future we will inhabit?[8]

This opens up a whole domain of speculation on disembodied rationality, tele-existence, the pleasures of the interface, cyborg identity, and so on. Of course, these issues are not without interest. But, at the same time, there is the exclusion of a whole set of other issues that also pertain to what it is to be human now and what future humans can look forward to. It is as if the social and political turbulence of our time – ethnic conflict, resurgent nationalism, urban fragmentation – had nothing at all to do with virtual space. As if they were happening in a different world. I think it is time that this real world broke in on the virtual one. Consider the cyberspace vision in the context of the new world disorder and disruption. The technological imagin-ary is driven by the fantasy of rational mastery of humans over nature and their own nature. Let us consider these fantasies of mastery and control in the context of what Cornelius Castoriadis has called the 'dilapidation of the West',[9] involving a crisis of the political and the erosion of the social fabric. In looking at cyberspace and virtual reality from this different vertex, we can try to re-socialise and re-politicise what has been posed in an abstract, philosophical sense as the question of technology and what it means to be human in today's world.

CYBERSPACE AND SELF-IDENTITY

Let us first consider the question of self-identity, which has become a pervasive theme in all discourses on cyberspace and virtual reality. In this new techno-reality, it is suggested, identity will be a matter of freedom and choice:

> In the ultimate artificial reality, physical appearance will be com-pletely composable. You might choose on one occasion to be tall and beautiful; on another you might wish to be short and plain. It would

be instructive to see how changed physical attributes altered your interactions with other people. Not only might people treat you differently, but you might find yourself treating them differently as well.[10]

Identities are composable in so far as the constraints of the real world and real-world body are overcome in the artificial domain. The exhilaration of virtual existence and experience comes from the sense of transcendence and liberation from the material and embodied world. Cultural conditions now 'make physicality seem a better state to be from than to inhabit':

> In a world despoiled by overdevelopment, overpopulation, and time-release environmental poisons, it is comforting to think that physical forms can recover their pristine purity by being reconstituted as informational patterns in a multidimensional computer space. A cyberspace body, like a cyberspace landscape, is immune to blight and corruption.[11]

In cyberspace, 'subjectivity is dispersed throughout the cybernetic circuit . . . the boundaries of self are defined less by the skin than by the feedback loops connecting body and simulation in a techno-bio-integrated circuit'.[12] In this accommodating reality, the self is reconstituted as a fluid and polymorphous entity. Identities can be selected or discarded almost at will, as in a game or a fiction.

This question of technology and identity has been taken up in quite different ways, and we should take good care to distinguish them. At the banal end of the spectrum are invocations of a new world of fantasy and imagination. When they suggest that 'in VR we can choose to represent ourselves as anything we wish', Sherman and Judkins have in mind the idea that we might want to represent ourselves as 'a lobster or a book-end, a drumstick or Saturn'.[13] The guru of the virtual-reality industry, Timothy Leary, has similar powers of imagination. In the electronic domain, he says, 'anything you can think of, dream of, hallucinate can be created. And communicated electronically. As Jimi Hendrix sang, "I'm a million miles away and I'm right here in your windowpane as Photon the Clown with a 95-foot-long triple penis made of marshmallows."'[14] In less grandiose fashion, Howard Rheingold describes how electronic networks 'dissolve boundaries of identity':

> I know a person who spends hours of his day as a fantasy character who resembles 'a cross between Thorin Oakenshield and the Little Prince', and is an architect and educator and bit of a magician aboard an imaginary space colony: By day, David is an energy economist in Boulder, Colorado, father of three; at night he's Spark of Cyberion City – a place where I'm known only as Pollenator.[15]

New identities, mobile identities, exploratory identities – but, it seems, also banal identities. Only the technology is new: in the games and encounters in cyberspace, it seems, there is little that is new or surprising. Rheingold believes that they have their roots 'deep in that part of human nature that delights in storytelling and playing "let's pretend"'.[16] Michael Benedikt develops the same point:

> Cyberspace's inherent immateriality and malleability of content pro-
> vides the most tempting stage for the acting out of mythic realities,
> realities once 'confined' to drug-enhanced ritual, to theatre, painting,
> books, and to such media that are always, in themselves, somehow less
> than what they reach for, mere gateways. Cyberspace can be seen as an
> extension, some might say an inevitable extension, of our age-old
> capacity and need to dwell in fiction, to dwell empowered or en-
> lightened on other, mythic planes.[17]

All this rhetoric of 'age-old' dreams and desires – which is quite common among the cyber-visionaries – is unspeakably vacuous and devoid of inspiration. It is a familiar old appeal to an imaginative space in which we can occupy new identities and create new experiences to transcend the limitations of our mundane lives. It is the aesthetic of fantasy-gaming; the fag-end of a Romantic sensibility.

The imagination is dead: only the technology is new. The visions are bereft (lobsters and drumsticks), but the point is that the technology will, supposedly, let us experience them *as if they were real*. Another self-styled seer, Jaron Lanier, reveals why the technology is the crucial element. Which particular identity one inhabits is of less importance than what is common to all identities in virtual existence. As we grow up in the physical world, Lanier argues, we have to submit to the dictates of its constraining and frustrating reality. We discover 'that not only are we forced to live inside the physical world, we are made of it and we are almost powerless in it':

> We are actually extremely limited. We can't get to our food easily, we
> need help. The earlier back into my childhood I remember, the more I
> remember an internal feeling of an infinite possibility for sensation and
> perception and form and the frustration of reconciling this with the
> physical world outside which was very very fixed, very dull, and very
> frustrating – really something like a prison.[18]

The new technology promises to deliver its user from the constraints and defeats of physical reality and the physical body. It provides the opportunity to go back and to explore what might have been, if we had been able to sustain the infantile experience of power and infinite possibility. Virtual reality is, or is imagined as, 'a combination of the objectivity of the physical world with the unlimitedness and the uncensored content normally associated with dreams or imagination'.[19] The technology is invested by omnipotence fantasies. In the virtual world, it is suggested, we shall receive all the gratifications that we are entitled to, but have been deprived of; in this world, we can reclaim the (infantile) illusion of magical creative power.

All this appears rather familiar and unexceptional. Familiar and unexceptional, because this discourse on virtual futures constitutes no more than a mundane, commonsense re-formulation of the (Kantian) transcendental imagination, rooted in a coherent and unified subjectivity, in the unity of mind and body, the '"transcendental synthesis" of our sensible and intelligible experience'.[20] *Plus ça change* . . . . There are more radical and challenging encounters with cyberspace, however. These other discourses can no longer accept the ontological status of the subject, and take as their premise the fractured, plural, decentred condition of contemporary subjectivity. They take very seriously the argument that the postmodern condition is one of fragmentation and dissolution of the subject. Continuing belief, or faith, in the essential unity and coherence of the personal self is held to be ideological, illusionary and nostalgic. In the postmodern scheme of things, there is no longer any place for the Kantian (even less the Cartesian) anthropology. Virtual technology is welcomed as the nemesis of the transcendental ego and its imagination. In cyberspace, there are possibilities for exploring the complexities of self-identity, including the relation between mental space and the bodily Other. We are provided with a virtual laboratory for analysing the postmodern – and perhaps post-human – condition.

Weaving together a blend of post-structuralist theory and cyberpunk fiction, this other discourse charts the emergence of cyborg identities. In the new world order, old and trusted boundaries – between human and machine, self and other, body and mind, hallucination and reality – are dissolved and deconstructed. With the erosion of clear distinctions, the emphasis is on interfaces, combinations and altered states. David Tomas writes of the 'technologising' of ethnic and individual identities: 'The continuous manipulation . . . of the body's ectodermic surface and the constant exchange of organic and synthetic body parts can produce rewritings of the body's social and cultural form that are directly related to the reconstitution of social identities.'[21] In an already hybrid world, it introduces 'another *technologically* creolised cultural laminate with a different set of ethnic-type rules of social bonding'. But, more than this, through the configurations of electronic and virtual space, 'it presents an all-encompassing sensorial ecology that presents opportunities for alternative dematerialised identity compositions'.[22] In its most sustained form – a kind of cyborg schizoanalysis – the collapse of boundary and order is linked to the deconstruction of ego and identity and the praise of bodily disorganisation, primary processes and libidinal sensation.[23]

This critical and oppositional discourse on cyberspace and virtual reality has been developed to great effect within a feminist perspective and agenda. The imaginative project was initiated by Donna Haraway in her manifesto for cyborgs as 'an effort to contribute to a socialist-feminist culture and theory in a post-modernist, non-naturalist mode, and in the utopian tradition of imagining a world without gender'. Cyborg identity represented an 'imaginative resource' in developing an argument for *pleasure* in the confusion of boundaries and for *responsibility* in their construction'.[24] Subsequent cyberfeminists have tended to place the emphasis on the moment of pleasure and confusion. Claudia Spinger draws attention to the 'thrill of escape from the confines of the body': 'Transgressed boundaries, in fact, define the cyborg, making it the consummate postmodern concept. . . . It involves transforming the self into something entirely new, combining technological with human identity.'[25] Virtual-reality environments allow their users 'to choose their disguises and assume alternative identities', Sadie Plant argues, 'and off-the-shelf identity is an exciting new adventure. . . . Women, who know all about disguise, are already familiar with this trip.' In this context, engagement with identity is a strategic intervention, intent on subverting masculine fantasies; it is 'a disturbance of human identity far more profound than pointed ears, or even gender bending, or becoming a sentient octopus.'[26]

This political edge is not always sustained, however, and it is not all that there is to cyborg feminism. It is accompanied by other desires and sentiments, reminiscent of – though not entirely the same as – the fantasies of omnipotent gratification evoked by Jaron Lanier. Cyberspace is imagined as a zone of unlimited freedom, 'a grid reference for free experimentation, an atmosphere in which there are no barriers, no restrictions on how far it is possible to go'; it is a place that allows women's desire 'to flow in the dense tapestries and complex depth of the computer image'.[27] Claudia Springer evokes 'a microelectronic imaginary where our bodies are obliterated and our consciousness integrated into the matrix'. Observing that the word 'matrix' derives from the Latin '*mater*', meaning both 'mother' and 'womb', she suggests that 'computers in popular culture's cyborg imagery extend to us the thrill of metaphoric escape into the comforting security of the mother's womb'.[28] There is an idealisation of the electronic matrix as a facilitating and containing environment. Like the original, maternal matrix, 'the silently active containing space in which psychological and bodily experience occur', this other, technological, matrix seems to offer the space for unconstrained, omnipotent experience, as well as providing a 'protective shield' affording 'insulation from external reality'.[29]

It is time that we let this reality intrude into the discussion again. We should consider these various, and conflicting, discourses on cyberspace and self-identity in the context of wider debates on identity and identity crisis in the real world.[30] It is, of course, in accounts of the 'postmodern condition' that the question of identity has been problematised, with the idea of a central and coherent self challenged and exposed as a fiction. The argument, as Stephen Frosh observes, is that 'if the reality of modernity is one of fragmentation and the dissolution of the self, then belief in the integrity of the personal self is ideological, Imaginary, fantastic ... whatever illusions we may choose to employ to make ourselves feel better, they remain illusory, deceptive and false.'[31] No longer stable and continuous, identity becomes uncertain and problematical. Carlo Mongardini takes note of the inconsistency of the ego-image in the postmodern era, and of the disturbing consequences of that inconsistency:

> A capacity for resistance in the individual is what is lacking here and above all *a historical consciousness which would permit him to interpret and thus control reality.* The individual becomes a mere fraction of himself, and loses the sense of being an actor in the processes of change.[32]

The loss of coherence and continuity in identity is associated with the loss of control over reality.

This crisis of self-identity is, then, more than a personal (that is, psychological) crisis. As Christopher Lasch has argued, it registers a significant transformation in the relationship between the self and the social world outside. It is associated with 'the waning of the old sense of a life as a life-history or narrative – a way of understanding identity that depended on the belief in a durable public world, reassuring in its solidity, which outlasts an individual life and passes some sort of judgement on it'.[33] This important cultural shift involves a loss of social meaning, and a consequent retreat from moral engagement. Mongardini observes a loss of the ethical dimension of life, which requires precisely continuity and stability of individual identity and social reality. There is now, he argues,

> a greater sense of alienation that makes it increasingly difficult to have relationships that demand more of the personality, such as love, friendship, generosity, forms of identification. . . . The loss of ability to give meaning to reality is also the product of psychic protection, the desire of the individual not to put himself at risk by exposing himself to the stimulus of a reality he can no longer interpret.[34]

There is dissociation and disengagement, withdrawal and solipsism. 'Change acts like a drug', argues Mongardini, 'It leads individuals to give up the unity and coherence of their own identity, both on the psychological and social level.'[35]

In the discourses on cyberspace and identity, however, things do not appear so problematical or bad. This is because the technological realm offers precisely a form of psychic protection against the defeating stimulus of reality. Techno-reality is where identity crisis can be denied or disavowed, and coherence sustained through the fiction of protean imagination; or it is where the stressful and distressing consequences of fragmentation can be neutralised, and the condition experienced in terms of perverse pleasure and play.

Cyberspace and virtual reality are not new in this respect. Mary Ann Doane describes the psychic uses of early cinematographic technologies in a way that is strikingly similar:

> One could isolate two impulses in tension at the turn of the century – the impulse to rectify the discontinuity of modernity, its traumatic disruption, through the provision of an illusion of continuity (to resist modernity), and the impulse to embody (literally give body to) discontinuity as a fundamental human condition (to embrace modernity). The cinema, in effect, does both.[36]

The new virtual technologies now provide a space in which to resist or embrace postmodernity. It is a space in which the imperatives and impositions of the real world may be effaced or transcended. In the postmodern context, it might be seen in terms of the turn to an aesthetic justification for life: 'Morality is thus replaced by multiple games and possibilities of aesthetic attitudes.'[37] Lost in the funhouse. Through the constitution of a kind of magical reality and realism, in which normal human limits may be overcome and usual boundaries transgressed, the new technological medium promotes, and gratifies, (magical) fantasies of omnipotence and creative mastery.

The technological domain readily becomes a world of its own, dissociated from the complexity and gravity of the real world. Brenda Laurel thinks of it as a virtual theatre, in which we can satisfy 'the age-old desire to make our fantasies palpable'; it provides 'an experience where I can play make-believe, and where the world auto-magically pushes back.'[38] We might also see it in the context of what Joyce McDougall calls 'psychic theatre', involving the acting out of more basic and primitive instincts and desires.[39] The techno-environments of cyberspace and virtual reality are particularly receptive to the projection and acting out of unconscious fantasies. In certain cases, as I have already argued, this may involve receptiveness to narcissistic forms of regression. Narcissism may be seen as representing 'a retreat from reality into a phantasy world in which there are no boundaries; this can be symbolised by the early monad, in which the mother offers the new-born infant an extended period of self-absorption and limitless, omnipotent contentment'.[40] In this context, the virtual world may be seen as constituting a protective container within which all wishes are gratified (and ungratifying encounters with the frustrations of the real world 'auto-magically' deferred). In other cases, as I have again suggested, the created environment may respond to psychotic states of mind. Peter Weibel describes virtuality as 'psychotic space':

> This is the space of the psychotic that stage-manages reality in hallucinatory wish-fulfilment, uttering the battle-cry 'VR everywhere'. . . . Cyberspace is the name for such a psychotic environment, where the boundaries between wish and reality are blurred.[41]

In this psychotic space, the reality of the real world is disavowed; the coherence of the self deconstructed into fragments; and the quality of experience reduced to sensation and intoxication. It is what is evoked in the fiction of cyberpunk, where 'the speed of thrill substitutes for affection, reflection and care', and where, as 'hallucinations and reality collapse into each other, there is no space from which to reflect'.[42]

Marike Finlay argues that such narcissistic and psychotic defences are characteristic of postmodern subjectivity, representing strategies 'to overcome the ontological doubt about one's own status as a self by retreating to the original omnipotence of the child who creates the breast by hallucinating it'.[43] Virtual subjectivity – one crucial form through which the postmodern subject exists – may be understood in this light. The new technological environments of virtual reality and cyberspace confuse the boundaries between internal and external worlds, creating the illusion that internal and external realities are one and the same. Artificial reality is designed and ordered in conformity with the dictates of pleasure and desire. To interact with it entails suspension of the real and physical self, or its substitution by a disembodied, virtual surrogate or clone. Under these conditions of existence, it appears as if there are no limits to what can be imagined and acted out. Moreover, there are no Others (no other bodies) to impose restrictions and inhibitions on what is imagined or done. The substantive presence of (external) Others cannot be differentiated from the objects created by the projection of (internal) fantasies. Virtual empowerment is a solipsistic affair, encouraging a sense of self-containment and self-sufficiency, and involving denial of the need for external objects.

Such empowerment entails a refusal to recognise the substantive and independent reality of others and to be involved in relations of mutual dependency and responsibility. As Marike Finlay argues, 'Only in phantasy can one be omnipotent without loss or reparation.'[44] Such a reality and such a subjectivity can only be seen as asocial and, consequently, amoral. 'Floating identities', Gérard Raulet observes, 'are in the realm of schizophrenia or neo-narcissism.'[45] The sense of unrestricted freedom and mastery belongs to disembodied identities. Such a fantasy, when it is socially institutionalised, must have its consequences for a real world of situated identities. As Michael Heim argues, the technological systems that convert primary bodily presence into tele-presence are also 'introducing a remove between *re*presented presences'. They are changing the nature of interpersonal relationships. 'Without directly meeting others physically', says Heim, 'our ethics languishes.' Indeed, the machine interface 'may amplify an amoral indifference to human relationships . . . [and] often eliminate the need to respond directly to what takes place between humans.'[46] We are reminded of the reality of our embodied and embedded existence in the real world, and of the ethical disposition necessary for coexistence to be possible in that world. It is the continuity of grounded identity that underpins and underwrites moral obligation and commitment.

It is not my intention to deny the imaginative possibilities inherent in the new technologies, but rather to consider what is the nature of the imagination that is being sustained. From this perspective, it is useful to look at experiences in and of cyberspace and virtual reality in the light of Winnicott's notion of potential space: the 'third area of human living', neither inside the individual nor outside in the world of shared reality, the space of creative playing and cultural experience.[47] In elaborating his ideas, Winnicott drew attention to the continuity between the potential space that supports infantile illusions of magical creative power, and that which is associated with mature aesthetic or spiritual creativity. In virtual environments, this link between infantile and imaginative illusion becomes particularly apparent, as I have already indicated, and it seems appropriate to think of them in terms of the technological institution of potential or intermediate space. This magical–aesthetic aspect of the technologies is clearly that which has gathered most interest.

But we cannot be concerned with creative illusion alone (which is precisely what the new romancers of cyberspace do). In his discussion of potential space, Winnicott also put great emphasis on the moment of disillusionment, which involves 'acknowledging a limitation of magical control and acknowledging dependence on the goodwill of people in the external world'.[48] As Thomas Ogden points out, the infant then 'develops to capacity to see beyond the world he has created through the projection of internal objects'. The individual thereby becomes

> capable of entering into relationships with actual objects in a manner that involves more than a simple transference projection of his internal object world . . . mental representations acquire increasing autonomy from [their] origins and from the omnipotent thinking associated with relations between internal objects.[49]

Potential space is a transitional space. It is in this intermediate space, through the interaction of both internal and external realities, that moral sense is evolved. Transitional experience involves the differentiation of internal and external worlds – it is on this basis that aesthetic transgression becomes possible – and the acknowledgement of 'a world of utilisable objects, i.e., people with whom [one] can enter into a realm of shared experience-in-the-world outside of [oneself]'.[50] This enables the development of capacities for concern, empathy and moral encounter. Potential space is, in this sense, transitive. We should hold on to this point in our discussions of the cultural aspects of cyberspace and virtual-reality technologies. When it seems as if the new technologies are responding to regressive and solipsistic desires, we should consider the consequences and implications for moral-political life in the real world.

VIRTUAL COMMUNITY AND COLLECTIVE IDENTITY

This takes us to the question of collective identity and community in virtual space. Many of those who have considered these issues have made the (perverse) assumption that they are dealing with a self-contained and autonomous domain of technology. I shall argue, again, that the new technological developments must be situated in the broader context of social and political change and upheaval. The world is transforming itself. The maps are being broken apart and re-arranged. Through these turbulent and often conflictual processes of transformation, we are seeing the dislocation and re-location of senses of belonging and community. The experience of cultural encounter and confrontation is something that is increasingly characteristic of life in our cities. Virtual communities do not exist in a different world. They must be situated in the context of these new cultural and political geographies. How, then, are we to understand the significance of virtual communities and communitarianism in the contemporary world? What are their possibilities and what are their limitations?

Virtual reality and cyberspace are commonly imagined in terms of reaction against, or opposition to, the real world. They are readily associated with a set of ideas about new and innovative forms of society and sociality. In certain cases, these are presented in terms of some kind of utopian project. Virtual reality is imagined as a 'nowhere–somewhere' alternative to the difficult and dangerous conditions of contemporary social reality. We might consider this in the context of Krishan Kumar's observations about the recent displacement of utopia from time back to space. The postmodern utopia, he suggests, involves 'returning to the older, pre-18th century, spatial forms of utopia, the kind inaugurated by More'.[51] Virtual space, which is on a continuum with other hyperreal utopian spaces – from Disneyland to Biosphere 2 – is a space removed. As in utopian thinking more generally, there is the belief or hope that the mediated interaction that takes place in that other world will represent an ideal and universal form of human association and collectivity. Michael Benedikt sets it in the historical context of projects undertaken in pursuit of realising the dream of the Heavenly City:

> Consider: Where Eden (before the Fall) stands for our state of innocence, indeed ignorance, the Heavenly City stands for our state of wisdom, and knowledge; where Eden stands for our intimate contact with material nature, the Heavenly City stands for our transcendence of both materiality and nature; where Eden stands for the world of unsymbolised, asocial reality, the Heavenly City stands for the world of enlightened human interaction, form and information.[52]

The elsewhere of cyberspace is a place of salvation and transcendence. This vision of the new Jerusalem very clearly expresses the utopian aspirations in the virtual-reality project.

Not all virtual realists are quite so unrealistic, however. There are others with a more pragmatic and political disposition who have more to contribute to our understanding of the relation between cyberspace and the real world. There is still the sense of virtual reality as an alternative reality in a world gone wrong. Techno-sociality is seen as the basis for developing new and compensatory forms of community and conviviality. Networks are understood to be 'social nodes for fostering those fluid and multiple elective affinities that everyday urban life seldom, in fact, supports.'[53] Virtual communities represent:

> flexible, lively, and practical adaptations to the real circumstances that confront persons seeking community. . . . They are part of a range of innovative solutions to the drive for sociality – a drive that can be frequently thwarted by the geographical and cultural realities of cities. . . . In this context, electronic virtual communities are complex and ingenious strategies for *survival*.[54]

But this involves a clear recognition that such communities exist in, and in relation to, everyday life in the real world: 'virtual communities of cyberspace live in the borderlands of both physical and virtual culture'.[55] Virtual interaction is about adjustment and adaption to the increasingly difficult circumstances of the contemporary world. We may then ask how adequate or meaningful it is as a response to those circumstances.

The most sustained attempt to develop this approach and agenda is that of Howard Rheingold in his book *The Virtual Community*. While there is something of the utopian in Rheingold (west-Coast style), there is also a clear concern with the social order. If we look at his arguments in a little detail, we can perhaps see some of the appeal of the pragmatic approach to virtual community, but also identify its limitations and weaknesses. Like other virtual communitarians, Rheingold starts out from what he sees as the damaged or decayed state of modern democratic and community life. The use of computer-mediated communications, he argues, is driven by 'the hunger for community that grows in the breasts of people around the world as more and more informal public spaces disappear from our real lives'.[56] Rheingold emphasises the social importance of the places in which we gather together for conviviality, 'the unacknowledged agorae of modern life'. 'When the automobilecentric, suburban, fast-food, shopping mall way of life eliminated many of these "third places" from traditional towns and cities around the world, the social fabric of existing communities started shredding.' His hope is that virtual technologies may be used to staunch such developments. Rheingold's belief is that cyberspace can become 'one of the informal public places where people can rebuild the aspects of community that were lost when the malt shop became the mall.'[57] In cyberspace, he maintains, we shall be able to recapture the sense of a 'social commons'.

The virtual community of the network is the focus for a grand project of social revitalisation and renewal. Under conditions of virtual existence, it seems possible to recover the values and ideals that have been lost to the real world. Through this new medium, it is claimed, we shall be able to construct new sorts of community, linked by commonality of interest and affinity rather than by accidents of location. Rheingold believes that we now have 'access to a tool that could bring conviviality and understanding into our lives and might help revitalise the public sphere'; that, through the construction of an 'electronic agora', we shall be in a position to 'revitalise citizen-based democracy'.[58] It is envisaged that on-line communities will develop in ways that transcend national frontiers. Rheingold thinks of local networks as 'gateways to a wider realm, the worldwide Net-at-large'.[59] In the context of this 'integrated entity', he maintains, we will be in a position to build a 'global civil society' and a new kind of international culture.

Like many other advocates of virtual existence, Rheingold is a self-styled visionary. His ideas are projected as exercises in radical imagination. It is this preachy posture that seems to give cyberspace ideology its popular appeal. There is another aspect to Rheingold's discourse, however, and I think that this has been an even more significant factor in gaining approval for the project of virtual sociality. For all its futuristic pretensions, Rheingold's imagination is fundamentally conservative and nostalgic. He is essentially concerned with the restoration of a lost object: community:

> The fact that we need computer networks to recapture the sense of cooperative spirit that so many people seemed to lose when we gained all this technology is a painful irony. I'm not so sure myself anymore that tapping away on a keyboard and staring at a screen all day by necessity is 'progress' compared to chopping logs and raising beans all day by necessity. While we've been gaining new technologies, we've been losing our sense of community, in many places in the world, and in most cases the technologies have precipitated that loss. But this does not make an effective argument against the premise that people can use computers to cooperate in new ways.[60]

The Net is seen as re-kindling the sense of family – 'a family of invisible friends'. It re-creates the ethos of the village pump and the town square. Rheingold can envisage 'not only community but true spiritual communion' in what he describes as 'communitarian places online'.[61] The electronic community is characterised by commonality of interests, by the sense of 'shared consciousness' and the experience of 'groupmind'.[62] The images are of maternal–familial containment. The ideas are of unity, unanimity and mutualism. Rheingold's image of virtual community turns out to be no more than an electronic variant of the 'Rousseauist dream' of a transparent society in which 'the ideal of community expresses a longing for harmony among persons, for consensus and mutual understanding'.[63] It is a social vision that is grounded in a primal sense of enclosure and wholeness.

Rheingold's *The Virtual Community* is a good condensation of the pragmatic case for association and collectivity in cyberspace. In a manner that contrasts with the otherworldliness of cyber-utopianism, Rheingold is intent on connecting virtual solutions to real-world problems. A sustained case is made for the possibilities of applying virtual and network technologies for the purposes of social and political amelioration (while, at the same time, there is an awareness of the dangers of 'misapplication'). There is a growing recognition that electronic media have changed the way that we live in the world. Joshua Meyrowitz has observed how much television has altered the logic of the social order by restructuring the relationship between physical place and social place, thereby 'liberating' community from spatial locality.[64] Anthony Giddens describes a process of 'reality inversion', which means that 'we live "in the world" in a different sense from previous eras of history':

> The transformations of place, and the intrusion of distance into local activities, combined with the centrality of mediated experience, radically change what 'the world' actually is. This is so both on the level of the 'phenomenal world' of the individual and the general universe of social activity within which collective social life is enacted. Although everyone lives a local life, phenomenal worlds for the most part are truly global.[65]

In the light of these very significant developments, virtual communitarianism assumes a clear resonance and appeal. It appears to have a philosophy of social action appropriate to the conditions of the new technological order.

Because virtual experiences and encounters are becoming increasingly prevalent in the contemporary world, I believe we must indeed take very seriously their significance and implications for society and sociality. What I would question, however, is the relevance of techno-communitarianism as a response to these developments. Let us consider what is at issue. That which is generally presented in terms of technological futures is much more a matter of social relations and representations of social life in the present. In a period of turbulent change, in part a consequence of technological innovations, the nature of our relation to others and to collectivities has become more difficult and uncertain. 'The old forms of solidarity were internalised within the extended family and the village community,' argues Edgar Morin, 'but now these internalised social bonds are disappearing.'[66] We must search for new senses and experiences of solidarity, he maintains, though these must now be at more expansive scales than in the past. And, of course, this is what virtual community seems to be all about. Solidarity in cyberspace seems to be a matter of extending the security of small-town *Gemeinschaft* to the transnational scale of the global village. There is, however, something deceptive in this sense of continuity and fulfilment. In considering another postmodern space, Disneyland, Michael Sorkin suggests that it 'invokes an urbanism without producing a city . . . it produces a kind of aura-stripped hypercity, a city with billions of citizens ... but no residents'.[67] Jean Baudrillard says that it is 'an entire synthetic world which springs up, a maquette of our entire history in cryogenised form'.[68] We might see virtual and network association in the same light. There is the invocation of community, but not the production of a society. There is 'groupmind', but not social encounter. There is on-line communion, but there are no residents of hyperspace. This is another synthetic world, and here, too, history is frozen. What we have is the preservation through simulation of the old forms of solidarity and community. In the end, not an alternative society, but an alternative to society.

We might go so far as to see a particular affinity between virtual technologies and this communitarian spirit. As Iris Marion Young argues, the idealisation of community involves denial of the difference, or basic asymmetry, of subjects. Proponents of community

> deny difference by positing fusion rather than separation as the social ideal. They conceive the social subject as a relation of unity or mutuality composed by identification and symmetry among individuals within a totality. Communitarianism represents an urge to see persons in unity with one another in a shared whole.[69]

Existence in cyberspace – a space in which real selves and situations are in suspension – encourages the sense of identification and symmetry among individuals. De-materialised and de-localised, says Gérard Raulet, 'subjectivities are at once interchangeable and arbitrary. . . . The subject is reduced to pure functionality.'[70] The sense of unity and mutuality in a shared whole is 'artificially' created through the institution of technology.

The new technologies seem responsive to the dream of a transparent society. Communitarianism promotes the ideal of the immediate co-presence of subjects:

> Immediacy is better than mediation because immediate relations have the purity and security longed for in the Rousseauist dream: we are transparent to one another, purely copresent in the same time and space, close enough to touch, and nothing comes between us to obstruct our vision of one another.[71]

It is precisely this experience of immediacy that is central to the advocacy of virtual reality and relationships. According to Barrie Sherman and Phil Judkins, virtual reality 'can transmit a universal "language". . . . It is a perfect medium through which to communicate in what will be difficult times. . . . Common symbols will emphasise common humanity, expose common difficulties and help with common solutions.'[72] Jaron Lanier puts particular emphasis on this quality of virtual encounter. He likes to talk of 'post-symbolic communication' and a 'post-symbolic world'. He believes that it will be possible 'to make up the world instead of talking about it', with people 'using virtual reality a lot and really getting good at making worlds to communicate with each other'. The frustrations of mediated communication will be transcended in an order where 'you can just synthesise experience'.[73] These virtual ideologies are perpetuating the age-old ideal of a communications utopia. Immediacy of communication is associated with the achievement of shared consciousness and mutual understanding. The illusion of transparency and consensus sustains the communitarian myth, now imagined at the scale of global electronic *Gemeinschaft*. It is an Edenic myth.

Techno-community is fundamentally an anti-political ideal. Serge Moscovici speaks of the dialectic of order and disorder in human societies. Order, he maintains, has no basis in reality; it is a 'regressive phantasy'. A social system is only viable if it can 'create a certain disorder, if it can admit a certain level of uncertainty, if it can tolerate a certain level of fear'.[74] Richard Sennett has put great emphasis on this need to provoke disorder in his discussion of urban environments. In arguing that 'disorder and painful dislocation are the central elements in civilising social life',[75] Sennett makes the 'uses of disorder' the basis of an ethical approach to designing and living in cities. He is in opposition to those planners – 'experts in *Gemeinschaft*' – who 'in the face of larger differences in the city ... tend to withdraw to the local, intimate, communal scale'.[76] Sennett believes that this denial of difference reflects 'a great fear which our civilisation has refused to admit, much less to reckon':

> The way cities look reflects a great, unreckoned fear of exposure . . . . What is characteristic of our city-building is to wall off the differences between people, assuming that these differences are more likely to be mutually threatening than mutually stimulating. What we have made in the urban realm are therefore bland, neutralising spaces, spaces which remove the threat of social contact.[77]

What is created is the blandness of the 'neutralised city'. Disneyland is no more than the parodic extension of this principle. Here, too, 'the highly regulated, completely synthetic vision provides a simplified, sanitised experience that stands in for the more undisciplined complexities of the city'.[78] I have already noted the continuity between postmodern spaces like Disneyland and electronic virtual spaces. Virtual community similarly reflects the desire to control exposure and to create security and order. It also is driven by the compulsion to neutralise.

Cyberspace and virtual reality have generally been considered as a technological matter. They have seemed to offer some kind of technological fix for a world gone wrong, promising the restoration of a sense of community and communitarian order. It is all too easy to think of them as alternatives to the real world and its disorder. Containing spaces. I am arguing that we should approach these new technologies in a very different way. We must begin from the real world, which is the world in which virtual communities are now being imagined. And we must recognise that difference, asymmetry and conflict are constitutive features of that world. Not community. As Chantal Mouffe argues, the ideal of common substantive interests, of consensus and unanimity, is an illusion. We must recognise the constitutive role of antagonism in social life and acknowledge that 'a healthy democratic process calls for a vibrant clash of political positions and an open conflict of interests'.[79] For that is the key issue: a political framework that can accommodate difference and antagonism to sustain what Mouffe calls an 'agonistic pluralism'. This is so even in the matter of virtual association and collectivity.

The question of technology is not primarily a technological question. In considering the development of techno-communities, we must continue to be guided by social and political objectives. Against the wishful optimism of virtual communitarianism, I have chosen to emphasise those aspects of virtual culture that are inimical to democratic culture (in the sense of political thinkers like Young, Sennett and Mouffe). I have argued that virtual space is being created as a domain of order, refuge, withdrawal. Perhaps I have overstated my case. Maybe. The point has been to shift the discussion into the realm of social and political theory. Hopes for cyber-society have drawn their legitimacy from a metaphysics of technological progress – whatever comes next must be better than what went before. I am arguing for a different kind of justification, concerned with questions of pluralism and democracy now. We might then ask, for example, whether, or how, virtual technologies could be mobilised in pursuit of what Richard Sennett calls the 'art of exposure' (which I would consider to be the opposite of the science of withdrawal). Julia Kristeva considers the idea of a 'transitional' or 'transitive' space as important in thinking about national communities in more open ways.[80] We might consider what a transitional (as opposed to autistic) logic might mean in the context of imagining virtual communities. The point is to broaden and to politicise the debate on community and collectivity in cyberspace. Those who will, of course, continue to work for this new form of association should not be allowed to set the agenda on their own narrow, and often technocratic, terms.

THE WORLDS WE LIVE IN

We can all too easily think of cyberspace and virtual reality in terms of an alternative space and reality. As if it were possible to create a new reality which would no longer be open to objections like that which has been left behind. As if we could substitute a reality more in conformity with our desires for the unsatisfactory real one. The new technologies seem to offer possibilities for re-creating the world afresh. We can see virtual culture, then, in terms of utopia: as expressing the principle of hope and the belief in a better word. That is the most obvious response. It is the one that virtual marketing and promotion always peddles. But we can also see virtual culture from an opposite perspective: instead of hopes for a new world, we would then see dissatisfactions about, and rejection of, an old one. This would have the more apocalyptic sense of looking back on the end of the world; what would be more significant would be the sense of an ending. This is how I am inclined to see virtual culture – because there is something banal and unpersuasive about its utopian ideal, and because what is more striking to me about it is its regressive (infantile, Edenic) mood and sentiments. It is what I have discussed in terms of omnipotence fantasies (at the individual level) and familial communitarianism (at the group and collective level). Regression as transcendence. Dieter Lenzen interprets contemporary society in terms of redemption through the totalisation of childhood. He sees a project of cultural regeneration through regression:

> A regression from adults to children could cause people to disappear completely in the end, opening the way to a renewal of the world. We can see from this that the phenomenon of expanding childhood observable on all sides can be interpreted as an apocalyptic process. Correspondingly, the disappearance of adults could be understood as the beginning of a cosmic regeneration process based on the destruction of history.[81]

We could see virtual discourse as drawing on this mythology (as well as the more familiar metaphysics of technological progress) when it imagines the possibility of new individuals and new communities.

The mythology of cyberspace is preferred over its sociology. I have argued that it is time to re-locate virtual culture in the real world (the real world that virtual culturalists, seduced by their own metaphors, pronounce dead or dying). Through the development of new technologies, we are, indeed, more and more open to experiences of de-realisation and de-localisation. But we continue to have physical and localised existences. We must consider our state of suspension between these conditions. We must de-mythologise virtual culture if we are to assess the serious implications it has for our personal and collective lives. Far from being some kind of solution for the world's problems – could there ever be a 'solution'? – virtual inversion simply adds to its complexities. Paul Virilio imagines the coexistence of two societies:

> One is a society of 'cocoons' . . . where people hide away at home, linked into communication networks, inert. . . . The other is a society of the ultra-crowded megalopolis and of urban nomadism. . . . Some people, those in the virtual community, will live in the real time of the world-city, but others will live in deferred time, in other words, in the actual city, in the streets.[82]

In the first society, you may be transported by the pleasures of 'fractal dreaming'. The other society will accumulate the reality that has been repressed. We know that what is repressed cannot be kept out of the dreams.

Chapter 5

CONSUMING IMAGES

From the symbolic to the psychotic

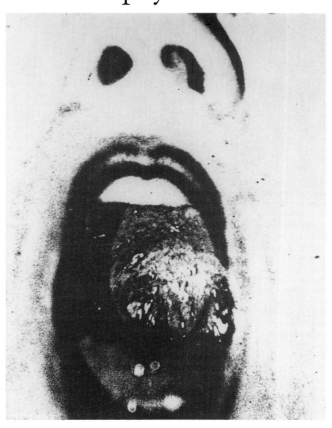

5

CONSUMING IMAGES
From the symbolic to the psychotic

The soft machine is the human body under constant siege from a vast hungry host of parasites with many names but one nature being hungry and one intention to eat.

(William Burroughs, *The Soft Machine*)

When our knowledge is hard to bear with, our only escape is to treat it the way we treat things that offend us: we sweep such things away, put them at a distance from which their stench or repulsive sight is less likely to affect us; we hide them. Offensive thoughts must be *suppressed*.

(Zygmunt Bauman, *Mortality, Immortality and Other Life Strategies*)

How strange it is. We have these deep terrible lingering fears about ourselves and the people we love. Yet we walk around, talk to people, eat and drink. We manage to function. The feelings are deep and real. Shouldn't they paralyse us? How is it we can survive them, at least for a while? We drive a car, we teach a class. How is it no one sees how deeply afraid we were, last night, this morning? Is it something we all hide from each other, by mutual consent? Or do we share the same secret without knowing it? Wear the same disguise.

(Don DeLillo, *White Noise*)

SOCIOLOGIES OF CONSUMPTION

In his book *Captains of Consciousness* written in the mid-1970s, Stuart Ewen analysed the growth of consumer culture in terms of the extension of corporate control over ways of life. 'Far-sighted businessmen', he argued, 'began to see the necessity of organising their business not merely around the production of goods, but around the creation of a buying public [and of] a psychic desire to consume.'[1] This project involved the construction of a 'mass individual': 'by transforming the notion of "class" into "mass", business hoped to create an "individual" who could locate his needs and frustrations in terms of the consumption of goods rather than the quality and content of his life (work)'.[2] The advertising industry 'increasingly offered mass-produced solutions to "instinctive" strivings', though this could include 'mass produced visions of individualism by which people could extricate themselves from the mass'.[3] Ewen paints a bleak picture in which authentic (popular) culture is overwhelmed by the false and fetishistic order of the market. The consumer believes that new freedoms are on offer, but is cruelly deceived in that belief. What is on offer is no more than the illusion of freedom: 'The linking of the market-place to utopian ideals, to political and social freedom, to material well-being, and to the realisation of fantasy, represents the spectacle of liberation emanating from the bowels of domination and denial.'[4] The spectacle is the device of corporate interests.

Two decades later, in the mid-1990s, the critique of consumer culture developed by Stuart Ewen seems to belong to another era. Neither his deterministic tone, which sees capital as all-powerful and consumers as passive victims, nor his moralistic attitude, which judges commodified identity in the light of authentic identity, fits easily with our times. Our attitude to consumer culture has changed significantly. During the 1980s, we experienced the fierce promotion of enterprise and market culture under successive Thatcher and Reagan governments. We also witnessed the dramatic collapse of an alternative to capitalist values. As a consequence of these developments there has been a growing acceptance of the need to live with, and to work within the parameters of, consumer culture. The world has become the world of commodities and, it is argued, we must accommodate ourselves to this reality (and its pleasures). This was precisely the context within which the 'New Times' project sought to develop a radical alternative to the neo-liberal market ideology. In this post-Marxist agenda, the issue was about commodities and lifestyles and the empowerment of the consumer; it was a question of creating markets that would respond to the diversity of consumer needs and preferences. What was argued was that capitalist societies were actually undergoing a process of transformation, characterised in terms of the shift from Fordism to post-Fordism, and that the logic of this transformation was opening up new possibilities for a more democratic (and more pleasurable) consumer culture. Post-Fordism was about the construction of more complex, segmented markets that would permit more flexible and plural lifestyles. Consumption was seen as a creative and transformative act, with the real promise of freedom. Here was the spectacle of liberation without the bowels of domination and denial.

In the development of cultural and media studies, there has been this same shift of concern and perspective. More deterministic accounts of media influence have generally given way to ideas about the active audience. Moralistic responses to the media have generally been replaced by a more detached, or ethnographic, stance. Alan Tomlinson notes the progression from an older generation of cultural critics who saw consumerism as a 'Corrupting Other' ('a sad, dislocated, elitist, and perhaps menopausal, critique') to a younger generation that recognises that 'consumer culture can be exciting novel, convenient and fun; it can be energising rather than enervating'.[5] Martyn Lee describes the same trajectory of change in terms of the evolution from an older generation with 'totalising and wholly negative definitions' of cultural consumption, to a new generation for whom 'popular culture is transformed into a marvellously subversive space in which its forms and artefacts are seen, not as the reason for melancholic denigration as objects of ontological alienation and exploitation, but precisely the reverse: a cause for celebration'.[6] The new generation validates the experience of consumption, and is concerned to explore how it relates to questions of self-expression, identity and pleasure. Moral denunciation has ceded to the more dispassionate survey of the micro-practices of cultural consumption.

This trajectory of development is familiar to us all, and provides the familiar context for contemporary sociological debates around cultural consumption. I want to make some brief preliminary observations on these sociological perspectives before going on to consider some alternative approaches to the phenomenon of consumption. My focus, in this and in the following sections, will be primarily on the consumption of media and media products.

Sociological and ethnographic studies of media consumption developed very much out of a kind of oedipal struggle against an older generation of cultural critics and all they stood for. Where the older generation deplored what it considered to be the corrupting nature of the market, the younger took commercial culture seriously, arguing in favour of its enabling and empowering potential. Where the older generation veered towards elitism and moralism, the younger was convinced of the active and creative capacities of audiences, and risked succumbing to relativism and populism. What I am suggesting is that the agenda of consumption studies was defined against what it rejected in the older generation. In this sense, we can say that what it stands for has been determined, in a negative sense, by that older generation: its almost exclusive emphasis on pleasure and symbolic gratification was in defiance of what it saw as a puritanical and instrumentalist understanding of the consumption of popular media.

Let us be clear that, as a consequence of this process of self-definition through opposition and rejection, consumption studies have made a valuable contribution to our understanding of individual and social uses of the media. However, the historical process through which they have become defined in their interests and scope has not been without cost. There is the sense of continual vigilance, occasionally with overtones of political correctness, in the face of possible counter-attack from 'determinism' or 'elitism'. Indeed, one sometimes has the feeling that the 'other' of cultural determinism or elitism is necessary to the realisation of a sense of purpose and momentum. There is also the problematical consequence that the research agenda has tended to become focused around a rather narrow conceptual repertoire (meaning, identity, distinction, pleasure). This has meant that consumption and audience studies have remained somewhat detached from many of the agendas and debates that have been of concern within the broader field of media studies. Take as an example the question of media and democracy. This, too, raises the issue of media consumption – though it does so within a quite different intellectual perspective – and one might expect cultural studies of consumption to cast some light, from their perspective, on the behaviour of the rational citizen-consumer posited within theories of the mediated public sphere. Should they not have something to say about the processes of cognition, understanding and judgement that are supposed to be occurring in this particular sphere of media consumption? Or take media coverage of war and conflict, of Bosnia, say. What might the idea of the active audience contribute to our understanding of such a viewing experience? What are we to think about pleasure or identity in a context where anguish, despair or compassion might be more appropriate responses? I am suggesting that the 'consumer self' remains a rather limited concept, which needs to be related to broader aspects of human behaviour and motivation. I also think that there is a need to achieve a better accommodation between theoretical elaboration and responsiveness to the world's events and issues. At a time when its agenda should be opened up, there is the danger that consumption and audience studies will be content to occupy a small and self-contained island within the field of media and cultural studies. The risk is that they will become stuck in the repetitive defence of their own *status quo*.

Over the past three or four years we have seen a gathering dissatisfaction with consumption and audience studies. What we are beginning to see is the reassertion, against the idea of the active audience, of old arguments about media power and control. As David Morley observes, critiques of 'active audience theory' are all too predictably resulting in 'clarion calls for the return to the "old certainties" of political economy and conspiracy theory and to models of imposed "dominant ideologies"'.[7] And so we find ourselves still caught up in the stalemate encounter that has affected media and cultural studies for so long: the false polarisation that opposes those concerned with the shaping force of structural and 'macro' processes against those interested in questions of agency and in 'micro' processes. Morley argues, quite rightly, that we must resist the temptation of this old confrontation. The imperative is to find a way of 'steering between the dangers of an improper romanticism of "consumer freedoms", on the one hand, and a paranoiac fantasy of "global control", on the other'. 'The challenge', he proposes, 'lies precisely in the attempt to construct a model of television consumption that is sensitive to both the "vertical" dimension of power and ideology and the "horizontal" dimension of television's insertion in, and articulation with, the context and practices of everyday life.'[8]

It is in the spirit of this proposal that the following arguments and discussion are elaborated. I shall accept the idea of the active audience as the starting point for my reflections. What will concern me are the nature and the motivations of audience activity. Within cultural and media studies, great emphasis has been put on the symbolic, expressive and affirmative nature of consumption. This very much reflects the general association now of consumer culture with human freedom. In consumer ideology, Zygmunt Bauman observes, capitalism seems to have found the secret of the philosopher's stone.

110

All customers may be free and happy at the same time; identities and pleasures are not scarce goods. 'For the consumer', he suggests, 'reality is [no longer] the enemy of pleasure. The tragic moment has been removed from the insatiable drive to enjoyment. Reality as the consumer experiences it, *is* a pursuit of pleasure.' 'As if this was not a sufficiently formidable achievement', Bauman argues, 'the world of consumption seems to have cured freedom from another affliction: insecurity. In its consumer version, individual freedom may be exercised without sacrificing that certainty which lies at the bottom of spiritual security.'[9] It is within this framework that ideas about active consumers and audiences have been elaborated.

But it is possible to consider consumer activity and activeness in a quite different light. In this light, we are still very far from reconciling ourselves with the difficult and intractable principle of reality, and insecurity remains a powerful motivating force in our conduct. Consumption may then be seen as one of the institutionalised strategies of social defence that we have developed to cope with the real world; it serves to evade or to insulate against the anxieties or fears provoked by our relation to that world. It is precisely this relation of consumption to anxiety that concerns Don DeLillo in his novel *White Noise*:

> Pain, death, reality, these are all unnatural. We can't bear these things as they are. We know too much. So we resort to repression, compromise and disguise. This is how we survive in the universe. This is the natural language of the species.[10]

This matter of how we survive in the universe seems to me to be quite crucial, and I now want to consider its significance in more detail. In doing so, I shall argue that, as well as its symbolic aspects, we should also take into account what I would call the psychotic temptation of consumption.

THE SOFT MACHINE

For Elias Canetti, fear and anxiety are fundamental to human experience, and strategies for living with fear and anxiety are fundamental to human cultural life. 'Man's body is naked and vulnerable in its softness to every assault,' writes Canetti.

> With care and cunning he may be able to fend off things which come near, but it is easy to reach him from a distance; spears and arrows can transfix him. He has invented shields and armour, and built walls and whole fortresses around himself; what he most desires from all these precautions is a feeling of invulnerability.[11]

What Canetti is saying about physical defences can help us to understand culture as a strategy of defence. Cultural barriers and containers have also been constructed to 'fend things off'; forms of cultural organisation and expression have been mobilised to sustain the sense of invulnerable existence.

In *Civilisation and Its Discontents*, Freud provides some important clues for understanding these mechanisms of cultural defence and insulation. Emphasising how much unhappiness and suffering constantly threaten our well-being, he argues that the avoidance of unpleasure may be a more significant motivating force in human behaviour than the obtaining of pleasure. Freud's observations suggest that evasive strategies may take the form of screening or filtering painful realities, or, alternatively, they may work towards the transformation or even the substitution of reality. In the first case, it is a matter of diminishing the impact of incoming stimuli. 'In the last analysis,' Freud maintains, 'all suffering is nothing else than sensation; it only exists in so far as we feel it.'[12] This being the case, one must find the means to contain and control the pain of reality, to keep suffering at a distance: what is called for is some form of narcosis of the senses. In the second case, it is a question of making oneself independent of the external world. Satisfaction may be obtained from illusions, for example, 'which are recognised as such without the discrepancy between them and reality being allowed to interfere with enjoyment'. More than this, 'one can try to re-create the world, to build up in its stead another world in which its most unbearable features are eliminated and replaced by others that are in conformity with one's own wishes'.[13] Freud describes this as the 'delusional remoulding of reality', which may be undertaken either individually or collectively.

In the context of modernity and the modern world, this struggle between culture and reality assumes new and heightened forms. Susan Buck-Morss (following Benjamin, Simmel and Freud) describes how 'the technologically altered environment exposes the human sensorium to physical shocks that have their correspondence in psychic shock', such that 'shock is the very essence of modern experience'.[14] Protection against stimuli then becomes more important than their reception. Consciousness must become 'a shield protecting the organism against stimuli':

> The ego employs consciousness as a buffer, blocking the openness of the anaesthetic system, thereby isolating present consciousness from past memory. Without the depth of memory, experience is impoverished. The problem is that under conditions of modern shock – the daily shocks of the modern world – response to stimuli *without* thinking has become necessary for survival.[15]

What have been the cultural responses to shock? One tendency has been to develop the means to diminish sensation. 'Its goal', says Buck-Morss 'is to *numb* the organism, to deaden the senses, to repress memory: the cognitive system of synaesthetics has become, rather, one of anaesthetics.' Anaesthesia is associated with the change 'from a cognitive mode of being "in touch" with reality to a way of blocking out reality'.[16] Another tendency has been to create an alternative, illusory or delusory, reality through 'sensory distraction'. In the case of such 'sensory addiction to a compensatory reality', the objective is 'manipulation of the synaesthetic system by control of environmental stimuli. It has the effect of anaesthetising the organism, not through numbing, but through flooding the senses.'[17] In both tendencies, it is technology that mediates between the human sensorium and the shocks of modern existence; technological shields and technological fortresses are made to fend off the things of the modern world.

I want to propose that these aspects of human culture and experience are very significant for understanding the cultural meaning of consumption. In general, the consumer has been conceived as a rational-aesthetic being, concerned with how best to satisfy needs, confirm identity or achieve pleasure. I am suggesting that vulnerability and anxiety, and the consequent motivation to avoid discomfort and unpleasure, are also significant factors that should be taken into account. Don DeLillo has described modern consumption as a form of 'mass anaesthesia', a means 'by which the culture softens the texture of real danger'.[18] We must acknowledge how much consumption is linked to protection of the emotional and bodily self. In so far as modern consumption involves the mobilisation of anaesthetising strategies, we might consider it in the context of what Giorgio Agamben (again following Walter Benjamin) describes as 'the destruction of experience'. The modern world is characterised, he argues, by the 'expropriation of experience' and the subsequent 'imposition of a form of experience as controlled and manipulated as a laboratory maze for rats'. 'Standing face to face with one of the great wonders of the world', he suggests, 'the overwhelming majority of people have no wish to experience it, preferring instead that the camera should.'[19] This touristic attitude is precisely that of the consumer. Here I want simply to note this transformation of experience (without becoming involved in debates about the validity and value of different kinds of experience).

In considering the modification and control of experience as central to the nature of consumption, it is appropriate to raise the question of drugs and addiction. A recent newspaper article compares computer games to drugs, arguing that 'next to crack, the video game is probably the most addictive product yet invented'.[20] The image is common and familiar, and it does not surprise us; it seems banal and predictable. There is, indeed, a spontaneous and commonsense association of consumerism with the imagery of drugs and addiction. Excessive and deviant forms of consumption seem to reveal something to us about the meaning of 'normal' consumption. What is particularly significant is the loss of the sense of reality. In his discussion of strategies for coping with the frustrations of external reality, Freud describes the effects of intoxication and 'intoxicating media' for 'keeping misery at a distance'. In addition to the immediate yield of pleasure, he argues, such media also afford 'a greatly desired degree of independence from the external world .... One can at any time withdraw from the pressure of reality and find refuge in a world of one's own with better conditions of sensibility.'[21] It is this taking refuge in a world of one's own that meets with social disapproval. Drugs are prohibited because of the way their consumers are deemed to lose their sense of reality. Society holds against the drug-taker the fact 'that he cuts himself off from the world, in exile from reality, far from objective reality and the real life of the city and the community; that he escapes into a world of simulation and fiction.'[22] Video games are compared to drugs because they too seem to encourage withdrawal and independence from the real world. However much we might criticise such an idea, however much we might emphasise their very obvious differences, the comparison of crack with computer games still appeals to the popular imagination; there is, I would suggest, a certain reason and resonance in the comparison.

'Drug addiction is characteristic of modernity', argues Susan Buck-Morss, 'It is the correlate and counterpart of shock.'[23] In it we can see something about the broader transformation in our relation and attitude to the external world. Drug experience – which has become 'the discarding of all experience'[24] – is the most intense expression of the overall destruction of experience. Today, indeed, we can say that the continuity between 'normal' and 'pathological' transformations of experience is resulting in the increasing difficulty of identifying a specific 'drug problem'. It is increasingly difficult to police the frontier between drug experiences and other forms of technological suppression or enhancement of our senses and feelings.[25] What is raised is the general question of the technological mediation of our senses and feelings.

FEAR AND KNOWLEDGE

I want, at this point, to turn to the consumption of media, and particularly television. In so doing, I want to focus, not on questions of pleasure, entertainment or identity consolidation, but rather on processes of cognition and intellection. More particularly still, I shall be concerned only with the most painful kinds of knowing and thinking. To watch television in our culture is to be exposed to violence, suffering and death. Across both documentary and fictional modes of programme, it is difficult to avoid the sight of actual or contrived dying. And yet this is occurring in a context in which the real experience of death is increasingly sequestered. In our culture, the personal and existential questions of death are denied and repressed. How are we to make sense of this apparent paradox? What motivates this kind of consumption? What are the uses and gratifications of watching people die? How can the vision of such terrible things be borne?

Slavenka Drakulić describes television coverage of the death of a small child in Sarajevo. The camera zooms in on the death scene; it shoots a close up of her father's eyes ... 'the camera returns to it several times'; the camera seeks out the wounded mother in the hospital:

> This is the end, this has to be the end. The camera can't go any further than the inhuman suffering of the mother who has lost her child.... This has to stop, I repeat to myself while the camera rolls on.... I don't want the camera to enter under that cover hiding her small body. But someone's hand surpasses my thoughts and lifts the white sheet.... We see a close-up of death. Then cut.[26]

In Bosnia we have seen it all: 'beheaded corpses being eaten by pigs and dogs. Eyes gouged out, scattered bodily parts that do not belong to anyone, anything. Skeletons and half-rotten skulls, children without legs, babies killed by sniper fire. A 12-year old rape victim talking about it on camera.'[27] We have seen all that on everyday television. We have watched chat shows, sport, MTV, but we have also watched all that. We have consumed this terrible 'pornography of the dying'. Through the medium of television we have, willingly it seems, exposed our reason and our emotions to the shock of these traumatic happenings of necrophiliac television.[28]

What can be our motivations for entering the war zone of television? How are we consuming, that is to say incorporating, the reality of such television? These are hopelessly difficult questions to answer. Of course, the straightforward search for knowledge about what is going on in the world must be an important factor. As Régis Debray quite rightly reminds us, such television has 'opened hearts and minds to suffering and oppression that was previously invisible, and in so doing, it has created a sort of global public opinion with some influence in the world'.[29] Opinion may be turned into compassion and compassion into active concern. But it does not seem that this is true in all cases, or that this is all that is going on in those who respond in such a way. Perhaps there are other factors to be taken into account. Zygmunt Bauman pays attention to the sense of survival, suggesting that, in a certain sense, we 'live through the deaths of the others, and their death gives meaning to our success: we have not died, *we* are *still* alive'.[30] Elias Canetti, too, puts emphasis on the pleasure of survival, claiming that 'Horror at the sight of death turns into satisfaction that it is someone else who is dead.'[31] Philip Mellor and Chris Shilling believe that what is significant is the way in which the meaning of death is fragmented and individualised:

> The thousands of deaths people tend to see on television during their lives also have this effect: they see the individual causes of the deaths of individual people, in individual circumstances, thus encouraging the view of death as avoidable and contingent. These deaths are therefore reassuring rather than threatening, since they orientate people towards strategies of survival rather than making them aware of the futility of all strategies in the face of mortality.[32]

In the context of this general discussion, it is only possible to speculate on the psychic processes that are mobilised. One must assume that audience engagement with the material of pain and death contains such elements of motivation. It is difficult otherwise to understand how such sights could be tolerated, and tolerated on such a continuous and repetitive basis.

Such material is surely the most shocking that can be imagined. The viewer should be devastated by the intense shock of such realities. The consumer of suffering and terror should be traumatised by the incorporation of such vision. But, for the most part at least, this is not what seems to happen. Audiences appear to be relatively unscathed by their encounters with the violence of war. How this could be so is something that stands in need of explanation. If it is difficult to fully understand why viewers choose exposure to pain and dying, perhaps we can say a little more about how, having once exposed themselves, they are able to escape the emotional and moral consequences of seeing and knowing. It is a question of identifying the mechanisms through which the reality of such things is blocked out, or is held at a distance. That we continue to walk around, to talk to people, to eat and drink, demonstrates that such means must exist. How is it, then, that such realities can be defused?

First, we should consider what the viewing and consuming of such images is about. Here there is the need to reorientate ourselves concerning the nature and the motivations of information gathering and opinion formation. We take for granted the desire to know (though, as I have suggested above, that we should desire to see and know certain things defies our rational comprehension). We generally do not take account of, or even recognise the existence of, the equally strong desire to *not* know, to *evade* knowledge. Knowledge may have disturbing or frightening consequences, so there may be reason to fend off things we do not want to see or hear. We may feel the hopelessness of knowing: to know some awful truth without the possibility of changing it can lead to utter despair. As Slavenka Drukulić argues, the fact that 'it is possible to watch war from so near in its most macabre details, makes sense only if, because of that, something can change for the better'.[33] Without that possibility, there is a certain obscenity to knowing. Alternatively, it may be the case that knowing about such things would entail making some change in ourselves. And because such change would be painful to both the individual and the social group, defensive organisations may be formed to resist and refuse knowledge and its consequences. As Wilfred Bion emphasises, strategies of evasion and dissimulation are as important in understanding human motivation as is the pursuit of clarity and truth.[34] We may evade knowledge, but we may also seek to contain its disruptive possibilities. What is known may be withheld from the processes of thinking; it may exist as the 'unthought known'.[35] Bion supposes that 'a primitive "thinking", active in the development of thought, should be distinguished from the thinking that is required for the use of thoughts'.[36] We can do other things with thoughts, he argues, than to think them. We might see the 'response to stimuli without thinking' that Susan Buck-Morss[37] sees as crucial to survival in the modern world, in terms of this inhibition of the kind of thinking required for the *use* of thoughts.

We must also consider how the medium through which such images are viewed and consumed might also be implicated in defusing their painful reality. I want to suggest that the screen plays a significant part in the compromising accommodation between the drives to know and to not know. 'Never before has an age been so informed about itself,' observed Siegfried Kracauer, some seventy years ago, in a discussion of photography and illustrated magazines. But immediately there is a qualification to this observation: 'Never before has a period known so little about itself. . . . The "image-idea" drives away the idea; the blizzard of photographs betrays an indifference toward what things mean.'[38] This is even more the case in the age of television and video technologies, when images of the world proliferate as never before. The television screen presents us with a wealth of information, but equally it functions to screen out the reality of what is seen and to inhibit knowledge. 'In the illustrated magazines', Kracauer wrote, 'people see the very world that the illustrated magazines prevent them from seeing.'[39] With television, this paradoxical relation between what is seen and what is consequently not seen is massively intensified. What is achieved is a condition in which exposure to the world's events is maximised, whilst, at the same time, exposure to their consequences is minimised. The screen that provides us with information about the world's realities is also a screen against the shock of seeing and knowing about those realities.

Through this technological form of seeing, it is possible to maintain a distance from what is seen. What it permits is an anaesthetised kind of knowing. 'We have seen', says Régis Debray (1992: 380), 'how miniaturisation through the image can render acceptable, and even picturesque, distant war and slaughter that would not be tolerable in its true nature and scale.'[40] A certain reality is perceived but its significance is de-realised. 'To reduce a column of civilian vehicles or a bombarded city to the size of a video screen', Debray continues, 'is not the best way to "realise" the human costs of a bombing expedition.'[41] The weightlessness of the image induces a sense of detachment and remoteness from what is seen. What is at issue is the condition of knowledge in the context of the transformation, or destruction, of experience. The point is 'not . . . that today there are no more experiences, but they are enacted outside the individual. And it is interesting that the individual merely observes them, with relief.'[42] The observer is outside, and protected from, the experience. The screen is a shield insulating him or her from the bombardment of experience.

Television seduces us with 'an undreamed of extension of impressions, experiences and fantasies', but at the same time it brings about 'the loss of the corporeal' and the 'desensualisation' of experience.[43] Television, says

François Brune, is about 'the flight from reality' and the attainment of a certain 'euphoria by evasion'. This involves the substitution of '*le vécu*' for '*le vivant*', where *le vécu* amounts to the 'simulation of others' experiences'.[44] Within the domain of mediated senses, the catastrophic and the banal are rendered homogeneous and consumed with equal commitment: 'Everything is cultural, everything is moral, everything is ethical, everything is aesthetic, everything is banal, everything is positive.'[45] This is the binding of experience into consumption. The media world 'renders most fundamental conditions of social existence invisible', argues Zygmunt Bauman, and at the same time it is tending to become 'the only reality against which the experience of the free consumer can and ought to be tested'.[46] What is comforting about this world is that it is possible to be simultaneously 'in touch' with reality and fending off its disturbing or threatening actuality.

In trying to think about media consumption and cognition as I have, I am not claiming to describe how individual viewers watch television. I am concerned, rather, with the cultural and technological context in, and sometimes against, which the viewing process occurs. It is a context that promotes a kind of schizophrenia, 'allowing us, on the one hand, to magically control our position *vis à vis* the world and its spectacles, and, on the other, to maintain a distance, never becoming actors in it and therefore never having to assume responsibilities'.[47] This kind of knowing has, it seems to me, enormous moral, emotional and existential implications. We may consider this agenda in terms of how our relation to the world is transformed through such technological mediation. We should also consider how media technologies are also, and at the same time, responding to more basic and continuous psychic demands.

The significance of these matters is confirmed, poignantly and humorously, in the fiction of Don DeLillo. DeLillo is drawn to televised images of death and disaster, concerned with what their consumption might tell us about our political and cultural unconscious. *Mao II* describes the television experience of Tiananmen Square, of Ayatollah Khomeini's funeral, of the Hillsborough stadium tragedy. One figure, Karen, watches Hillsborough with the sound switched off, gazing at an accumulation of images. 'They show men standing off to the side somewhere, watching sort of half interested. She sees a great straining knot of people pressed to a fence, forced massively forward.' The images pile up:

> In people's faces she sees the hopelessness of knowing. They show men calmly looking on. They show the face from a distance, bodies piling up behind it, smothered, sometimes only fingers moving, and it is like a fresco in an old dark church, a crowded vision of a rush to death as only a master of the age could paint it.[48]

DeLillo describes the numbed quality of witness in the age of television. Dispassionate proximity, intimate detachment. As one commentator on

DeLillo's work observes, 'television neither satisfies desire nor makes for catharsis. Its effect is anaesthetic.'[49] We can replay the events over and over again, watch them endless times. Repetition numbs further: 'By isolating the event and repeating it, its content, its horror evaporates. What we have before us is its form and rhythm. The event becomes aesthetic and the effect upon us anaesthetic.[50]

DeLillo is concerned with the perverse desire that people have to consume such images. In *White Noise*, the Gladney family settles down to Friday evening entertainment, 'watching houses slide into the ocean, whole villages crackle and ignite in a mass of advancing lava. Every disaster made us wish for more, for something bigger, grander, more sweeping.'[51] How can this intrigue with catastrophe be explained? At one level, it may be that 'we need an occasional catastrophe to break up the incessant bombardment of informa-tion. . . . Only a catastrophe gets our attention. We want them, we need them, we depend on them.'[52] But there is perhaps a deeper reason. As Tom LeClair observes in his analysis of *White Noise*, 'the effect of televised death is, like consumerism, anaesthetising. A seeming confrontation with reality is actually a means of evading one's own mortality.'[53] The consumption of such images is blocking out profound existential fears. (Siegfried Kracauer, inter-estingly, considers the consumption of news photographs in the same light: 'That the world devours them is a sign of the *fear of death*.'[54])

CONSUMING AND REALITY

Susan Buck-Morss draws our attention to the significance of phantasmagoric effects in both the experience of, and the defences against, the modern world.[55] In the nineteenth century, such effects were provided by bourgeois household interiors, by the glamour of shopping arcades, by the World Fairs, and also by panoramas and dioramas. Subsequently, in the twentieth century, they have been created through shopping malls, theme parks, video arcades, through the environment of the airplane, the phenomenon of the 'tourist bubble', the soundscape of the 'walkman', the visual surround of advertising, and so on. All of these may be described as environments of consumption, and, of course, historians and sociologists of consumption have written extensively about the exciting and giddy experience of these environments of modernity.

Through the effects of phantasmagoria, Buck-Morss argues, 'a narcotic was made out of reality itself'. In the case of arcades and of bourgeois interiors which 'immersed the home-dweller in a total environment, a privatised fantasy world that functioned as a protective shield for the sense and sensibilities of this new ruling class', this is, indeed, so.[56] So, too, with the urban *flâneur*, skilled in the 'capacity of distancing oneself by turning reality into a phantasmagoria: rather than being caught up in the crowd, he slows his pace and observes it, making a pattern out of its surface. He sees the crowd as a reflection of his dream mood, an "intoxication" for his senses.'[57] But in other cases, what is at issue is narcosis through immersion in *alternative* realities. Through technological means, it became possible to create an 'altered world', a 'compensatory reality', an 'appearance of reality that tricks the senses through technical manipulation'.[58] We may see it, following Freud, in terms of the aspiration to re-create the world, to build in its stead another world in which its most unbearable features are eliminated and replaced by others in conformity with one's own wishes (we might now call it 'user-friendly').

Both of these modes of phantasmagoric experience constitute responses to the shock of modern existence, not in terms of the numbing or deadening of sensation, but rather through the control and management of stimuli. It is precisely a question of the technological mediation and enhancement of senses and emotions. There is the possibility of generating soothing and euphoric feelings. Zoë Heller, for example, reports the growth in the United States of New Age 'consciousness tech', that is, of 'brain machines' for promoting relaxed and de-stressed states of being.[59] Here the womb-like and containing environment of technology is intended to respond to the body's desire for equilibrium or entropy. Alternatively, there is the possibility of creating environments which bombard the senses and actually make a pleasure out of shock. Lieven de Cauter describes the 'synergetic pleasure' in using machines – cars, planes, speedboats, video and computer games – to experience speed, vertigo, disorientation.[60] In either case, the effect is that of anaesthetising the organism, not through numbing, but through flooding the senses. A 'compensatory reality' is used to achieve 'sensory distraction', blocking out competing stimuli of a more threatening kind. What is signifiant, in both cases, is that it is possible to regulate and control the sensorium.

I want now to consider this kind of consumption experience (or relation to experience) specifically with respect to television and post-television technologies. Image and vision technologies raise interesting issues because of their borderline condition between representation and phantasmagoria. We generally think about them in realist terms, in terms of their representational and referential qualities, in terms of how they give us sight of the world and its events (this was precisely the point of concern in the preceding section). But we may equally consider these technologies in terms of sensory distraction and sensory involvement in compensatory realities, that is to say, in terms of the intoxication of phantasmagoria. Already in the nineteenth century, one aspect of visual culture reflected 'a retreat from modernity which took the form of a withdrawal from the complexities of both experiencing and registering the changing nature of modern life'.[61] This retreat was associated with attempts to construct alternative realities, and, more than this, to immerse the viewer in these presenting realities. Through the subsequent evolution of image and vision media, it can be argued, it is this phantasmagoric dimension that has become increasingly significant. Indeed, writers like Paul

Virilio and Jean Baudrillard have famously and frequently argued that this is precisely what characterises postmodern experience. Gianni Vattimo believes that what now prevails is 'the world of merchandise and images, the phantasmagoria of the mass media', and that 'the proliferation of images of the world entails that we lose our "sense of reality"'. It is the 'loss of reality', the 'genuine erosion of the principle of reality', that, in his view, distinguishes the postmodern world.[62] What it reflects, I shall argue, is actually the desire to take refuge from the shocking and exhausting reality of the modern world.

Let us consider media consumption in this context, beginning with television. Our relation to the television screen seems to contradict the postmodern thesis, so much has it been associated historically with the representation and documentation of the real world. And yet increasingly, I think, there is reason and justification for thinking about screen watching in the light of phantasmagoric defences. Reality shows provide an excellent focus for exploring phantasmagoric experience, precisely because they seem to reveal a growth, even, in concern about the real world, real people, real problems. In one respect this is, indeed, the case. No doubt, viewers feel that reality shows are engaging them directly – without the mediation of professional commentators and interpreters – in contemporary social issues. But there is more to be said. We must take account of the nature of audience engagement, and particularly of the immediacy of involvement and participation. What are being mobilised by reality shows are feelings and sensations, at the expense of reason, analysis, reflection. Engagement is about flooding the senses and shocking the emotions. 'On the one hand', writes François Brune, 'there is a world that can no longer be understood or mastered, and, on the other, there is the primacy of the visual and of its euphoric and dramatised signs. . . . The substitutes of image and emotion are offered to those who have lost their hold on the real world.'[63] In this respect, reality shows may be seen in terms of phantasmagoric experience: a narcotic is made out of reality itself; there is sensory distraction through a compensatory reality.

Alain Ehrenberg argues that reality shows 'push back representation in favour of presence' and that they should be seen in the context of an overall shift in audiovisual culture 'from the era of representation to that of sensation and stimulation'. Interactivity is the key phenomenon. Ehrenberg sees the consumption of reality television in terms of the pleasures of submitting to vertiginous experiences and controlled shocks of the kind that may be mastered and controlled. They are part of the same domain of experience as drugs and synergetic pleasures. Reality shows 'plunge the consumer into a bath of sensations . . . transforming the screen from being a receiver of images to being a producer of corporeal shocks'.[64] They are precisely about pleasure, and at the same time anaesthesia, through intoxication of the senses.

Reality television may be seen as anticipating, ahead of any technological transformation, the experience of post-television, and particularly of virtual-reality systems. Virtual reality – given the undeveloped state of the technology at the present time, we are, in fact, talking about the desire for, and psychic investment in, virtual experience – presents itself as the ultimate in sensation and stimulation, the most perfect of vertigo machines. Virtual reality – the scientific project and the science fiction that idealises it – is inspired by the dream of an alternative and compensatory reality, a factitious world that will surround us and incorporate us. We may think of it as the fulfilment of television or computer technologies; in terms of a screen which may be entered, a screen world in which we can be immersed. Alternatively, it may be seen as an electronic simulation of the shopping mall or theme park or 'tourist bubble'. It is also possible to see this technological enhancement of senses and emotions in the context of drug experience. Virtual reality is strongly associated with psychedelic counter-culture (Timothy Leary is one of its most vocal ideologists). As the entrepreneurial guru of virtual culture, Jaron Lanier, puts it, virtual reality 'has the fun of the Sixties' idea of what drugs were, along with the safety and insulation you have with computers'.[65] Virtual reality might be considered the ultimate consumer environment.

In this (still putative) world, the complexities and intractabilities of the real world are screened out. The culture of virtual reality reflects 'the desire to escape both the human body and the human world'.[66] Here it is possible to exist as a virtual self, an aetherial and protean entity, rid of the density of being that afflicts our real self and body. Here there is the possibility of doing 'virtually' things that are impossible, or are prohibited, in real life; there is the chance to overcome the physical and moral restrictions that limit the expression of imagination and fantasy. There is the belief that this other reality 'will be richly complex and yet somehow ouchlessly transcendent of the messy contradictions of our Euclidean space and fleshy groundedness'.[67] This is a world of perfect illusion and intoxication, a world that is in conformity with our wishes. We can have oceanic and womb-like experiences of floating comfort, or we can take pleasure in the eroticism of cybersex, which will be 'like having sex while doing the best designer drugs, without the hangover and without having to negotiate limits with partners'.[68] Virtual reality is so attractive because it combines entertainment and thrills with comfort and security. This is the pleasure of the interface and of interactive consumption. The pleasure of uninhibited consumption.

If the perfection of image technologies is associated with perfecting the pleasures of consumption (making it more active), it may equally and simultaneously be associated with the avoidance, the fending off, of un-pleasure and unhappiness. That modern prototype of the consumer, the *flâneur*, is commonly thought of in terms of freedom and pleasure. But, as Elizabeth Wilson reminds us, he was also driven by profound insecurity and anxiety.[69] The pleasures of the postmodern consumer of video and computer games are equally implicated in the mastering of anxiety.[70] Behind the pleasures of consumption, then, it is possible to detect a sense of anxiety about the real world and its assaults on the consumer. We must also take account of more primordial anxieties, those associated with our own bodies and mortality (and this is just what Don DeLillo takes so seriously). Jaron Lanier, who is now a great celebrity of virtual-reality culture, makes the point quite clearly when he argues that technology is 'kind of a flight from death ... [it] has the promise of transcending the body, depending of what you think a body is, because it brings with it tremendous objective power'.[71] Virtual reality blocks out the fear of death:

> There's a tendency to think about technology in terms of the gadgetry aspect of it, but actually the cultural component in technological products is every bit as important. In a virtual reality system the only part you can perceive is the cultural component. The whole character reverses itself, becomes very warm, takes on a feeling of intimacy. You make up a world, and somebody else goes into the world. It feels very close, very human.[72]

Flight from the fear of death takes the consumer of virtual reality into a womb-like environment which responds to infantile desires for omnipotence and immortality.

The consumption of media technologies and products raises questions about our – ever more troubled, it seems – relation to reality and the real world. John Steiner alerts us to how 'different mechanisms of defence affect our contact with reality in different ways'. In certain cases, with repression for example, 'a symbolic connexion with reality is retained'; at the other extreme, in psychotic forms of defence, contact with reality may be lost, and 'the very structures required to perceive reality [may be] attacked and impaired'.[73] We might consider image technologies and their consumption in the light of this spectrum of possibilities. Here, of course, it is not a question of individual disorders, but, rather, of the whole institution of visual culture, of what has become an institutionalised and normalised technological order. Generally, we may see image technologies as still being 'in touch' with reality. But they may also be mobilised as intoxicating and narcotic distractions or defences against the vicissitudes of reality. And, at their most extreme, they may be used to construct alternative and compensatory realities. In contemporary society, Carlo Mongardini argues,

> It is as if, under pressure from the intense material of experience, individuals activated a *psychic defence*, distanced others more and isolated with greater indifference their own interior worlds. The loss of ability to give meaning to reality is also the product of this psychic protection, the desire of the individual not to put himself at risk by exposing himself to the stimulus of a reality he can no longer interpret.[74]

We might see virtual reality as the perfected technological response to this postmodern condition of alienation from physical and social engagement. We might see consumption through virtual reality as a psychotic form of consumption, even as it becomes an ordinary and mundane phenomenon of consumer culture.

CONCLUSION

It's reality itself that's been destroyed.
(Don DeLillo)

The sociology of consumption and audiences has established itself as a significant area of research within cultural and media studies. In opposition to earlier attitudes, which suggested the passivity of consumers, and which involved some degree of moral disapproval of 'consumerism', it has emphasised the active and creative nature of consumption; it has taken seriously the question of pleasure; and it has shown how, through mechanisms of differentiation and distinction, consumption is associated with the formation of identity. Research over a decade or so, drawing on the disciplines of sociology, anthropology and history, has contributed greatly to our understanding of the symbolic meanings of consumption. It has also helped to illuminate processes of economic and cultural transformation in western capitalist societies.

Recently, there have been stirrings of criticism and reaction, however, involving both accusations of populism and the reassertion of more structural sociological perspectives, centred around questions of power, ideology and constraint. In some respects, we might see this in terms of a necessary corrective to the biases of concern and focus within consumption studies. In the context of British media and cultural studies, however, there is more to it than this. What is activated is an old rift within the 'discipline', which has divided, even polarised, those who emphasise the importance of political economy and those privileging cultural and symbolic processes.[75] Originally organised around the dichotomy of base and superstructure, it has subsequently been re-cast in terms of other (binary) oppositions (structure versus agency, macro-processes versus micro-processes). Although criticisms have frequently been made of this theoretical dualism, it has actually proven extremely difficult to overcome and still remains a powerful factor in the way in which culture and media are understood and researched (one consequence being that we remain caught up in a theoretical impasse which offers us the too-simple choice between 'passive' or 'active' notions of consumers and viewers). It would be a great misfortune, as David Morley says, if the recent revival of structural theories were simply to amount to the reassertion of old truths about cultural domination, with the real achievements of consumption studies being denied or dismissed (on account of some of the most extreme and voluntaristic formulations). It would be equally regrettable, though, if, in retaliation against such deterministic criticism, the sociology of consumption were to end up in defensive self-justification of 'active audience' theory.

It seems to me that there is still a great deal more to be said about the nature, and relation, of freedom and constraint in the consumption process, and I have sought in this chapter to raise some preliminary issues through a consideration of media consumption specifically. In doing so, I have accepted the idea of the active audience as my starting point, aiming to add some complexity to this too-simple premiss. This complexity involves recognising the possibility that freedom may, in fact, be exercised in ways that might seem 'perverse' or 'regressive' (and may involve the choice, for whatever reason, to impose limits on one's own freedom). To understand the conditions of freedom, we must take into account the social and the historical context of consumption, in all its contradictoriness. 'The prevailing hedonism has us think and say that happiness is at hand for everyone,' comments François Brune. 'And, at the same time, everyone is persuaded by the treatment of the news that the reality surrounding us is always in crisis.'[76] In the former case, it makes sense to talk of the pursuit of symbolic gratification and differentiation. In the latter, something more complex is at issue: what is mobilised is a sense of vulnerability and insecurity that may draw on basic and primitive fears. In this context, consumption activities may be driven by the desire to create defensive barriers and to avoid or minimise anxiety.

In exploring such mechanisms, I have taken account of the consumption of violent material (rather than the soaps or music television that are the usual fare of consumption studies), and I have drawn attention to the cognitive aspects of consumption activity. It is generally assumed that watching war coverage, for example, is driven by a desire to see, know and, consequently, form an opinion. Of course this is occurring, but so too are other processes. There may, at the same time, be inhibitions on the capacity to know or on the capacity to think what is known. Such resistances will serve to screen out the reality of what is seen and known. What is achieved is a kind of borderline attitude in which reality is simultaneously acknowledged and evaded. What concern me are the mechanisms – cognitive, in this case – through which the consumer deadens the shock of real violence.

I have taken this discussion of consumption and reality further by looking at post-television technologies, where it is no longer a case of blocking out the shock of reality, but rather of creating alternative and compensatory realities with better conditions of sensibility. Through such technologies, of which virtual reality is no doubt the most significant, there is the possibility of combining pleasure and security in consumption processes. The real world, with all its unpredictability and intractability, may be cancelled out in favour of a simulated copy that responds to the omnipotent desires and fantasies of its consumer. This leads me to suggest that such 'postmodern' environments of consumption contain a psychotic element.[77] The combined pleasure and security of such consumption environments is a consequence of severance from reality and the real world. This is not a matter of individual psycho-pathology, but rather of a collective experience which is institutionalised as the social norm. In the postmodern imagination this may be seen in terms of emancipation and liberation from the burden of reality; I see the flight into virtuality in terms of escape from, and thereby defence against, a reality and a real world that have become increasingly dangerous and difficult to manage.

My concern has been with what might be called existential aspects of consumption. This is not intended to represent an alternative to sociological accounts of the consumption process, but rather to complement them. The point is that there are aspects of consumer motivation which have not been taken into account in discussions of pleasure or identity-formation, but which are also fundamental to understanding the active, and often creative, consumer and audience member. I have taken account of emotions associated with vulnerability, anxiety and also ontological insecurity. Of course, these feelings and fears are 'in the background' much of the time – we carry on walking around, talking to people, eating and drinking – but they are always there and they are significant in our behaviour. In considering them, I have raised the question of how consumption relates to reality and its vicissitudes. In one sense, I believe, the institution of consumerism (activities, environments, technologies) may justifiably be seen in terms of strategies of insulation and protection against the shocks of the real world. If this is the case, then it is appropriate that our now quite advanced understanding of the symbolic dimensions of consumption should be complemented by a greater awareness of its psychotic tendencies and temptations.

'Random Access Memory, Acquired Immune Deficiency Syndrome, Mutual Assured Destruction.'[78]

Chapter 6

THE CITY IN THE FIELD OF VISION

6

THE CITY IN THE FIELD OF VISION

Things are disappearing. If you want to see anything, you have to hurry.
(Wim Wenders, quoting Cézanne)

Here, I am concerned with different ways in which we see the surrounding world and envisage our involvement in it. I am concerned with how vision is implicated in the creation of a world of meaning and imaginary significations. And I have chosen to pursue my inquiry in relation to how vision is brought to bear on the city and the urban scene – for, as James Donald argues, we may think of the city in terms of a 'mode of seeing', a 'structure of visibility'.[1] First, I shall discuss the cinematic projection of the city and of urban modernity, and then I shall turn to a consideration of television and video technologies in relation to the contemporary city. In choosing this particular focus, in contrasting two distinctive ways of envisioning the city, I am wanting to suggest something of the complexity and scope of our visual relation to the world.

In my discussion of the institution of cinema, I shall suggest that there is an imaginative richness: that the urban world is suffused with meaning and symbolism, and in a way that helps us to expand and extend our 'experiential repertoire'.[2] In the case of television and video images, I believe that we have to do with less substantial images, ones that do not sustain our attention or nourish our interpretative capacities. Vincent Amiel describes the difference in terms of the loss of cinematic gesture and iconicity. 'The weight of the gesture,' he argues, 'which is what gave time to [cinematic] images, is what is missing from our screens today.'[3] With electronic images, we are involved in a more problematical relation to the urban realm. In developing my narrative, I do not intend to suggest that it is simply the development of new media that has provoked or caused the weakening of the urban imagination: what is at issue is clearly a broader transformation of the city as imaginary institution, and we must then consider the significance of vision in the changing institution of that imaginary. But I do recognise that what I am developing is a narrative of decline and also of loss. 'It is already clear,' says Donald, 'that both "the city" and "cinema" are ... slipping into history.'[4] Clearly, we

129

must turn our attention – and let it be our critical attention – to what is now in the process of succeeding them. At the same time, we should be reflecting on what is becoming lost to us, and on the consequences – both social and individual – of this loss. And by what necessity is it, we should ask, that we are relinquishing an urban vision?

THE CITY AND THE DREAM SCENE

> Hey, Mister Sandman.
> Life is a dream
> But I remember it like a movie.
> (Laurie Anderson, *Stories from the Nerve Bible*)

The city is an imaginary signification; in James Donald's words, 'the city is the way we moderns live and act, as much as where'.[5] The city exists around us, and it also lives within us. It is a place for experience, above all for group experience. 'Human beings go into groups as they go into dreams,' says Didier Anzieu.[6] They want a space of encounter and of pleasure, they want to be contained and protected, they have fantasies of fusion with the crowd. But it is also a space where they must confront their fears and anxieties. The group may be experienced as threatening and persecutory, individuals may feel that they will be overwhelmed by the collectivity and will lose their own identities in it. The city can be seen, then, in terms of a kind of psycho-geography: it is the scene of collective emotional life.

And in this we must figure the importance of vision. The city gives prominence to the activity of the eye. It is a place of visual encounter and experience: the City of Light. It is through its visibility that we know the city. Particular forms of vision relate to particular ways of apprehending and making sense of it. This raises the question of the technological means through which we have our visual experiences. To see, to know, and thereby to have control. Vision and light against the forces of darkness, against the obscure labyrinth in which we might lose ourselves. But nothing is sure; there is always unease. Whatever is visible always contains within it the potential to be lost from view.

Let us first consider the experience of the modern city, starting from its most elemental and 'primitive' energies. We must begin with what Lewis Mumford described as 'the realities of human antagonism and enmity'. Urban culture is associated with the experience of aggression and violent behaviour. Even when this is contained, there is fear and anxiety. Mumford refers to 'the deepened collective anxieties' that characterise urban culture, suggesting that urban life encourages a 'paranoid psychal structure': urban life is about 'struggle, aggression, domination, conquest – and servitude'; the city is 'the container of disruptive internal forces, directed towards ceaseless destruction and extermination'.[7] Urban culture may be seen (in Hobbesian terms) as a constant state of hostility and struggle. Feelings of anxiety and fear are, then, constitutive of urban life.

The fundamental question is how to contain and articulate such passions and aggressions. We may say that the quality of urban culture is a function precisely of the capacity to *civilise* those primitive forces. Urbanity depends on holding the forces of order and disorder in creative tension. In the modern city a productive accommodation was achieved: the energy and dynamism of collective emotions were harnessed and given imaginative expression. Modern urban experience involved encounter and contact, the challenge of strangers and of the unknown; the modern city was a place of psychological shock and excitement, a kind of vertigo machine. It was possible to sustain an urban culture that could admit a certain level of danger and tolerate a certain degree of fear. In vision, it involves the glance, the look, the sexual gaze – the eye caught up in the 'intersubjective visual relations' that characterise the psychic and eroticised space of the city.[8]

But against these fluid and chaotic tendencies, there has been a countervailing force in modern urban culture. There has been the aspiration to an encompassing order and rationality. This was represented in the ideal or fantasy of the 'concept city', to be found in modern urban utopianism: it articulated the desire to make the city a comprehensible and a governable space. Against the perceived threat of disorder and fragmentation, urban planning has stood for order and integrity. Le Corbusier was perhaps the most epic and authoritarian exponent of such a project. The architect and planner, he believed, must stand for clarity and cohesion in the face of the dark and formless flows – the magma, the miasma – that threaten their dissolution. Cities are planned when they are coherent, when they are 'legible' and 'imageable'. The city should be transparent. This involves another kind of vision: the distanced perspective of the panorama and panopticon, the encompassing gaze of the survey and of surveillance, through which the city is visually possessed.

What was vital to the dynamism of the modern city was the creative tension between immersion and detachment. The dynamism of modern cinema was also charged by this tension, the movement between immersed vision and detached vision. Cinema provided complex representations of modern urban experience. It took its audiences into the labyrinth, exposed them to the dangers, the fears, the eroticism of the streets; but it could also put them above and beyond the threats of the city, affording them the security of panoramic vision, the view of the angels. Not only did cinema give representation to the urban scene, it also embodied the visual experience of the city. The medium of film, as Vivian Sobchack says, 'makes visible not just the objective world, but the very structure and process of subjective embodied vision'. The cinema is able to constitute visual/visible space 'as always also motor and tactile space – a space that is deep and textural, that can be materially inhabited, that provides not merely a ground for the visual/visible, but also a particular *situation*'.[9] The movie camera provides the close-up experience of intersubjective vision, embodied vision, but it can also withdraw to the distanced perspective of rational vision. People went into movie houses as they went into dreams. They entered into the scene of fantasy and desire, they took pleasure in the thrill of immersion. But they were aware that they were all the time screened from actual dangers. The film as an object for vision, the projected images, divided the pleasures of fear from the reality. The psychic space of the screen matched that of the urban imaginary.

The modern city and its cinematic projection can be seen in terms of a dramatic encounter between the irrational and instinctual forces, the fearful elements of the city, the unconscious and the uncanny, on the one hand, and the powers of reason, vision, control, that is to say conscious powers, on the other. A theatre of the mind. That, at least, is our contemporary sense of the modern city as the ideal containing environment. The image of the dream, the oneiric, is integral to it. The city becomes implicated in the human need for the dreaming experience. The dream space may be seen as 'the intrapsychic equivalent of transitional space where a person "actualises certain types of experiences". The dream space contains, for the purpose of personal elaboration, what might otherwise be acted out – or, rather, evacuated – in "social space".'[10] In this case we have a public dream. The psychic space is mapped onto the social space. The city becomes a transitional space in which to actualise experiences. The good city, the good dream.

But now, it seems, it is the lost city, the lost dream. There is an elegiac note in James Donald's paper. 'Spatial organisation', he says 'is increasingly determined by global information flows; the analytics and oneirics of cinema are becoming less powerful than the apparatus of visibility inscribed in and by television, video and multimedia.'[11] A particular imaginary configuration – the 'classic' modern city, 'classical' cinema – is losing its imaginative hold. It is not that something has replaced it: the term 'postmodern' can only be understood in a negative sense, as marking an emptiness, a loss, a lack, in urban culture. When we think about cities now, we are likely to talk in terms of fragmentation, disintegration, disenchantment, disillusionment: in terms of something that is falling apart or losing its imaginary charge. The image of the city no longer works so readily as a topographical projection. No longer does it function as a transitional space for the collectivity. The city is no longer imageable. It is becoming lost from view.

THE CITY IN THE FIELD OF VISION

I now want to go on to think about what has happened in and to the urban imaginary. We may approach this question through the visual sense, considering what has happened to the city in the field of vision. Johannes Birringer writes of 'the disappearance of identifiable cities ... the end of the city as an imaginative or emotional focus even of cultural alienation'. This he describes as 'a crisis of visual space'.[12] I shall consider the shift in the imaginary signification of the city in terms of a dislocation in the structure of its visibility.

Let us consider vision in terms of our relationship to the city, in terms of how we are connected to the urban scene. What has happened, or is happening, to that visual relation and connection? What is being lost or gained? How are we to understand the significance for us of what is happening? 'We can speak of a city', says Donatella Mazzoleni, 'as long as the totality of those who live in a collective construction constitute a collective anthropoid body, which maintains in some way an identity as a "subject". The city is therefore the site of an identification.' She describes the city as 'the body's Double':

> The city takes shape as a body which is much bigger than that of the individual living person, yet similar in its metabolic functions (of production, of assimilation, of self-control), in its organisation, and also, more or less covertly, in its form – with which latter it is possible to establish a two-way relationship, of mutual belonging and of mutual independence.[13]

Seen in this way, the city may exist as a space of potentiality. But now, Mazzoleni argues, it has become difficult to make an identification. The metropolis has assumed an 'alien subjectivity' which it is difficult to relate to:

> Metropolises are no longer 'places', because their dimensions exceed by far the dimensions of the perceptive apparatus of their inhabitants. The widest sensory aperture, that of light, is shattered. It was the visual field, in some respect, which defined the city dimensionally: in the metropolis there is no longer pan-orama (the vision of all), because its body overflows beyond the horizon. In the metropolitan aesthetic the eye fails in its role as an instrument of total control at a distance[14]

The city now exceeds the field of vision. Its visibility has receded. It no longer reflects our identity back to us. Mazzoleni describes this in terms of the experience of immersion, loss of self, regression to a condition of pre-separation: 'the most elementary distinction of space – the distinction between "inside" and "outside", which is the distinction between "I" and "the world" – grows weaker'.[15]

In contemporary scenarios of the postmodern and information city, we may locate a similar narrative of transformation in visual experience (though in such accounts its significance is generally denied or disavowed; an underlying teleologism encourages submission – which may assume a euphoric and triumphalist guise – to the new order). In these discourses, it is said that cities are now becoming nodes in the new global communications networks. They are being subsumed within the deterritorialised hyperspace of information and image flows. 'The virtual city of today exists in real time but not in real space,' writes Paul Virilio. 'The city is no longer a geographical entity: with today's telecommunications it is everywhere, it is a world-city.'[16] The city expands to a global scale. Its localised integrity has disintegrated. It has become a non-place. It seems to have lost its reality, and now is experienced as unreal, derealised. In postmodern discourses, the city is imagined in terms of hyperreality, virtual reality, the simulacrum. There is the idea (though already it is a cliché) that we are lost in this hyperspace. Again the sense of being overwhelmed or immersed. Again the collapse of distance, detachment, perspective. There is the experience of not being able to separate the self from the environment: the experience of interface, fusion, the blurring of boundaries. 'In the past', Virilio observes, 'there was a difference between man and his environment: today, the capacity for instantaneous action at a distance means that habitat has become a *habit* [clothing] of the interactive individual.'[17] We may consider the nature of this changed relationship (from a different point of view than the postmodern urbanists). As Louis Sass notes:

> The very idea that something real might pre-exist the image or the simulacrum and remain beyond its grasp begins to fall away. So does the idea of some idiosyncratic or private realm that would be the locus of a true or inner self. Instead of the old pathos of distance, with its sense of inwardness and detachment, the condition of an inner self cut off from some unattainable reality, we enter into a universe devoid of both objects and selves, where there is only a swarming of 'self-objects', images and simulacra filling us without resistance.[18]

Again, there is the collapsing of distinction between 'inside' and 'outside', 'I' and 'the world': the pre-separated state of the self-object.

There is the sense, then, of a significant transformation in our visual relation and connection to the (urban) world. Though I recognise the dangers of nostalgia, it is difficult not to think about it in terms of a loss: a loss of perspective, a loss from view. Let us now consider more precisely what it is that (it seems) is being lost. To do so, it is necessary to think a little more about the nature and meaning of visual experience (as we have become surrounded by images and simulacra – heteronomous vision – there seems to have been a loss of interest in the existential significance of seeing and looking).

First, we should take account of the structure of vision: vision in terms of subject locations, that is to say. Vision involves our presence in the world, which is a double presence. In Merleau-Ponty's terms:

> The enigma is that my body simultaneously sees and is seen. That which looks at all things can also look at itself and recognise, in what it sees, the 'other side' of its power of looking. It sees itself seeing; it touches itself touching; it is visible and sensitive for itself. It is not a self through transparence, like thought, which only thinks its object by assimilating

it, by constituting it, by transforming it into thought. It is a self through confusion, narcissism, through inherence of the one who sees in that which he sees, and through inherence of sensing in the sensed.[19]

(It seems that we all too easily now conceive of seeing according to the model of thinking.) In Merleau-Ponty's formulation, the structure of vision involves the dual location of subjectivity: the double experience of both immersion and detachment. Visual experience is created through the connection between these two locational poles: 'when the spark is lit between sensing and sensible'.[20] On the basis of this structure of vision, we can then begin to comprehend visual meaning and signification. Meaning is generated through a reciprocating motion between subject positions: between immersion in the visible, which is open to the indeterminacy of the world, and the detachment of elucidation, reflection, interpretation. Through vision – which is always invested by our affects and desires (as well, of course, as by our more rational capacities) – we animate the world, discover it, respond to it, give it shape, pattern, order. Visibility is filled with signification.

In this context, we might return again to the question of dreams and the dream experience. We may consider dream as a particular dimension of visual experience and culture, and then the dream quality also as something that is used to endow waking vision with new resonance and significations. Dreaming may be a transformative process. Thomas Ogden describes it as 'an experience of de-integrating one's experience and re-presenting it to oneself in a new form and a new context'.[21] It is a continuous process of de-integration and re-integration of experience. Christopher Bollas describes the dream experience in the same terms that we have been using to understand visual experience generally. 'Dream life mirrors an important feature of self experience,' he maintains, 'particularly that essential split between two subjective locations: the place of the initiating subject who reflects upon the self, and the position of that subject who is reflected upon.'[22] The dualism of 'experiencing self' and 'reflecting self' allows the individual 'to process life according to different yet interdependent modes of engagement: one immersive, the other reflective'.[23] The dream space is a space of experience. In entering it,

> I am transformed from the one who holds the internal world in my mind to the one who is experientially inside the dramaturgy of the other. . . . I live in a place where I seem to have been held before: inside the magical and erotic embrace of a forming intelligence that bears me. To be in a dream is thus a continuous reminiscence of being inside the maternal world when one was partly a receptive figure within a comprehending environment.[24]

But there is always the moment of being transformed back into the one who again holds the internal world in his or her mind. One then re-enters the space of interpretation or understanding. The reflecting self then endeavours 'to objectify as best as possible where one has been and what is meant by one's actions'.[25] The whole experience, involving mobility between the two subject locations, encapsulates the structure of vision.

But the dream space is not simply an alternative and self-enclosed space. It also inheres in the waking space; it can suffuse the whole field of vision with a particular aura. Dreaming is a quality of seeing–feeling. 'It can certainly be said that contemplation of the dream-image inspires us,' Wittgenstein observes, 'that we just *are* inspired. . . . The dream affects us as does an idea pregnant with possible developments.'[26] The dream affords an aura (enchanting, haunting, erotic, uncanny), and this aura may attach itself and adhere to objects and places in the real world. Aspects and details of the world become vivid, stand out, because they become charged with meaning. We endow things with psychic states, says Christopher Bollas: we 'travel in a rendered world of psychic signifiers that light up in the subject clusters of feeling, imagery, somatic states, and memories, and reawaken the sexual states that partly drove the initial investiture'.[27] In this way we see and relate to a world that lives. We may think of what is created as an atmosphere, mediating between seer and seen. 'Atmosphere is the common reality of perceiver and perceived,' observes Gernot Böhme. Atmospheres are 'affective powers of feeling, spatial bearers of moods'; they are 'what are experienced in bodily presence in relation to persons and things or in spaces'.[28] Atmospheres vitalise and animate the spaces of the city.

Dreaming may be a private and personal experience (another person will not then be inspired by what stimulates or excites me). But, as I have already suggested, it is also possible for the dream phenomenon to transcend individual experience (for there to be a collective oneirics, above and beyond the separate life of each individual consciousness and unconsciousness). What the modern city did was precisely to provide a means – an imaginary focus – for this to occur. It was Freud who showed how the city could provide an imaginary focus – Rome was the city of his dreams – for thinking and analysing psychic processes (the psycho-archaeological dig).[29] But in and through the city, there was also the potential to achieve a collective form of what Christopher Bollas calls 'the projective subjectification of reality'. Freud himself suggests this when he says that urban landmarks may function as shared 'mnemic symbols'.[30] We may see *lieux de mémoire* as anchoring and condensing the collective imagination of the city.[31] But there are also more intangible phenomena: the myths and narratives that accumulate within urban culture, giving scope to our collective emotions. It is here that cinema has functioned so significantly and meaningfully. The filmic city has figured prominently in the dream work of urban collective life. It has permitted the *mise-en-scène* of the fears and anxieties, the fantasies and desires, of the group. In the urban imaginary, the mere appearances of the city became endowed with collective meaning. An urban aura was created; it could be said that urban spaces were '"tinctured" through the presence of things, of persons or environmental constellations, that is, through their ecstasies'.[32] This was the oneiric space of the city.

Vision may develop, then, as something far more rich and expressive than the rationalistic seeing – sight as a form of thinking – that we have come to mistake for it. We may see urban vision in terms of the accumulation of meanings and atmospheres. We should also see it in relational terms, as a process of engagement and involvement with the urban scene. Vision is transitive, mediating between the inner world of psychic meaning and the outer world of the urban environment. The collectivity both invests meaning in the city and discovers meaning there: the collectivity creates the city and the city creates the collectivity. It may be seen in terms of the institution of a potential space. 'The differentiation of symbol, symbolised, and interpreting subject creates the possibility of triangularity within which space is created,' says Thomas Ogden. 'That space . . . is the space in which creativity becomes possible and is the space in which we are alive as human beings as opposed to being simply reactive beings.'[33] (It is the antithesis, then of Mazzoleni's image of pre-separation.) Visual meaning and signification are instituted within a particular structure of visual space. Within such a resonant space, imaginative and creative possibilities can be envisioned.

But no more, it appears. All this now seems a lost ideal. The mediation between outer reality and inner reality is more problematical. The city no longer functions readily as a potential space. The analytics and oneirics of cinema are becoming less powerful. There is a sense of imaginary collapse, which is at the same time a collapse of visual relationship and connection to the city. The city is slipping from view, from visual meaning and visual possibility.

THE CITY LOST FROM VIEW

One evening they walked past a department store, just out strolling, and Marina looked at a television set in the window and saw the most remarkable thing, something so strange she had to stop and stare, grab hard at Lee. It was the world gone inside out. There they were gaping back at themselves from the TV screen. She was on television. Lee was on television, standing next to her, holding Junie in his arms. Marina looked at them in life, then looked at the screen.

(Don DeLillo, *Libra*)

Of course, we must be clear that there are still the same drives, the same passions, the same needs: these have not changed. We must still come to terms with the emotional and collective experience of the city. Still we must find ways to process the flux of representations, affects and desires. And in this respect vision and visibility remain crucial. 'Would the most unbearable loss be the loss from view?' asks J.-B. Pontalis. 'Above all we must see. Not only see but see above all in order to calm the anguish caused by absence, to reassure ourselves that the loved object is within our field of vision, reflecting our identity back to us.' 'Why do we dream', he asks, 'if not to see what has *disappeared* (worlds, places, people, faces) each night, to verify its permanence, and to try to join the ephemeral and the eternal?'[34] The city should not be lost from view. We still (surely?) have a need to see our identity (individual and collective) reflected back to us. We still need the urban scene to be a visible focus of experience and meaning (conscious and unconscious). We should sustain our visual relationship to the city.

How is this being pursued now? How is it being pursued, we should ask, now that the technological means have devolved from cinema to television and video? We must consider how these technologies involve us (as viewers) in urban life, how they permit us to process urban experience, how they affect the ways in which we imagine (dream) the city, what they mean for collective urban identity. Let us, then, reflect on how urban culture finds representation – or now, more exactly, presence – on the electronic screen. We must try to understand the post-cinematographic structure of vision and visibility in relation to the 'postmodern' city.

Cameras proliferate in the (postmodern) urban environment. All around us – in streets, in public buildings, in department stores, in corner shops – their lenses watch us, creating a new scanscape. A growing number of city centres are monitored by an extensive network of cameras recording everything that moves. We see images of ourselves as we pass shop windows, as we walk through shopping malls, as we stand in banks or post-offices. Everything is video-recorded, continuously, indiscriminately. It is the distributed panopticon, the dispersed panorama of the city. Consider its symbolic resonance in our urban culture, brought out with awful poignancy at the time of the murder of 2-year-old James Bulger in Liverpool in February 1993. Melanie Phillips and Martin Kettle described it then in terms of 'the lost child who wanders off only to be "rescued" by evil forces'. This death appals, they wrote, 'because it exposes once again our society's growing indifference and our own increasing isolation'. And the fact that the abduction was recorded on a security camera made all this even worse: 'we are therefore doubly affronted, both by being made complicit in this terrible tragedy and by the demonstrable fact that such "security" devices are anything but'.[35] There is the expectation – the fantasy – of visibility and transparency in the urban scene, but this is overwhelmed by the sense of urban alienation, violence and horror.

Surveillance is not just something that is now undertaken by public and official agencies. It is an activity that thousands of individual urban citizens are increasingly involving themselves in. 'People behave in the third person', observes Don DeLillo. 'They are becoming their own espionage agencies, their own television agencies, their own television stations. They are filming police beatings and babysitters slapping their kids.'[36] What began when

Abraham Zapruder recorded John F. Kennedy's fatal motorcade ride through Dallas came of age with George Holliday's recording of Rodney King being beaten up by the Los Angeles police. We can speak, albeit ironically, of the increasing democratisation of surveillance. *Newsweek* magazine writes of the proliferation of 'video vigilantes' in US cities:

> Part accidental tourists, part masked avengers, part high-tech snoops, they are out there waiting, 14 million owners of video cameras, fingers on the pause button, prepared to get the goods on hated neighbours, suspicious babysitters or brutal cops.[37]

The city now constitutes a mosaic of micro-visions and micro-visibilities. With the camcording of the city, we have the fragmentation and devolution of vision-as-control to the individual level. Vigilante taping is a means through which individuals strive to protect themselves against the lurking and encroaching threats of the city. Through the video camera, they aspire to keep dangers at a distance (though the danger is always there, of course, right there in the camera's field of vision).

Visual detachment and perspective are difficult to achieve: these cameras also draw the observer into the urban scene, providing a new directness, intimacy and intensity of vision. Beatrix Campbell describes the young men who recorded their own violent behaviour during the urban riots in Britain in 1991. Racing stolen cars round the streets, the joyriders also video-recorded their displays and circulated their cassettes around a samizdat network. 'Just as the domestication of the means of visual reproduction revolutionised the production of pornography,' Campbell argues, 'so it occasioned another metamorphosis in the witnessing and worshipping of the car and the joyride.' Their riotous behaviour is endowed with an added narcissistic intensity: 'The night boys who loved being seen, who needed to be seen, could now see themselves.'[38] Yves Eudes describes another group of young men, in Los Angeles, who also experience a certain pleasure – this time professional: they are freelance stringers – in capturing scenes of urban violence. Equipped with video gear, a fast vehicle, and a radio to listen into police messages, their endeavour is to record the violence of the streets – not the consequences of violence, but the very acts of violence themselves. On one occasion, they come across a man who has been shot, a crowd of adolescents begins to laugh and provoke: 'They pose and demand to be filmed. . . . Silent and efficient, the ambulance crew takes away the wounded man, no longer moving. The young men who have been filmed want to know what channel they will appear on.'[39] Again there is the shock of immediacy, of immersion in the reality of the streets, and again narcissistic thrill and pleasure are inherent in it. Visual detachment is (must be) achieved too: though it is now a kind of anaesthetis-ation and numbing of the (moral) senses, not the detachment of perspective and reflection.

These kinds of video images – camcorder shots, vigilante documentation, shock reportage, reality voyeurism – have become the basis now of a new form of public entertainment. It has been called neo-television, or, more fittingly, reality television. It is a television of the city, and of what goes on in its streets, neighbourhoods, homes. Viewers watch themselves, their neighbours and the strangers and aliens that surround them. Ordinary people are its stars, and frequently it is they who have produced its images. It is a television of the misfortunes, disasters and crimes that afflict urban life. But also a television of how ordinary people cope with and survive them, everyday heroes of the urban scene. Reality television is a kind of morality television, publicising the private and intimate lives of its viewers in order to help them to deal with the complexities and contingencies of the perilous city. 'After being considered for a long time as a window on the world,' Alain Ehrenberg observes, 'television is more and more becoming a window on the self, on the internal conflicts of the subject, and on the difficulties of life.'[40] Reality shows communicate the shock of living, assuming that in making ordinary people's lives transparent they are making the pain easier to live with. No longer is the objective to represent the real world in order to allow for imaginative identification, contemplation and reflection: the point is, rather, to plunge the watcher into direct and immediate emotional involvement. 'In place of reason', argues Michel Maffesoli, 'we now see something which is more nearly emotional or "affectual", which puts greater accent on the image and its "contaminating" quality, which is much more sensible than intelligible.'[41] The intention, moreover, is that we should relate to the image as to the object itself. In reality television, the structure of representation is giving way to the simulation of presence. As Jean Louis Weissberg points out, this new televisual form is seeking to respond to the increasing desire 'to participate in experience, rather than to observe it at a distance'. The fictional nature of the image is denied: 'it is no longer truthfulness that is laid claim to, but rather a more authentic experience of participation'.[42] To have the experience, to lose oneself in the experience: this is how reality television seeks to connect us visually to the postmodern urban scene.

So, we have moved a long way from the analytics and oneirics of cinema to these new forms of karaoke television. Clearly they are associated with new ways of looking, new ways of envisaging and observing the city. Let us now consider the nature of this new mode of seeing, this new structure of visibility, in urban culture. What, we must ask, does it mean for urban experience, and for making sense of that experience? How might it change the ways in which we seek to imagine and give form to our collective life? What are its implications for the possibility space of the city? Let us consider how far we have moved away from the cinematographic imagination.

The new structure of visibility in fact represents the fulfilment of what was initiated by television. In the purer form of the video image, we may see more clearly what differentiates and distinguishes tele-vision from cinematic vision. Dallas, 1963, the Lee Oswald of Don DeLillo's *Libra* sees his own assassination as a television image: 'He could see himself shot as the camera caught it. Through the pain he watched TV. . . . Lee watched himself react to the augering heat of the bullet.' Reality had been sucked into the television screen. 'He was in pain. He knew what it meant to be in pain. All you had to do was see TV.'[43] The world had gone inside out. This is no longer a representation of the world, but its facsimile. The space between experience and detachment has imploded. The seeing self has collapsed into the seen self; the reflecting self has disappeared into the immersed self. From Lee Oswald we progress perhaps to Pangborn in J. G. Ballard's story 'Motel Architecture': Pangborn who is eager 'to merge with the white sky of the screen . . . [to] merge forever into the universe of the infinite close-up'.[44] There is something psychically compelling about the fantasised loss of bodily reality (and the substitution of a proxy reality).

What is it, then, that distinguishes the electronic image from the cinematic image? According to Vivian Sobchack,

> electronic 'presence' is at one remove from previous connections between signification and referentiality – neither asserting an objective possession of the world and self (like the photograph), nor a centred and subjective spatio-temporal engagement with the world and others accumulated and projected as a conscious and embodied experience (like film).[45]

It is more appropriate to think of electronic presence than of electronic representation. The viewer is incorporated into a quasi-disembodied 'meta-world', experiencing 'a purely spectacular, kinetically exciting, often dizzying sense of bodily freedom'.[46] The temporality of the electronic image is that of the instant – which can also be, countless times, instantly re-run. As Pascal Bonitzer argues, the television and video image is characterised by reiteration and repetition (and, consequently, it produces not memory, but forgetfulness).[47] In this placeless and timeless meta-world, one may feel intensities of affect – the euphoria of electronic presence – but at the same time, there is a weakening – numbing – of the real emotions that depend on a grounded and embodied existence and connection with, and commitment to, a real world of objects. As Sobchack says, the superficiality of electronic space 'at once disorients and liberates the activity of consciousness from the gravitational pull and orientation of its hitherto embodied and grounded existence'.[48] There is thrill, but not morality.

Television struggles to represent and relate to the urban world (and we should hang on to whatever is still possible in this respect). In this sense, we can regard reality television as a descendent of *cinéma vérité*. But it is also driven by another logic – one that is quite antithetical to this kind of social engagement. Jean Louis Weissberg considers reality television to be the 'last frontier' between spectacle and experience. Though it still functions in terms of the old technology of television, it anticipates the new technology of virtual reality, 'seeking to efface the real, to displace representation, in favour of the simulation of pure presence'.[49] Alain Ehrenberg makes the same point. Reality television should be seen in terms of the logic of interactivity, he argues. Anticipating virtual interactive environments, it aspires to collapse the distance between image and viewer/user, immersing him or her in a flood of corporeal shocks and sensations.[50] We should consider it in the context of the long history of vertigo machines. Lieven de Cauter describes the introduction of such machines into world exhibitions at the turn of the century. They were machines which transformed the panoramic pleasure into physical pleasure: 'The preponderance of the visual was transferred to the tactile ... not the gaze (vastness), but the sense of dizziness (depth) formed the main characteristic.'[51] It has been a continuing aspiration through the century (cinema was, of course, submitted to a whole series of experimentations involving intensification of the image, and also the mobilisation of other senses than the visual). It has been an aspiration with serious and problematical consequences. 'Vertigo machines, in all their different guises,' argues de Cauter, 'led to one thing: the disappearance of the horizon. This in turn was intimately linked to the disappearance of a coherent representational system.'[52] These machines have been associated with the implosion of the representational system.

This new structure of vision and visibility, I would suggest, has significant implications for the structure of experience and meaning. Earlier, in considering cinematic representation, I made use of the distinction between the experiencing self and the detached, reflective self, arguing that it is through their dialectical interaction that structures of meaning are created, and then developed into personal and collective narratives (the projective subjectification of the world). In the case of electronic images (in their vertiginous aspect, at least), this distinction is subverted, collapsed. The imaginative space of representation is replaced by the (euphoric) immediacy of presence and experience. There is immersion (shock, stimulus, emotion), but there is no subjective location from which to effect the (psychic or creative) transformation of experience. Distance is achieved only through the muting of sensation, through the anaesthetisation of the senses. Pain is deferred through the derealisation and devitalisation of the image (through repetition, for example: think of Zapruder's, endlessly re-played, footage of the Kennedy assassination). There is no place for perspective, only the possibility of modulating intensity of affect.

We must consider what implications this has for the processing and transformation of experience. In the case of cinema, we may think of the screen as a transitive or transitional space, mediating between the outer (urban) world and the inner world of conscious and unconscious life. It is a space, as I have already suggested, in which the world is invested with meaning and signification; one mechanism through which human subjects may do the dream work of their own lives. We may think of it (following

Thomas Ogden's re-working of Kleinian categories) in terms of an interplay between experience in the paranoid-schizoid position ('a self that is buffeted by thoughts, feelings, and perceptions as if they were external forces or physical objects occupying or bombarding oneself') and the more detached experience of the depressive position (involving symbol formation and processes of 'integration, resolution and containment').[53] In the post-cinematographic developments, something quite other seems to be at work. I would describe it in terms of the interplay between paranoid-schizoid experience and what has been called experience in the autistic-contiguous position. The latter is a more primitive experience of sensory domination, and can involve 'a feeling of entrapment in a world of sensation that is almost completely unmediated and undefined by symbols'; it can also entail withdrawal into 'non-experience', a 'state in which there is a cessation or paralysis of attributing meaning to experience'.[54] Transformative experience involves differentiation. In Ogden's terms, 'it is the differentiation of symbol, symbolised, and interpreting subject that creates the possibility of triangularity, within which potential space is created'. When there is de-differentiation – when the distinction between symbol and symbolised is collapsed, and when there is only the self of unmediated experience – there is no possibility of triangularity. There is then only autistic experience – which is precisely the antithesis of transitional experience. With the breakdown of 'threeness', 'there are only objects, and no subjects'.[55] There is only reactiveness, and not the transformation of experiences.

Reality television: images of urban life, so close and intimate in one sense, but so far away, so lacking in resonance, so denuded of meaning. Images that blindly confront us, intransitive images. Is Krysztof Wodiczko's Alien Staff a parodic response? At the top of the Staff there is a small video monitor, and there is the expectation that what is happening on it will incite curiosity: 'Those who really want to see will have to come up close and then they'll realise the two faces are the same. Perhaps they'll remain up close for several seconds to hear what's being said, facing the user who won't necessarily speak.'[56] The means of visual production (of a kind) are increasingly disseminated around the urban scene. We may think in terms of a molecular vision of the city now. Neo-television is about making the lives of urban citizens transparent. It is about the publication of private worlds (turning the world inside out). A proliferation of images. But, indeed, we don't know what is being said. There is an accumulation of meaninglessness, just images.

These images no longer mediate effectively between our private worlds and the public world of the city. There is no longer a space of representation, no longer a transitional space, an analytical space, a dream space. There is consequently no space for exploring and transforming the relationship between the inner self and the object world. The dream space of cinema has given way to what we may see as a worry space. 'Compared with the extraordinary invention of the dream,' says Adam Phillips, 'the ordinary worry seems drab':

> Compared with the dream, the worry is almost pure, uncooked day-residue; indeed it is addicted to reality. There is apparently little condensation or displacement; there seems to be no question of intelligibility, although there is a noticeable intensity of feeling. Worrying, that is to say, often has the appearance, the screen, that we associate with a certain version of reality.[57]

Where the dream draws on the power of metaphor, the worry has the flat quality of literalness. Where the dream mobilises narrative, the worry is circular and repetitive. And what is true at the individual level, also applies at the collective level. There is no collective analytical space, no collective dream space. Reality television has been described as a kind of collective therapy,[58] and in this respect it does, indeed, seek to transcend molecular isolation. But in doing so, it makes clear the collapse of sociality: the problems (and heroisms) that it depicts are those individuals in a fragmented city, individuals who no longer seem to have values and a sociality in common. And when it does so, it is through emotional identification – emotional identification with the experience of countless individuals – and not analysis (imaginative or rational). Urban culture is experienced as no more than the serial and random flow of emotional encounters.

WILL WE LET CINEMA DIE?

Developments in television and neo-television (and beyond, into the realm of virtual and simulation technologies) seem to be incrementally weakening the hold that cinema has in our culture and imagination. Pascal Bonitzer expresses this perception when he laments the decline, and perhaps the demise, of the institution of cinema. 'We like the cinema less now,' he writes, 'we hardly like it at all, hardly anybody likes it anymore.' In his view, television has brought about the dissolution and devaluation of the image: it has become 'degraded, washed out, effaced,' he argues, it is 'as far as possible from the *dream* and the *charm* that once seemed the *raison d'être* of the image as such'. For Bonitzer, the image has become void of meaning and resonance: 'the twentieth-century image grimaces'.[59] Cinema no longer seems viable as a form of visual expression and relation to the world.

The 'death of cinema': should we not, indeed, feel a sense of loss and regret? This is not to indulge in nostalgia for 'old' images. We can also recognise the need to continually transform – to de-integrate – structures of vision and visibility. Of course it is the case that new technologies – and let us remember that cinema was once one of these – can play a crucial role here (though I would emphasise that they do not necessarily – of themselves – change ways of seeing, and that there are other than technological means by which we may come to see anew). To acknowledge loss and feel regret may entail, rather, an expression of resistance to the teleological techno-imagination: to that triumphalist, and often manic, way of thinking that tells us that, in vision as in all other things, the future is always superior to the past, seeking to make us contemptuous of the forms of representation we already have, telling us to disown and forget 'old' ways of seeing (nostalgia is the residue of this progressivist logic). As Gilles Deleuze argues, with the arrival of television, cinema was still at the beginning of its creative project: there was no question of it dying a natural death.[60] If we are witnessing the 'death of cinema', it is because cinema is being put to death. And there is loss and regret for the imaginative and creative possibilities in cinema, which are now, increasingly, denied to us.

Will we let cinema die? (What means do we have to stop it?) The demise of cinema would be a great cultural loss. It would be to lose a particularly rich and complex way of viewing the world: the world would, in a significant way, be lost from view. Italo Calvino describes how, for him, the cinema 'satisfied a need for disorientation, for the projection of my attention into a different space, a need which I believe corresponds to a primary function of our assuming our place in the world'. Cinematic vision constituted 'an expansion of the boundaries of the real'.[61] It is an experience (increasingly it might be dismissed as nostalgic) that has been experienced by millions of people (film culture is ordinary). Can we afford to lose it?

It is in the context of the urban world, and urban culture particularly, that cinema has been crucial as a way of seeing – of seeing, and also of imagining, understanding and relating. Writing about Naples, Giuliana Bruno notes the affinity between the cinematic and the urban imaginary ('As film was implanted in the cityscape, the cityscape was implanted within film'). She compares the film spectator to the urban *flâneur*: 'The "dream web" of film reception, with its geographical implantation, embodies *flânerie*'s mode of watching and its public dimension.'[62] There is an affinity between modes of perception, one in which the joy of watching affords access (for both women and men) to the pleasure of a dream space ('dream-*rêverie*'). Again, it is an experience that has been enjoyed by millions, in all modern cities. Is there now a nostalgic sense of distance in its recollection? But what should we do, where would we be, without it?

Shall we have to be without it? For the moment, at least, we still have access to cinematic vision. There is even a renewed interest in cinematic modernity (as there is in urban modernity). In this we see expressed a sense of loss and distance. But perhaps also it shows that we do not easily relinquish our imaginary investment in cinematic vision. Cinema can still figure in the way we relate to our (urban) world. In *Wings of Desire* there is still a complexity of vision and imaginative engagement. In the images of O. J. Simpson's Ford Bronco ride to Rockingham, however, there is something less. Quentin Curtis tells of how he saw the latter:

I was watching in London, flipping between two channels carrying shots from different helicopters, between images that were grimy but close-up, and ones that were clearer but further away. Sitting in my armchair, editing the century's most wrenching chase sequence, I began to feel I was watching the future of film – or, perhaps, its death.[63]

Will we let film die? Can we do without the structure of cinematic visibility? Shall we have to make do with the reality show of O. J.'s ride? We should heed Walter Benjamin's warning: 'every image of the past that is not recognised by the present as one of its own concerns threatens to disappear irretrievably'.[64] What do we think that images are for?

Chapter 7

WILL IMAGES MOVE US STILL?

7

WILL IMAGES
MOVE US STILL?

Also if we are moved by a photograph it is because it is close to death.
(Christian Boltanski, interview in *Creative Camera*)

THE 'DEATH OF PHOTOGRAPHY'

The death of photography has been reported. There is a growing sense that
we are now witnessing the birth of a new era, that of post-photography. This,
of course, represents a response to the development of new digital electronic
technologies for the registration, manipulation and storage of images. Over
the past decade or so, we have seen the increasing convergence of photographic technologies with video and computer technologies, and this convergence seems set to bring about a new context in which still images will
constitute just one small element in the encompassing domain of what has
been termed hypermedia. Virtual technologies, with their capacity to origin-
ate a 'realistic' image on the basis of mathematical applications that model
reality, add to the sense of anticipation and expectation.

What is happening to our image culture – whatever it may amount to – is
generally being interpreted in terms of technological revolution, and of
revolutionary implications for those who produce and consume images.
Philippe Quéau describes it as 'the revolution of "new images"', claiming that
it is 'comparable with the appearance of the alphabet, the birth of painting,
or the invention of photography'. It constitutes, he says, 'a new tool of
creation and also of knowledge'.[1] This notion of technocultural revolution
has been widely accepted and celebrated by cultural critics and practitioners,
and such ready acceptance has tended to inhibit critical engagement with post-
photography. Indeed, it has encouraged a great faith in the new digital
technologies, based on the expectation that they can empower their users and
consumers. A great deal of what passes for commentary or analysis amounts
to little more than a simple and unthinking progressivism, unswerving in its
belief that the future is always superior to the past, and firm in its conviction
that this superior future is a spontaneous consequence of technological
development. The fact that technological development is seen as some kind

149

of transcendent and autonomous force – rather than as what it really is, that is to say embedded in a whole array of social institutions and organisations – also works to reduce what is, in reality, a highly complex and uneven process of change to an abstract and schematic teleology of 'progress'. The idea of a revolution in this context serves to intensify contrasts between past (bad) and future (good), and thereby to obscure the nature and significance of very real continuities.

From such a perspective, old technologies (chemical and optical) have come to seem restrictive and impoverished, whilst the new electronic technologies promise to inaugurate an era of almost unbounded freedom and flexibility in the creation of images. There is the sense that photography was constrained by its inherent automatism and realism, that is to say, by its essentially passive nature; that the imagination of photographers was restricted because they could aspire to be no more than the mere recorders of reality. In the future, it is said, the enhanced ability to process and manipulate images will give the post-photographer greater 'control', while the capacity to generate (virtual) images through computers, and thereby to make images independent of referents in 'the real world', will offer greater 'freedom' to the post-photographic imagination. What is supposed to be superior about the post-photographic future becomes clear, then, through contrast with what is seen as an inferior, and obsolete, photographic past.

The new technologies are associated with the emergence of a wholly new kind of visual discourse. This, it is argued, has profoundly transformed our ideas of reality, knowledge and truth. For William Mitchell, 'an interlude of false innocence has passed':

> Today, as we enter the post-photographic era, we must face once again the ineradicable fragility of our ontological distinctions between the imaginary and the real, and the tragic elusiveness of the Cartesian dream.[2]

Jonathan Crary conceives of the new order in terms of a new 'model of vision':

> The rapid development in little more than a decade of a vast array of computer graphics techniques is part of a sweeping reconfiguration of relations between an observing subject and modes of representation that effectively nullifies most of the culturally established meanings of the terms *observer* and *representation*. The formalisation and diffusion of computer-generated imagery heralds the ubiquitous implantation of fabricated visual 'spaces' radically different from the mimetic capacities of film, photography, and television.[3]

We are, says Crary, 'in the midst of a transformation in the nature of visuality probably more profound than the break that separates medieval imagery from Renaissance perspective'.[4]

The technological and visual revolution associated with new digital techniques is understood, furthermore, to be at the very heart of broader cultural revolution. There is the belief that the transformation in image cultures is central to the historical transition from the condition of modernity to that of postmodernity. Digital imaging is seen as 'felicitously adapted to the diverse projects of our postmodern era'.[5] The postmodern order is considered to be one in which the primacy of the material world over that of the image is contested, in which the domain of the image has become autonomous, even in which the very existence of the 'real world' is called into question. It is the world of simulation and simulacra. Gianni Vattimo writes of the erosion of the principle of reality: 'By a perverse kind of internal logic, the world of objects measured and manipulated by techno-science (the world of the *real*, according to metaphysics) has become the world of merchandise and images, the phantasmagoria of the mass media.'[6] In the face of this 'loss of reality', we must come to terms with 'the world of images of the world.'[7] The discussion of post-photography is caught up in this projection of the world as a 'post-real' techno-sphere – the world of cyberspace and virtual reality. Within this postmodern agenda concerning reality and hyperreality, it is again philosophical questions (of ontology and epistemology) that are the focus of attention and interest. The sentiment that postmodern sophistications have now overtaken modern ingenuousness brings with it the sense of cultural and intellectual 'progress'.

What I have outlined here, in schematic form, constitutes the conceptual and theoretical framework for most accounts of the 'death of photography' and the birth of a post-photographic culture. It is the story of how the image has now progressed from the age of its mechanical production to that of its digital origination and replication. It is the story of how new technologies have provided 'a welcome opportunity to expose the aporias in photography's construction of the visual world, to deconstruct the very ideas of photographic objectivity and closure, and to resist what has become an increasingly sclerotic pictorial tradition'.[8] In this respect, we can say that the discourse of post-photography has been extremely effective, significantly changing the way in which we think of image and reality. It has managed to persuade us that photographs were once 'comfortably regarded as causally generated truthful reports about things in the real world', and it has convinced us of how unsophisticated we were in such a regard. It has convincingly argued that 'the emergence of digital imaging has irrevocably subverted these certainties, forcing us to adopt a far more wary and more vigilant interpretive stance.'[9] We are warned against the seduction of naive realism. Now we have become more reflexive, more 'theoretical', more 'knowing' in our relation to the world of images.

The death of photography, an image revolution, the birth of a postmodern visual culture: there is the sense of a clear historical trajectory of the image. The significance and implications of the 'image revolution' have already been discursively fixed and contained. The certainties of the photographic era have been deconstructed, and we are now ready, it seems, to come to terms with the fragility of ontological distinctions between imaginary and real. What more is there to be said? We could easily bring the discussion to an end at this point. Perhaps we should be satisfied that so much is already known about the future of images and image culture. Perhaps we should be content with this discursive organisation and ordering of post-photographic culture. But I am not. So, let us keep the discussion going. Digital culture as we know it is distinctly unimaginative and dismally repetitive. Despite its theoretical sophistication and even 'correctness', there is something restrictive and limiting in the organisation and order of its theoretical schema. Theoretical structures can work to actually inhibit or restrict our understanding; they may simply confirm and reinforce what is already known; they can function to invalidate or devalorise other ways of understanding and knowing. It is with this in mind that I want now to consider what is being commonly said about the historical trajectory of images.

Whatever might be 'new' about digital technologies, there is something old in the imaginary signification of 'image revolution'. It involves a metaphysics of progress: the imagination of change in terms of a cumulative process in which whatever comes after is necessarily better than what went before. Cornelius Castoriadis describes its general logic:

> On the one hand, it forbids judgement on any and all particular events or instances of reality, since they all form necessary elements of the Grand Design. At the same time, however, it allows itself to pass an unrestricted positive judgement on the totality of the process, which is, and can only be, good.[10]

It is a rationalistic schema, concerned with the project of rational mastery and empowerment (over nature and over human nature). In the next part of my argument, I shall be concerned with how the theory of the image is caught up in this teleological vision. In so far as it is implicated in the technological imaginary, I shall argue, it assumes an abstract and deterministic form, closing off alternative lines of inquiry and judgement.

Following this critique, I want to consider other ways in which we might look at what is happening in the culture of images. I take as my starting point, not the question of technologies and technological revolution, but rather the *uses* of photography and post-photography. Where the prevailing interest is in the information format of image technologies, my concern is with what might be called the existential reference of images to the world. Photographs have provided a way of relating to the world – not only cognitively, but also emotionally, aesthetically, morally, politically. 'The range of possible emotional expression through images is as wide as it is with words', says John Berger, 'We regret, hope, fear, and love with images.'[11] These emotions, guided by our reasoning capacities, provide the energy to turn images to creative and moral–political ends. Such sentiments and concerns are uncomfortably at odds with the new agendas of post-photographic culture. These uses of photography now seem to mean strangely little to those who are primarily concerned with exposing the aporias of photography's construction of the visual world. Shall we just forget about such uses? Will they have no place in the new order? Because they are so important, I shall argue, we must begin to find a new basis for making them relevant again.

The progressivist agenda constructs a false polarisation between past and future, between photography and digital culture. According to its grand design, the new technologies must be good technologies (it assumes, that is to say, the thesis of the rationality of the real). From such a deterministic perspective, it is no longer relevant to take seriously the virtues of photographic culture, nor is it meaningful to question the virtues of post-photographic culture. Should we not be challenging this affirmative logic? Is not the whole process more complex, and isn't the appropriate response one of greater ambivalence? What alternative principles are there that would allow us to evaluate and assess more critically the transformations in image culture?

THE RATIONALISATION OF THE IMAGE

John Berger makes the point that when the camera was invented in 1839 Auguste Comte was completing his *Cours de Philosophie Positive*. Positivism and the camera grew up together, and what sustained them as practices 'was the belief that observable, quantifiable facts, recorded by scientists and experts, would one day offer man such a total knowledge about nature and society that he would be able to order them both':

> Comte wrote that theoretically nothing need remain unknown to man except, perhaps, the origin of the stars! Since then cameras have photographed even the formation of stars! And photographers now supply us with more facts every month than the eighteenth century Encyclopaedists dreamt of in their whole project.[12]

Photographic documentations of the world were about its cognitive apprehension. For the positivist, photography represented a privileged means for understanding the 'truth' about the world, its nature and its properties. And, of course, such visual knowledge of the world was closely associated with the project for its practical appropriation and exploitation. In this respect, the camera was an instrument of power and control. Photography has other, more creative capacities, as I shall go on to argue in the next section, but this capacity for visual arrogation has been, and remains, a dominant factor.

In his book *The Reconfigured Eye*, William Mitchell reflects on this spirit of positivism in the context of his account and analysis of post-photographic technologies and culture. He intends to dissociate them from its legacy. The camera, Mitchell points out, has been regarded as 'an ideal Cartesian instrument – a device for use by observing subjects to record supremely accurate traces of the objects before them'.[13] In so far as there appears to be no human intervention in the process of registering and recording an accurate image, photography has been regarded as the model of impersonal and objective neutrality. As Mitchell notes, 'the photographic procedure, like . . . scientific procedures, seems to provide a guaranteed way of overcoming subjectivity and getting at the real truth'.[14] This idea of photographic documents as truthful reports about things in the real world may be seen as functional to the culture that invented it: 'Chemical photography's temporary standardisation and stabilisation of the process of image making effectively served the purposes of an era dominated by science, exploration and industrialisation'.[15] The uses of positivism were directly linked to the objectives of industrial capitalism.

Mitchell, like John Berger too, is highly critical of this aspect of photographic history. In considering other possibilities, however, his agenda is quite unlike that of Berger (to whom I shall return shortly). Mitchell's hopes and expectations are invested in the new digital technologies, which, he argues, are 'relentlessly destabilising the old photographic orthodoxy, denaturing the established rules of graphic communication, and disrupting the familiar practices of image production and exchange.'[16] The point is that they make the intentional processes of image creation apparent, such that 'the traditional origin narrative by which automatically captured shaded perspective images are made to seem causal things of nature rather than products of human artifice . . . no longer has power to convince us.'[17] Digital images now constitute 'a new kind of token', with properties quite different from those of the photographic image. These new images can be used 'to yield new forms of understanding', and they can also be made to 'disturb and disorientate by blurring comfortable boundaries and encouraging transgression of rules on which we have come to rely'.[18] They have subverted traditional notions of truth, authenticity and originality, compelling us to be more 'knowing' about the nature and status of images. It is in this particular respect that Mitchell considers digital imaging to be so 'felicitously adapted' to the structure of feeling of what we are pleased to call 'our postmodern era'.

I would concede that there is a certain justification for this idea of progression to a higher stage of visual sophistication and reflexivity, but only in the limited terms of what must be seen as essentially a scientific teleology of the image. Mitchell is concerned centrally with philosophical and formalist issues, with questions of theoretical and methodological 'progress'. In this respect, he makes his point. But images do not and cannot exist in a pure domain of theory. New images are, of course, substantively implicated in furthering the objectives of what is now called post-industrial or information capitalism (for it was the needs of this system that effectively summoned them into existence). The 'image revolution' is significant in terms of a further and massive expansion of vision and visual techniques, allowing us to see new things and to see in new ways. In this context, the teleology of the image may be seen precisely in terms of the continuing development of ever more sophisticated technologies for 'getting at the real truth'. The objective remains the pursuit of total knowledge, and this knowledge is still in order to achieve order and control over the world. (What would give us grounds to think that it was otherwise?) Though he does not pursue its real consequences, it is something that Mitchell is actually quite aware of:

> Satellites continue to scan the earth and send images of its changing surface back. . . . These ceaselessly shed skins are computer processed, for various purposes, by mineral prospectors, weather forecasters, urban planners, archaeologists, military-intelligence gatherers, and many others. The entire surface of the earth has become a continuously unfolding spectacle and an object of unending, fine-grained surveillance.[19]

More than the Encyclopaedists dreamt of, indeed! Wouldn't the positivists have jealously understood this? Doesn't it suggest the continuing desire, by scientists and experts, to record observable, quantifiable facts?

It is in the context of this teleological worldview that I would accept that the scientists and the experts now have a far more sophisticated attitude to what used to be called 'the facts'. The process of getting at the truth is considered to be vastly more complex than was assumed in the nineteenth century. New technologies have massively extended the range and power of vision, and also the techniques for processing and analysing visual information. They have also blurred the boundaries between the visible and the invisible. Fred Ritchin describes the advent of what he calls 'hyper-photography':

> One can think of it as a photography that requires neither the simultaneity nor proximity of viewer and viewed, and that takes as its world anything that did, does, will, or might exist, visible or not – anything, in short, that can be sensed or conceived.[20]

New dimensions of reality are opened up to the powers of observation. With computer-graphics work stations, it becomes possible to 'see' things that are otherwise inaccessible to the human gaze: 'The procedure is to employ some appropriate scientific instrument to collect measurements and then to construct perspective views showing what would be seen if it were, in fact, possible to observe from certain specified viewpoints.'[21] In this way, simulation technologies massively enhance scientific endeavour. It is now actually possible 'to visualise the interior of a dying star or a nuclear explosion. The mind can go places where no physical being will ever be likely to go':

> Astrophysicist Michael Norman sums up the wonder of it all as he stands before the projected video animation of a tumultuously swirling tip of an extragalactic jet that may be a million light-years long: 'Look

at that motion! The best telescope can only represent these evolving gigantic jets as frozen snapshots in an instant in time. My simulation lets me study them close up in any colour at any speed.'[22]

New technologies are not only amplifying the powers of vision, they are also changing its nature (to include what was previously classified as invisible or unseeable) and its functions (making it a tool for the visual presentation of abstract data and concepts). Techniques and models of observation have, indeed, been transformed in ways the positivists could scarcely have imagined.

On this basis, it is possible to construct a logic of development which is about the shift from a perceptual approach to images (seen as 'quotations from appearances'), to one more concerned with the relation of imaging to conceptualisation. The representation of appearances is ceasing to be the incontrovertible basis of evidence or truth about phenomena in the world. We are seeing the rapid devaluation of sight as the fundamental criterion for knowledge and understanding. Of course, this questioning of photographic meaning and veracity is by no means an entirely new occurrence. Allan Sekula reminds us that even at the high point of nineteenth-century positivism there was always 'an acute recognition of the *inadequacies* and limits of ordinary visual empiricism'.[23] Nonetheless this questioning has now reached a critical stage, opening the way to a new and more sophisticated model of vision and knowledge. Jean Louis Weissberg argues that we are in fact moving from an era of 'knowledge through recording' to one of 'knowledge through simulation'. In this latter case, he argues, 'the image no longer serves to re-present the object ... but, rather, signals it, reveals it, makes it exist'.[24] The aim is to create a 'double' of the reality, one that approximates to the referent, not only in terms of appearances, but also in terms of other (invisible) properties and qualities that it possesses. Through progression from simulation of the object by means of digital images to the higher stage of 'simulating its presence', it becomes possible 'to take the image for the object'.[25] It is possible, that is to say, to experience it and to interact with it as if it were an object in the real world. And when this becomes the case, we can say that we 'know' the object in a more complex and comprehensive sense. Experiential apprehension is grounded in conceptual and theoretical apprehension.

We should consider this logic in relation to the evolving accommodation between empiricist and rationalist aspects of Enlightenment thinking. The point, which Ernest Gellner makes very forcefully, is that there has always been a powerful symbiotic relationship between empiricism and rationalism in the modern world: 'The two seeming opponents were in fact complementary. Neither could function without the other. Each, strangely enough, performed the task of the other.'[26] Visual empiricism was no exception in this respect. If, in the history of photographic observation, there has always been the danger of a naive empiricism, there has also been an acute awareness that visual experience and evidence could only perform its task, for certain purposes at least, if it were incorporated within systems of rational procedure and analysis (this is precisely Allan Sekula's point). The advent of post-photography has simply served to make this all the more clear. Within the broader scientific and philosophical context, we have come to recognise that the compromise between rationalism and empiricism is increasingly on the terms of the former. Horkheimer and Adorno described it as 'the triumph of subjective rationality, the subjection of all reality to logical formalism'.[27] In the particular sphere of post-photography, too, it is apparent that rationality is the ascendant and dominant principle. We can describe its logic of development in terms of the increasing rationalisation of vision.

I have described these developments in terms of a 'logic', because that, it seems, is how our culture can make best sense of them. The idea of necessary (and inevitable) progression appeals to us, and our culture finds it entirely reasonable to interpret this trajectory in terms of increasing rationality. The project of rationalism, initiated by Descartes, has been about the pursuit of cognitive certainty and conviction. This entails, as Ernest Gellner observes, 'purg[ing] our minds of that which is merely cultural, accidental and untrustworthy'.[28] In so far as culture is associated with 'error' – 'a kind of systematic, communally induced error' – the Cartesian ambition involves 'a programme for man's liberation from culture'.[29] Reason must dissociate itself from cultural accretion; to realise its potential for enlightenment it must become self-sufficient and self-valorising.

We can make sense of the pursuit of photographic truth in the context of this rationalist programme, though we would have to acknowledge photography's spontaneous and desirous affinity with the cultural, the accidental and the untrustworthy. As John Berger argues, the Cartesian revolution created a deep suspicion of appearances: 'It was no longer the look of things which mattered. What mattered was measurement and difference, rather than visual correspondences.'[30] Its complicity with appearances, and thereby with the meanings cultures attach to appearances, always put photography on the side of 'error'. We may then understand developments in photographic technology and culture in terms of the ongoing struggle to purge the medium of its 'impurities'. Positivism may be seen as a preliminary attempt to rationalise the image (though now we will say that it lacked the means, and that its ideas of cognitive truth were simplistic). The 'digital revolution' (with its new means and new approach to cognition) takes the Cartesian project in image culture to a 'higher stage'. This is what Mitchell's 'reconfigured eye' represents. In characterising this supposed revolution, Jonathan Crary describes how the new technologies are 'relocating vision to a plane severed from a human observer'. The idea of a 'real, optically perceived world' has been undermined, he argues, and 'if these images can be said to refer to anything, it is to millions of bits of electronic mathematical data'.[31] What are these new – de-personalised, de-contextualised – 'techniques' of observation but the fulfilment of the rationalist programme? The rationalisation of the image has been a dominant force in the development of photography and post-photography, and accounts of that development (only) in terms of this particular 'logic' have come to seem both coherent and compelling.

In most recent discussion, digital culture has generally been accepted on its own terms. There has been broad assent to its agenda of progress, and growing interest in the new techniques of observation made possible by post-photographic technologies (because this coincides with what we expect of 'technological revolutions'). This has meant that it has not been considered as a *culture*. To do so would involve the de-familiarisation of the Cartesian programme. What is it, we would have to ask, that drives the rationalisation of vision (assuming that it surely cannot be reason alone)? We would have to consider not only what is positively desired and pursued, but also what is at the same time being denied and repressed. In general terms, how are we to understand the hostility to what is 'merely' cultural, accidental and un-trustworthy? What does it mean to seek 'liberation' from our culture? More particularly in relation to digital culture, how are we to make sense of the distrust of appearances, the 'look of things', and ultimately, perhaps even the visual itself?

LOOKING AT THE WORLD AGAIN

In posing such questions, I want now to change the focus of the discussion. The debate on post-photography has become obsessed with the 'digital revolution' and how it is transforming epistemological paradigms and models of vision. The overriding concern is with formal and theoretical issues concerning the nature and the status of the new images. Strangely, we seem now to feel that the rationalisation of vision is more important than the things that really matter to us (love, fear, grief . . .). Other ways of thinking about images and their relation to the world have been devalued (we are being persuaded that they are now anachronistic). There is even the danger that the 'revolution' will make us forget about what we want to do with images – why we want to look at them, how we feel about them, how we react and respond to them. In the discussion that follows, I want to identify some other possibilities inherent in a changing image culture. I shall begin from ex-periences of images (rather than from new technologies and techniques), and from ways of thinking about image culture that are grounded in such experiences. Then I shall seek to locate these in the broader contexts of those aspects of modern culture that have been concerned, not with scientific and technological rationalisation, but rather with imaginative and political free-dom. If the idea of postmodernity really means anything at all, surely it must be around such concerns of creative and democratic emancipation. It is in the context of these (modern and postmodern) agendas that we should now be thinking about the uses of images.

Are there ways, then, of proceeding constructively against the digital grain (without just becoming a counter-revolutionary)? For me, this is a matter of whether it is possible to introduce, or reintroduce, what might simply be called existential dimensions into an agenda that has become predominantly conceptual and rationalistic ('severed from a human observer'). It is about our capacity to be moved by what we see in images. Let us begin with a deliberatively 'primitive' view of photographic images. For Roland Barthes, in *Camera Lucida*, the preliminary question is 'what does my body know of Photography?'[32] Cognition is experienced here as a complex process, mediated through the body and suffused with affect and emotion. Where some images have left him indifferent and irritated, important others have 'provoked tiny jubilations, as if they referred to a stilled centre, an erotic or lacerating value buried in myself'.[33] Barthes's project is to explore the experience of photography 'not as a question (a theme) but as a wound: I see, I feel, hence I notice, I observe, and I think'.[34] One is in love with certain photographs, and one may be 'pricked' by pity at the sight of others. For Barthes, understanding the representational nature of these images cannot be separated from understanding the sensations – the touch – of desire or of grief that they provoke.

John Berger, who is similarly concerned with the nature of the relation between seer and seen, also works to (emotionally) deepen our understanding of photographic apprehension and cognition. Berger wants to explore other kinds of meaning than those valorised by reason. He is intent on reconnecting photography to 'the sensuous, the particular, and the ephemeral'.[35] Against the grain of rationalism, Berger puts great emphasis on the value of appearances: 'appearances as signs addressed to the living ... there to be *read* by the eye'. Appearances, he insists, are oracular in their nature:

> Like oracles they go beyond, they insinuate further than the discrete phenomena they present, and yet their insinuations are rarely sufficient to make any more comprehensive reading indisputable. The precise meaning of an oracular statement depends on the quest or need of the one who listens to it.[36]

The image reveals new possibilities: 'Every image used by a spectator is a going further than he could have achieved alone, towards a prey, a Madonna, a sexual pleasure, a landscape, a face, a different world.'[37] What Berger emphasises is the relation between sight and imagination. 'Appearances', he argues, 'are both cognitive and metaphoric. We classify by appearances and dream with appearances.' It is creative imagination that illuminates and animates our apprehension of the world: 'Without imagination the world becomes unreflective and opaque. Only existence remains.'[38]

Yet another aspect and quality of visual knowing is made apparent in Walter Benjamin's small history of photography. 'With photography', Benjamin argues, 'we encounter something new and strange.' Photographic technology can give its products 'a magical value'. Its beholder 'feels an irresistible urge to search such a picture for the tiny spark of contingency, of the Here and Now, with which reality has so to speak seared the subject'.[39] Benjamin understands the nature of this visual magic with the help of Freud. 'For it is another nature', he says, 'that speaks to the camera than to the eye: other in the sense that a space informed by human consciousness gives way to a space informed by the unconscious.'[40] Benjamin thinks of the 'optical unconscious' as being in continuity with the 'instinctual unconscious' discovered by psychoanalysis. His well-known formulation remains tantalisingly brief and elliptical. We can appropriate it, I think, to explore the conflictual nature of knowledge and of feelings about knowledge. Consider Thomas Ogden's concise and lucid observation on the nature of unconscious processes:

> The creation of the unconscious mind (and therefore, the conscious mind) becomes possible and necessary only in the face of conflicted desire that leads to the need to disown and yet preserve aspects of experience, i. e., the need to maintain two different modes of experiencing the same psychological event simultaneously. In other words, the very existence of the differentiation of the conscious and unconscious mind stems from a conflict between a desire to feel/think/be in specific ways, and the desire not to feel/think/be in those ways.[41]

We can see visual experience in terms of these processes of division. Visual cognition is grounded in feelings of both pleasure and displeasure: the desire to see coexists with the fear of seeing. The ambivalence in all object relations is, of course, apparent in our relation to the objects of visual knowledge.

These various and different meditations on the nature of photography all serve the present argument in so far as they contradict any idea of purely rational seeing and knowing. In their distinctive ways, they aim to show us how vision also serves psychic and bodily demands, and how much it is also needed in the cause of sublimation and imaginative transformation. These existential aspects of image use have been most keen, no doubt, in the encounter with death and mortality. Images have always been linked with death, and a particular kind of meditation on death has been a consistent theme in modern reflections on photographic culture. 'All photographs are *memento mori*,' says Susan Sontag. 'To take a photograph is to participate in another person's (or thing's) mortality, vulnerability, mutability.'[42] Death is 'what is utterly mysterious for man', Pierre MacOrlan observed, and the power of photography resides in its relation to this mystery:

> To be able to create the death of things and creatures, if only for a second, is a force of revelation which, without explanation (which is useless), fixes the essential character of what must constitute a fine

anxiety, one rich in forms, fragrances, repugnances, and, naturally, the association of ideas.[43]

Roland Barthes describes photographers as 'agents of Death', and photography as corresponding to the intrusion into modern societies of 'an asymbolic Death, outside of religion, outside of ritual, a kind of abrupt dive into literal Death'.[44] Photographs relate to anxieties and fears in the face of mortality, and may then enable the imaginative possession and modification of those feelings.

But it can be otherwise. Another kind of response, which has been closely associated with the project of modern rationalism, can be to deny or disavow our mortal nature. As Horkheimer and Adorno argue, the logic of rationality and rationalisation aimed at 'liberating men from fear' through the imperious force of reason: 'Nothing at all remains outside, because the mere idea of outsideness is the very source of fear .... Man imagines himself free from fear when there is no longer anything unknown.'[45] Through rational control and mastery (over both nature and human nature), rationalism and positivism, 'its ultimate product', have sought to occlude the sources of mortal fear. We may consider digital technology and discourse as being in continuity with this project of rational subjection. Electronic images are not frozen, do not fade; their quality is not elegiac, they are not just registrations of mortality. Digital techniques produce images in cryogenised form: they can be awoken, re-animated, brought 'up to date'. Digital manipulation can resurrect the dead. William Mitchell thinks of dead Elvis and the possibility now that we could be presented with 'a sharp, detailed "photograph" of him in a recognisably contemporary setting'.[46] 'Bringing back Marilyn' is the example that occurs to Fred Ritchin.[47] Death-defying simulation is linked to powerful fantasies of rational transcendence. 'To lose sight of the unbearable', says Régis Debray, 'is to diminish the dark attraction of shadows, and of their opposite, the value of a ray of light.' 'The death of death', he suggests, 'would strike a decisive blow against the imagination.'[48] Of course, there is reason to believe that the rationalist dream will always be cloyed. With Roland Barthes, we must inquire as to the anthropological place of death in our culture: 'For Death must be somewhere in society.'[49] Do we really think it could be nowhere?

I am concerned that we should hold on to a sense of the complexity of image cultures, and, particularly, that we should continue to recognise the significance of other than rational uses of the image. In the context of the emerging digital culture, however, such concerns can only appear to be perverse and problematical. From the austere perspective of post-photography, they will seem 'innocent' and nostalgic. This version of a 'postmodern' image culture is devoted precisely to the critique and deconstruction of such dubious notions. The new information format is understood in terms of the emancipation of the image from its empirical limitations and sentimental associations; it is a matter, that is to say, of purifying the image of what are considered to be its residual realist and humanist interests. This is, in fact, the programme of rationalisation masquerading in the drag of postmodernism. What is so striking about it is its arrogance (in the sense intended by W. R. Bion when he speaks of 'the arrogance of Oedipus in vowing to lay bare the truth at no matter what cost'[50]). With its singular commitment to the rationalisation of vision, digital culture has tended to deny or to devalue other uses of the image. It is no longer concerned with the image as transitional between inner and outer realities. If imagination means anything at all in this progressivist scheme, it is certainly not what John Berger calls 'the primary faculty of the human imagination – the faculty of being able to identify with another person's experience'[51] (which is all that could help Oedipus in his suffering). Belief in 'perfect' images seems to be inhibiting our relation to 'good enough' images. Consider Barthes's observation that ultimately 'in order to see a photograph well, it is best to look away or close your eyes'.[52] In a context of change (arrogantly called 'progress'), can we now sustain a vital *culture* of images?

The first question is whether we can see possibilities in this historical moment? Are we able to re-describe the context in which our image culture is being transformed, in such a way as to achieve a more radical understanding of what we could mean by 'postmodern'? It is a question of subverting the ideology of modernity (and postmodernity) as the progressive emancipation of rationality. We might begin from Horkheimer and Adorno's *Dialectic of Enlightenment* – in some ways a founding text of postmodernism – and its exploration of how, from the primordial 'cry of terror', a history of fear has shadowed the history of reason. The fear that is repressed returns as a cultural malady. For Horkheimer and Adorno, 'Enlightenment behaves like Sophocles' tragic hero, Oedipus: it surely did liberate the species from the awful power of nature but also brought with it a new plague.[53] The logic of rational mastery is always defeated by what still remains 'outside'. And mastery itself, moreover, may be associated with an (irrational) sense of loss, and with cultural undercurrents of melancholy and apocalyptic depression.[54] To say that we are postmodern would then involve recognition of how Enlightenment has failed by the same token that it has succeeded. We might understand postmodern sensibility in the way that Mladen Dolar intends, when he says that 'it doesn't imply a going beyond the modern, but rather an awareness of its internal limit, its split . . .'[55] Following his insight, we might see postmodernity, imagined in a fundamentally counter-teleological sense, in terms of possibilities for allowing the return of what modern culture has repressed or disavowed. The real question then is whether we could look those possibilities in the face. The story of Oedipus is one of the struggle to evade painful realities through 'turning a blind eye' and of the retreat into omnipotence.[56] There is a need to live with the unhappy conclusions that realistic insight would demand. A postmodern culture would have to look back at the repressed fears and unconscious forces that have haunted reason's progress.

And it should then be about their imaginative and political transformation. The modern world was not shaped by reason and Enlightenment alone. Johann Arnason reasserts the cultural and intellectual significance of Romanticism, emphasising the importance of the interrelation and interaction between these two cultural currents, and arguing that it is precisely 'this cultural configuration (rather than an irresistible logic or an uncompleted project of Enlightenment alone) [that] should be placed at the centre of a theory of cultural modernity'.[57] And of postmodernity, too. This other current is important in terms of the critique of Enlightenment (though, of course, there are as many problems with Romantic culture as with Enlightenment culture; each has come to our century in a debased form). It has been concerned with rationality's Other, with what was repressed by, and what remained 'outside', Reason's comprehension. It also drew attention to our embeddedness in human cultures (and consequently in the cultural, accidental and untrustworthy). We can only come to terms with our human 'condition' in the context of particular human cultures. As David Roberts argues, where Enlightenment pursued the principle of 'radical *abstraction from the given*', Romantic thinkers held on to that of cultural and historical '*incarnation*'.[58] And where Enlightenment aspired to rational transcendence, the Romantic emphasis was on the powers of creativity and imagination necessary for the achievement of human and political emancipation.

It is in this spirit that Cornelius Castoriadis opposes the openness of radical imagination against the closure of rationalist empire. What makes us human, he maintains, is not rationality, but 'the continuous, uncontrolled and uncontrollable surge of our creative radical imagination in and through the flux of representations, affects and desires.'[59] Castoriadis seeks a productive accommodation between unconscious, imaginative and reasoning powers (which also involves confronting the fear of death) in the cause of human autonomy. It is a matter of achieving 'a self-reflecting and deliberative subjectivity, one that has ceased to be a pseudo-rational and socially-adapted machine, but has on the contrary recognised and freed the radical imagination at the core of the psyche'.[60] This, of course, involves recognising the existence of other people, whose desires may be in opposition to our own. Consequently, the project of autonomy 'is necessarily social, and not simply individual.'[61] For Castoriadis, the project of bringing forth autonomous individuals and the project of an autonomous society are one and the same. What if we conceive the possibilities of postmodernism in this tougher and more radical way?

The point, let me reiterate, is to contest an overly rationalistic and imaginatively closed understanding of our changing image culture. It is to find other meaningful contexts in which to make sense of and make use of images. My suggestions of possibilities are intended to be brief and indicative only (and, surely, there are other lines of flight). What they aim to do is to (re)validate a world of meaning and action that is not reducible to rationality. Recall Barthes's individual encounter with the photographic image, moving from seeing and feeling, through attention and observation, to thought and elucidation. If you like, I am thinking of this kind of open sensibility in a social context, in terms of a broader culture of images. As Johann Arnason argues, in the terms of Merleau-Ponty, such a project would be about recovering an openness to the world, about 'relearning to look at the world'. Visual perception would be linked to 'a rediscovery and articulation of the opening to the world that is constitutive of the human condition'.[62] How we look at the world relates to our disposition towards the world.

At this point, we must finally come back to the question of how new images and new technologies fit into this. We should consider again whether or how they might change the way we look at the world. One possibility is opened up by those art and visual historians, working in a Foucauldian tradition, who have sought to identify significant discontinuities and disjunctures in regimes or models of vision. Thus, in relation to the birth of photography, Geoffrey Batchen argues that we must address ourselves 'not just to optics and chemistry but to a peculiarly modern inflection of power, knowledge, and subject'.[63] Now we are facing the imminent demise of this photographic 'assemblage': 'The desiring assemblage that incorporates both photography and the modern subject is by no means fixed and immutable. Indeed it may already be reconstituting itself along yet another line of flight.'[64] The death of photography now augurs a wholly new assemblage. This is what Batchen calls the 'postmodern prospect'. This kind of approach remains rather narrow in its focus, concerned almost exclusively with the relation between vision and knowledge/power (though, in inscribing epistemological change in some kind of social context, it provides us with a meaningful way of looking at the rationalisation of vision). Within these terms, however, it does show us how the look of things can be transformed, through the development of new forms of technological vision and new techniques of observation. At critical moments, it is argued, and usually through the advent of new technologies, the relation between vision and subjectivity can be dramatically changed. Older ways of seeing the world (in Mitchell's terms, 'sclerotic pictorial traditions') are dislodged, and at the same time new kinds of visual description become possible. There are possibilities for creative disruption. But at the same time, I would argue, these 'localised' shifts in techniques of observation may also make sense in the 'global' context of the developing rationalisation of vision. New ways of seeing may not be at odds with existing forms and relations of power in the visual field.

That is one way of thinking about the possibilities that may be available to us now (though it is still, I think, caught up in modernist notions of development and progress). Let me suggest another (which may be more postmodern, in the sense I am trying to elaborate). In this case, what are significant are not new technologies and images *per se*, but rather the re-ordering of the overall visual field and reappraisal of image cultures and traditions that they provoke. It is notable that much of the most interesting discussion of images now concerns not digital futures but, actually, what seemed until recently to be antique and forgotten media (the panorama, the camera obscura, the stereoscope); from our post-photographic vantage point these have suddenly acquired new meanings, and their re-evaluation now seems crucial to understanding the significance of digital culture. In this context, it seems productive to think, not in terms of discontinuities and disjunctures, but rather, on the basis of continuities, through generations of images and across visual forms.

In his critique of Foucauldian analysis (Crary's version), David Phillips recommends that we 'take into account the persistence and durability of older modes of visuality'. Against the idea of a sequential narrative of succeeding image cultures, and against the narrative logic of successive epistemological breaks, Phillips argues that 'vision operates instead as a palimpsest which conflates many different modes of perception – a model which applies both to the history of vision and to the perception of a singular observer'.[65] This seems to me a very productive metaphor (and one that can help us to resist both technological progressivism and epistemological evolutionism). Rather than privileging 'new' against 'old' images, we might then think about them all – all those that are still active, at least – in their contemporaneity. From such a perspective, what is significant is precisely the multiplicity and the diversity of contemporary images. In working against the grain of progessivist or evolutionary models, we can try to make creative use of the interplay of different orders of images. The coexistence of different images, different ways of seeing, different visual imaginations, may be seen as an imaginative resource.

This was the fundamental issue in the exhibition *Passages de l'Image*, held at the Centre Georges Pompidou in 1990. As Raymond Bellour expresses it in his contribution to the exhibition catalogue, it is 'the diversity of image forms that is now our problem', and the problem, by which he in fact means the solution, concerns the proliferation of *'passages'* or 'contaminations' between images.[66] The mixes, the relays, the *passages* or movements between images, he suggests, are taking shape in two ways: 'on the one hand, an oscillation between the mobility and immobility of the image; on the other, between maintaining photographic analogy and a tendency toward de-figuration'.[67] There is a sense in which 'we are now beyond the image'; a sense in which it is now more productive to think in terms of the hybridity of image forms. We must come to terms with new ways of 'seeing' through what might be called an-optical technologies. We can also recognise the potential of digital manipulation for effecting new forms of hybridisation (this is what William Mitchell refers to as 'electrobricolage'[68]). The artist, Esther Parada, talks about her attraction to digital technology in terms of the possibilities it offers for the 'shifting and blending' and the 'layering' of images (and texts); it allows, she says, 'the materialisation of linkages in time and space that enhance understanding'.[69]

At the same time, we can acknowledge the persistence of photographic vision, and recognise that it will continue to actually replenish itself. Take the work of Geneviève Cadieux, some of whose images featured in the *Passages* exhibition. Referring to its 'monumentality', Ingrid Schaffner has argued that Cadieux 'deploys the conventions of sculpture to upset the passivity of our encounter with the plane'.[70] Her photographic images revitalise our sense of seeing, and re-position it in relation to the senses of both touch and hearing (*Hear Me with Your Eyes* is the title of one of her pieces). Régis Durand emphasises the continuing possibilities – often, again, through the use of large-scale and 'heroic' formats, once associated with the 'fine arts' – for giving the 'force of evidence' inherent in the photographic image a renewed power to move and affect us.[71] Where we might easily be drawn into thinking in terms of 'emergent' versus 'residual' image forms, a cultivated sense of ambivalence may be more imaginatively productive. We should aspire to be open to the force of all modes of visual representation and presentation.

In re-describing the transformation of photography in terms of the layering of images or in terms of *passages* of the image, perhaps we can take a stand against the arrogance of (technological and cultural) modernity. Perhaps we can work towards a better context in which to explore the emotional, imaginative, moral and political aspects of a changing image culture. In an essay on 'Psychoanalysis and idolatry', Adam Phillips considers the significance of Freud's great collection of graven images. 'So what was Freud telling his patients and himself by displaying his collection in the rooms where he practised psychoanalysis . . .?' Phillips asks.[72] There are two speculative responses. Freud was saying that 'culture was history, and that this history . . . could be preserved and thought about'; 'the dead do not disappear', and on the recognition of this our psychic and cultural well-being may depend. And, second, Freud was also telling his patients and himself that 'culture was plural. . . . The figurines underlined the fact that there are all sorts of cultural conventions and worlds elsewhere, as many as can be found.'[73] Is not Freud's relation to his idols suggestive for how we might now think of our own relation to images? The archaeology of images is linked to psychological excavation. And images are a means of being open to cultural diversity; they represent Freud's 'wishful allegiance to alternative cultures'.[74]

We might inflect this disposition in more social and political ways. In contemporary political theory (of the anti-foundationalist kind) the idea of an absolute Truth is also called into question. In such a perspective, neatly summarised by Glyn Daly, the world can only be described through competing language games; it is 'permanently exposed to competing redescriptions', and, consequently '"truth" will always be conjuncturally put together as the result of a struggle between competing language-games/

discourses'. What is significant is precisely the interplay between these competing descriptions, all originating from particular (and limited) positions. Fundamental issues 'will be conjuncturally settled by those narratives – novels, ethnographies, journalist writings, etc. – with which we identify and express our solidarity'.[75] In this context, we could give some kind of political (rather than epistemological) meaning to the recognition that images can no longer be 'comfortably regarded as causally generated truthful reports about things in the real world' and that they might, in fact, be like 'more traditionally crafted images, which seemed notoriously ambiguous and uncertain human constructions'.[76] We would then consider our image culture in terms of its productive diversity, and we would be concerned with the possibilities (creative and also technological) for originating 'new' – insightful, open, moving – descriptions of the world.

* * * * *

Everyone recognises themselves in the photo album.
(Christian Boltanski, interview in *Creative Camera*)

There is a prevailing tendency to think of digital technologies as being 'revolutionary', and to suppose that they are so in their very 'nature'. Throughout this chapter, I have been arguing against such a position, suggesting that digital culture may, in fact, be seen in terms of the continuing rationalisation of vision (bringing this 'logic' to a new level of sophistication, and effecting a new accommodation between the rationalist and empiricist aspects of modern culture). I have endeavoured to move the discussion away from this predominantly theoretical and philosophical perspective, and to open up a more cultural and political agenda concerning the changing image culture. This has meant reasserting the importance of vision (appearances) in cultural experience – beginning from the uses of vision, that is to say, rather than from technological novelty. In emphasising the symbolic importance of images, we can consider their development in the context of the counter-rationalistic tendencies in modern culture (now being critically re-examined by those who are concerned to re-validate imagination and creativity in our culture). I think we can then go further, to consider the increasing multiplicity and diversity of ways of seeing in the context of new (postmodern) ways of thinking about political and democratic life. These ideas remain tentative and exploratory. They are intended to suggest pretexts and contexts through which to find more open and meaningful ways to reappropriate our culture of images. I am not denying the formidable capacities of the new technologies; I am trying to give them some more relevant cultural and political location.

The future of images is not (techno-logically) determined. Different possibilities exist – as long as we can resist the comforts of determinism. To make them exist, we must think very carefully about what it is that we now *want* from images. The 'death of photography' is one of those rare moments in which we are called upon to re-negotiate – and to re-cathect – our relation to images (old ones as much as new ones). In the end, images are significant in terms of what we can do with them and how they carry meanings for us. For some, this will indeed be a matter of exploiting the extraordinary power of the new technologies to 'see' the births and deaths of stars. Most of us, however, will have more mundane and personal concerns, because image culture – to adapt Raymond Williams's phrase – remains ordinary. Images will continue to be important – 'technological revolution' notwithstanding – because they mediate so effectively, and often movingly, between inner and outer realities.

NOTES

INTRODUCTION: IMAGE TECHNOLOGIES
AND VISUAL CULTURE

1 As such, it develops out of earlier critical analyses. See Frank Webster and Kevin Robins, *Information Technology: A Luddite Analysis*, Norwood, NJ, Ablex, 1986; Kevin Robins and Frank Webster, *The Technical Fix*, London, Macmillan, 1989; Les Levidow and Kevin Robins (eds), *Cyborg Worlds: The Military Information Society*, London, Free Association Book, 1989.

2 See Martin Jay, *Downcast Eyes: The Denigration of Vision in Twentieth-Century French Thought*, Berkeley, University of California Press, 1993; David Michael Levin (ed.), *Modernity and the Hegemony of Vision*, Berkeley, University of California Press, 1993.

3 On this, see *Passages de l'Image*, Paris, Centre Georges Pompidou, 1990, especially the essay by Jean-François Chevrier and Cathérine David, 'Actualité de l'image', pp. 17–36.

4 J.-B. Pontalis, 'Perdre de vue', *Nouvelle Revue de Psychanalyse*, 35, 1987, p. 235.

5 Margaret Iversen, 'What is a photograph?', *Art History*, 17 (3), 1994, p. 451.

6 Peter Benson, 'Freud and the visual', *Representations*, 45, 1994, p. 113.

7 Shiv Visavanathan, 'Bhopal: the imagination of a disaster', *Alternatives*, 11, 1986, p. 164.

8 Juan Goytisolo, *Quarantine*, London, Quartet, 1994, p. 69.

9 Kevin Robins and Les Levidow, 'Soldier, cyborg, citizen', in James Brook and Iain A. Boal (eds), *Resisting the Virtual Life: The Culture and Politics of Information*, San Francisco, City Lights, 1995.

10 Richard Kearney, *The Wake of Imagination*, London, Hutchinson, 1988, p. 390.

11 William J. Mitchell, *City of Bits: Space, Place and the Infobahn*, Cambridge, Mass., MIT Press, 1995, pp. 166, 167.

12 Bernard Sharratt, 'Communications and image studies: notes after Raymond Williams', *Comparative Criticism*, 11, 1989, p. 35.

1 THE TOUCH OF THE UNKNOWN

1 Max Horkheimer and Theodor W. Adorno, *Dialectic of Enlightenment*, London, Allen Lane, 1973, pp. 3, 16. Robert Hullot-Kentor describes the first essay in *Dialectic of Enlightenment* as presenting 'a history of fear from the primordial scream of terror in the face of overwhelming nature to positivism, in which thought is restricted to the standard of the mastery of nature and thus reduced to

169

nature . . .' 'Notes on *Dialectic of Enlightenment*: translating the Odysseus essay', *New German Critique*, 56, 1992.

2 Elias Canetti, *Crowds and Power*, Harmondsworth, Penguin, 1973, p. 15.

3 Steven Levy, 'TechnoMania', *Newsweek*, 27 February 1995, p. 15.

4 *Ibid.*, pp. 17, 14.

5 *Ibid.*, p. 17.

6 Roland Fischer, 'A story of the utopian vision of the world', *Diogenes*, 163, 1993, p. 21.

7 *Ibid.*

8 *Ibid.*

9 *Ibid.*

10 *Ibid.* Fischer is here quoting from R. W. Lucky, 'The urge of an ancient dream', *Scientific American*, 265, 1991, p. 138.

11 Zygmunt Bauman, 'Morality without ethics', *Theory, Culture and Society*, 11 (4), 1994, p. 12.

12 Louis Marin, 'The frontiers of utopia', in Krishan Kumar and Stephen Bann (eds), *Utopias and the Millennium*, London, Reaktion Books, 1993, p. 8.

13 *Ibid.*, p. 14.

14 *Ibid.*, p. 12.

15 *Ibid.*, p. 11.

16 *Ibid.*

17 Ralph Schroeder, 'Cyberculture, cyborg post-modernism and the sociology of virtual reality technologies', *Futures*, 26 (5), 1994, pp. 524–525.

18 Kiersta Fricke, 'Virtual reality: Venus return or vanishing point', *Leonardo*, 27 (4), 1994, p. 277.

19 Arturo Escobar, 'Welcome to cyberia: notes on the anthropology of cyberculture', *Current Anthropology*, 35 (3), 1994, p. 211.

20 Schroeder, 'Cyberculture', pp. 526–527.

21 Cornelius Castoriadis, 'Institution of society and religion', *Thesis Eleven*, 35, 1993, p. 12.

22 *Ibid.*, pp. 1–2.

23 Bauman, 'Morality without ethics', p. 4.

24 *Ibid.*, p. 11.

25 *Ibid.*, p. 4.

26 Michael Eigen, 'Towards Bion's starting point: between catastrophe and faith', *International Journal of Psycho-Analysis*, 66, 1985, p. 325.

27 Paul Hoggett, 'A place for experience: a psychoanalytic perspective on boundary, identity and culture', *Environment and Planning D: Society and Space*, 10 (3), 1992, p. 345.

28 *Ibid.*, p. 346.

29 Serge Moscovici, 'La crainte du contact', *Communications*, 57, 1993.

30 Canetti, *Crowds and Power*, p. 15.

31 Martin Jay, 'Scopic regimes of modernity', in Hal Foster (ed.), *Vision and Visuality*, Seattle, Bay Press, 1988, pp. 8, 10.

32 *Ibid.*, p. 10. Jay is here referring to Heidegger's critique of the modern technological worldview.

33 Anthony Vidler, 'Bodies in space/subjects in the city: psychopathologies of modern urbanism', *Differences: A Journal of Feminist Cultural Studies*, 5 (3), 1993, pp. 36, 34.

34 John Naughton, 'Smile, you're on TV', *Observer*, Life supplement, 13 November 1994, p. 40.

35 See Chapter 3 for a full discussion. See also David Morley and Kevin Robins, 'Cultural imperialism and the mediation of otherness', in Akbar S. Ahmed and

Cris N. Shore (eds), *The Future of Anthropology: Its Relevance to the Contemporary World*, London, Athlone Press, 1995.

36 Levy, 'TechnoMania', p. 15.

37 Shelley Rice, 'Boundless horizons: the panoramic image', *Art in America*, December 1993, p. 71.

38 Raymond Fielding, 'Hale's Tours: ultrarealism in the pre-1910 motion picture', in John L. Fell (ed.), *Film Before Griffith*, Berkeley, University of California Press, 1983, p. 117. Fielding describes these tours as 'one of the earliest examples in a long series of continuing attempts by film producers to duplicate or simulate certain aspects of perceived reality' (p. 129).

39 Niall Martin, 'Step into the cybercity', *Independent*, 18 January 1995.

40 Peter Hinssen, 'Life in the digital city', *Wired*, April 1995, p. 54.

41 George M. Taber, 'A whole new world', *Time*, 12 June 1995, p. 55.

42 'Holy Akira! It's Aeon Flux', *Newsweek*, 14 August 1995, p. 52.

43 W. R. Bion, *Learning from Experience*, London, Heinemann, 1962.

44 Hans A. Thorner, 'Notes on the desire for knowledge', *International Journal of Psycho-Analysis*, 62, 1981, p. 75.

45 Here I draw freely on the suggestive ideas developed in Thomas H. Ogden, *The Primitive Edge of Experience*, Northvale, NJ, Jason Aronson, 1989, ch. 8. Also suggestive in this context are Janet Riesenberg Malcolm's observations on the 'as-if' substitute formation. What is distinctive about this condition, she argues, is the 'attempt to keep a static position': 'A static situation acts for these people as a kind of reassurance, a kind of proof that they are all right, do not need any change, which they prove by perceiving themselves endowed with keen analytic perceptions and gifts and rich emotions.' All that is possible in this condition is 'an accumulation of meaninglessness'; Janet Riesenberg Malcolm, 'As if: the phenomenon of not learning', in Robin Anderson (ed.), *Clinical Lectures on Klein and Bion*, London, Tavistock/Routledge, 1993, pp. 121, 114, 117.

46 W. R. Bion, *Experiences in Group*, London, Tavistock, 1961.

47 David Armstrong, 'Names, thoughts and lies: the relevance of Bion's later writing for understanding experiences in groups', *Free Associations*, 26, 1992, pp. 269, 276.

48 Ogden, *Primitive Edge of Experience*, pp. 1–2.

49 Armstrong, 'Names, thoughts and lies', p. 270.

50 Eigen, 'Towards Bion's starting point', p. 329.

51 *Ibid.*, p. 326.

52 Christopher Bollas, *Being a Character: Psychoanalysis and Self Experience*, London, Routledge, 1993, p. 88.

53 Castoriadis, 'Institution of society and religion', pp. 12, 8. Cf. 'From that unsupervised and uncontrolled *elsewhere*, from that *otherwise than being*, comes the novelty and the unexpected; and in it all that is usual and homely sinks.' Bauman, 'Morality without ethics', p. 4. Bauman is here drawing on both Castoriadis and Emmanuel Levinas, to whom I shall refer below.

54 Cornelius Castoriadis, 'En mal de culture', *Esprit*, October 1994, p. 47.

55 An approach of particular interest, which I cannot pursue here, is that of Julia Kristeva, *Strangers to Ourselves*, New York, Harvester Wheatsheaf, 1991.

56 Emmanuel Levinas, 'Time and the Other', in Seán Hand (ed.), *The Levinas Reader*, Oxford, Blackwell, 1989, pp. 42–43.

57 Alphonso Lingis, *Foreign Bodies*, New York, Routledge, 1994, p. 177.

58 Emmanuel Levinas, 'Ethics as first philosophy', in Hand, *The Levinas Reader*, p. 83. On the ethical implications of Levinas's work, see also Zygmunt Bauman, *Postmodern Ethics*, Oxford, Blackwell, 1993, and also the text by Bauman cited above.

59 William J. Mitchell, *City of Bits: Space, Place and the Infobahn*, Cambridge, Mass., MIT Press, 1995, pp. 34.

60 *Ibid.*, p. 33.

61 This reflects a western arrogance that is utterly blind to other ways of seeing. We should take note of Daryush Shayegan's observation that 'the people living on our planet do not all have the same way of seeing the world'. 'The visionary man whose look is transfigured by the magic of the world', says Shayegan, 'does not see things in the same fashion as the visual man living in the disenchanted galaxy of Gutenberg.' Daryush Shayegan, *Le Regard Mutilé: Schizophrénie Culturelle – Pays Traditionnels Face à la Modernité*, Paris, Albin Michel, 1989, pp. 51, 140. In the context of a discussion of Jean Baudrillard's *America*, Shayegan makes clear, furthermore, the destabilising, and often destructive impact of western vision on non-western cultures. *Ibid.*, pp. 140–144. For an interesting, psychoanalytically oriented discussion of the difference between western and Islamic cultures of vision, see Jean-Michel Hirt, 'Photomaton', *Nouvelle Revue de Psychanalyse*, 44, 1991, pp. 210–222.

62 Mitchell, *City of Bits*, p. 100.

63 *Ibid.*, pp. 10, 24. 'You will become a modular, reconfigurable, infinitely extensible cyborg' (p. 30).

64 *Ibid.*, p. 19. 'Think of yourself on some evening in the not-so-distant future, when wearable, fitted, and implanted electronic organs connected by bodynets are as commonplace as cotton; your intimate infrastructure connects you seamlessly to a planetful of bits, and you have software in your underwear. It's eleven o'clock, Smarty Pants; do you know where your network connections are tonight?' (p. 31).

65 Mitchell displays no awareness that others might contest the self-evidence of his predictions. He does not recognise that there could be competing objectives, values or priorities. For him, 'the most crucial task before us is . . . one of imagining and creating digitally mediated environments for the kind of lives that we will want to lead and the sorts of communities that we will want to have' (*ibid.*, p. 5). Who is the 'we' that Mitchell invokes? Doesn't he recognise that there are still a great many non-cyborgs in this world?

66 Julian Stallabrass, 'Empowering technology: the exploration of cyberspace', *New Left Review*, 211, 1995, pp. 7, 5.

67 Mitchell, *City of Bits*, p. 105.

68 John Berger, 'Un spectacle nulle part contesté', *Le Monde Diplomatique*, March 1995, p. 25. This article is written in memory of Guy Debord.

69 Lingis, *Foreign Bodies*, p. 166.

70 Mitchell, *City of Bits*, pp. 184–185.

71 Richard Sennett, *Flesh and Stone: The Body and the City in Western Civilisation*, London, Faber & Faber, 1994, pp. 18, 21.

72 *Ibid.*, p. 17.

73 *Ibid.*, p. 21.

74 Mitchell, *City of Bits*, p. 167.

75 Sennett, *Flesh and Stone*, p. 17. On urbanity and bodily experience, see also Elizabeth Grosz, 'Bodies–cities', in Beatriz Colomina (ed.), *Sexuality and Space*, Princeton, Princeton Architectural Press, 1992.

76 Mitchell, *City of Bits*, pp. 43–44.

77 Alphonso Lingis, 'Bodies that touch us', *Thesis Eleven*, 36, 1993, p. 167.

78 Ian Craib, *The Importance of Disappointment*, London, Routledge, 1994, p. 42.

79 Canetti, *Crowds and Power*, p. 15.

80 Elizabeth Grosz, 'Merleau-Ponty and Irigaray in the flesh', *Thesis Eleven*, 36,

1993, p. 50. (The quotation is from Luce Irigaray, '*L'Ethique de la Différence Sexuelle*, Paris, Minuit, 1981, p. 155.)

81 *Ibid.*, p. 45.

82 Emmanuel Levinas, 'Time and the Other', p. 51.

83 Emmanuel Levinas, *Totality and Infinity*, Pittsburgh, Duquesne University Press, 1969, p. 258. On the caress, see also Zygmunt Bauman, *Postmodern Ethics*, pp. 92–98.

84 Alphonso Lingis, *Foreign Bodies*, p. 171 (my emphasis).

85 Maurice Merleau-Ponty, 'Eye and mind', in John O'Neill (ed.), *Phenomenology, Language and Sociology: Selected Essays of Maurice Merleau-Ponty*, London, Heinemann, 1974, pp. 281–282.

86 Maurice Merleau-Ponty, 'Cézanne's doubt', in *Sense and Non-Sense*, Evanston, Northwestern University Press, 1964, p. 19 (Merleau-Ponty's emphasis).

87 Vincent Amiel, 'Le corps en images (de Buster Keaton à John Cassavetes)', *Esprit*, February 1994, pp. 135–136.

88 Paul Virilio, 'Alerte dans le cyberespace!', *Le Monde Diplomatique*, August 1995, p. 28.

89 Julia Kristeva, 'The imaginary sense of forms', *Arts Magazine*, September 1991, p. 30 (Kristeva's emphasis).

2 THE SPACE OF THE SCREEN

1 William Leith, 'At home with Mr Hockney', *Independent on Sunday*, 21 October 1990, p. 37.

2 John Darius, *Beyond Vision*, Oxford, Oxford University Press, 1984, p. 17.

3 Stewart Brand, *The Media Lab: Inventing the Future at MIT*, New York, Viking, 1987, pp. 113–116.

4 Mike Laye, 'From today, is photography dead?', *Image*, 172, January 1990, pp. 11–12.

5 Philippe Quéau, Programme for Imagina 91, Tenth Monte Carlo Forum on New Images, 30 January to 1 February 1991. Subsequent programmes have assumed the same jubilant tone and attitude.

6 Gene Youngblood, 'The new renaissance: art, science and the universal machine', in Richard L. Loveless (ed.), *The Computer Revolution and the Arts*, Tampa, University of South Florida Press, 1989, p. 15.

7 *Ibid.*, p. 16.

8 *Ibid.*, p. 17.

9 Richard Wright, 'Computer graphics as allegorical knowledge: electronic imagery in the sciences', in *Digital Image – Digital Cinema: Siggraph '90 Art Show Catalog*, *Leonardo*, Supplemental Issue, 1990, p. 69.

10 Youngblood, 'The new renaissance', p. 15.

11 *Ibid.*, pp. 9–10.

12 Roger F. Malina, 'Digital image–digital cinema: the work of art in the age of post-mechanical reproduction', in *Digital Image–Digital Cinema: Siggraph '90 Art Show Catalog*, *Leonardo*, Supplemental Issue, 1990, p. 3.

13 For discussion, see Fred Ritchin, *In Our Own Image: The Coming Revolution in Photography*, New York, Aperture, 1990; Fred Ritchin, 'Photojournalism in the age of computers', in Carol Squiers (ed.), *The Critical Image*, Seattle, Bay Press, 1990; Karin Becker, 'To control our image: photojournalists meeting new technology', *Media, Culture and Society*, 13 (3), 1991.

14 Timothy Druckrey, 'L'amour faux', *Perspektief*, 37, December 1989 to January 1990, pp. 37, 41.

15 Don Slater, 'Image worlds', *Ten–8*, 22, 1986, p. 35.

16 Youngblood, 'The new renaissance', pp. 13–14.

17 Howard Rheingold, 'What's the big deal about cyberspace?', in Brenda Laurel (ed.), *The Art of Human–Computer Interface Design*, Reading, Mass., Addison-Wesley, 1990, p. 450.

18 John Walker, 'Through the looking glass', in Brenda Laurel (ed.), *The Art of Human–Computer Interface Design*, Reading, Mass., Addison-Wesley, 1990, p. 443.

19 *Ibid.*, pp. 446–447.

20 Timothy Leary, 'The interpersonal, interactive, interdimensional interface', in Brenda Laurel (ed.), *The Art of Human–Computer Interface Design*, Reading, Mass., Addison-Wesley, 1990, p. 232.

21 Rheingold, 'What's the big deal about cyberspace?', p. 452.

22 Sigmund Freud, *Civilisation and its Discontents*, London, Hogarth Press, revised edition, 1963, pp. 14–18.

23 Susan Sontag, *On Photography*, Harmondsworth, Penguin, 1979, pp. 8–9.

24 Scott Lash, *Sociology of Postmodernism*, London, Routledge, 1990, pp. 12–14.

25 Robert J. Stone, 'Virtual reality in telerobotics', in *Computer Graphics*, Proceedings of the Conference held in London, November 1990, Pinner, Middlesex, Blenheim Online, 1990, p. 32.

26 Scott S. Fisher, 'Virtual interface environments', in Brenda Laurel (ed.), *The Art of Human–Computer Interface Design*, Reading, Mass., Addison-Wesley, 1990, p. 430.

27 *Ibid.*, p. 453.

28 See Gregory MacNichol, 'What's wrong with reality?', *Computer Graphics World*, November 1990.

29 William Gibson, *Neuromancer*, London, Grafton Books, 1986, p. 67.

30 Regina Cornwell, 'Where is the window? Virtual reality technologies now', *Artscribe*, January–February 1991, p. 55.

31 John Perry Barlow, 'Being in nothingness', *Mondo 2000*, 2, 1990, p. 41.

32 Theodore Roszak, *The Cult of Information*, Cambridge, Lutterworth Press, 1986, pp. 146–150.

33 Quoted in Sioned Lewis and Karen Peet, 'It's real – virtually', *Wave*, Launch issue, Autumn 1990, p. 46.

34 Barlow, 'Being in nothingness', p. 36

35 Timothy Binkley, 'Digital dilemmas', in *Digital Image – Digital Cinema: Siggraph '90 Art Show Catalog*, *Leonardo*, Supplemental issue, 1990, p. 18.

36 Youngblood, 'The new renaissance', p. 18.

37 Michael Naimark, 'Realness and interactivity', in Brenda Laurel (ed.), *The Art of Human–Computer Interface Design*, Reading, Mass., Addison-Wesley, 1990, p. 457.

38 Joanna Pomian, 'A la recherche de la machine communicante', *Quaderni*, 5, Autumn 1988. For earlier discussions, see J. Bronowski, *The Identity of Man*, Harmondsworth, Penguin, 1967, ch. 1; Bruce Mazlish, 'The fourth discontinuity', *Technology and Culture*, 8 (1), 1967.

39 On Gibson, see David Tomas, 'The technophilic body: on technicity in William Gibson's cyborg culture', *New Formations*, 8, Summer 1989; Fred Pfeil, 'These disintegrations I'm looking forward to: science fiction from new wave to new age', in E. Ann Kaplan and Michael Sprinker (eds), *Cross Currents: Recent Trends in Humanities Research*, London, Verso, 1990. On the films, see Fred Glass, 'The "new bad future": *Robocop* and 1980s' sci-fi films', *Science and Culture*, 5, 1989; Giuliana Bruno, 'Ramble city: postmodernism and *Blade Runner*', October, 41, 1987.

40 Bill Nichols, 'The work of culture in the age of cybernetic systems', *Screen*, 29 (1), Winter 1988, p. 33.

41 Peter Emberley, 'Places and stories: the challenge of technology', *Social Research* 56 (3), 1989, p. 758.

42 *Ibid.*, p. 759.

43 Seymour Papert, *Mindstorms: Children, Computers and Powerful Ideas*, Brighton, Harvester, 1980, pp. 117, 119.

44 Morris Berman, 'Cybernetic dream of the twenty-first century', in Richard L. Loveless (ed.), *The Computer Revolution and the Arts*, Tampa, University of South Florida Press, 1989, p. 84; cf. 'VR [virtual reality] could be viewed as one step in the evolution toward the withering away of the body', Cornwell, 'Where is the window', p. 54.

45 Sherry Turkle, *The Second Self: Computers and the Human Spirit*, London, Granada, 1984, pp. 77–78.

46 Jean Baudrillard, *America*, London, Verso, 1988, p. 34.

47 Leary, 'Interpersonal, interactive, interdimensional interface', p. 232.

48 Philippe Dubois, *L'Acte Photographique*, Brussels, Editions Labor, 1983, pp. 134–148.

49 Christopher Lasch, *The Minimal Self*, London, Picador, 1985, p. 184.

50 Gilliam Skirrow, 'Hellivision: an analysis of video games', in Manuel Alvarado and John O. Thompson (eds), *The Media Reader*, London, British Film Institute, 1990, p. 336.

51 Sandra Sugawara, 'Tough times for trainers', *Washington Post–Washington Business*, 10 September 1990.

52 See Les Levidow and Kevin Robins (eds), *Cyborg Worlds: The Military Information Society*, London, Free Association Books, 1989; Kevin Robins and Frank Webster, *The Technical Fix*, London, Macmillan, 1989, ch. 8.

53 Colonel John Alexander, 'Antimaterial technology', *Military Review*, October 1989, pp. 38–39.

54 Paul N. Edwards, 'The closed world: systems discourse, military policy and post-World War II US historial consciousness', in Levidow and Robins, *Cyborg Worlds*, p. 154.

55 Paul N. Edwards, *Artificial Intelligence and High Technology War: The Perspective of the Formal Machine*, Working Paper No. 6, Silicon Valley Research Group, University of California, Santa Cruz, November 1986, p. 31.

56 See Joseph A. Kress, 'US army simulates SDI battle management', *Defence Computing*, July–August 1988.

57 Paul Virilio, *War and Cinema*, London, Verso, 1989, p. 65.

58 Evan Thomas and John Barry, 'War's new science', *Newsweek*, 18 February 1991, p. 21. Cf. 'The military is experimenting with pilot's helmets that display a computer-enhanced real-time landscape on the visor, with the pilot, in real or simulated flight, issuing voice commands like "select", "zoom", "god's eye", "fire". Instead of an arm for a pointer, the pilot points his eyes. "Fire": the definitive piercing glance.' Brand, *The Media Lab*, p. 139.

59 James Der Derian, 'The (s)pace of international relations: simulation, surveillance and speed'. Paper presented to the BISA/ISA Meeting, London, 28 March to 1 April 1989, p. 10. See also James Der Derian, *Antidiplomacy: Spies, Terror, Speed and War*, Oxford, Blackwell, 1992, ch. 8.

60 See, for example, Rupert Martin (ed.), *The View From Above*, London. Photographers' Gallery, 1983; Peter Mead, *The Eye in the Air*, London, HMSO, 1983.

61 Virilio, *War and Cinema*, p. 3.

62 William E. Burrows, *Deep Black: Space Espionage and National Security*, New York, Random House, 1986, p. 226.

63 Jeffrey T. Richelson, *America's Secret Eyes in Space: The U.S Keyhole Spy Satellite Program*, New York, Harper & Row, 1990; Jeffrey T. Richelson, 'The future of space reconnaissance', *Scientific American*, January 1991; Andrew Wilson (ed.), *Interavia Space Directory 1989–90*, Geneva, Interavia SA, 1989, pp. 288–291.

64 See Bhupendra Jasani and Toshibosmoi Sakata (eds), *Satellites for Arms Control and Crisis Monitoring*, Oxford, Oxford University Press, 1987; Michael Krepon, Peter Zimmerman, Leonard Spector and Mary Umberger (eds), *Commercial Observation Satellites and International Security*, London, Macmillan, 1990; Tomas Ries and Johnny Skorve, *Investigating Kola: A Study of Military Bases Using Satellite Photography*, London, Brassey's Defence Publishers, 1987; Peter Zimmerman, 'A new resource for arms control', *New Scientist*, 23 September 1989; Michael Krepon, 'Peacemakers or rent-a-spies?', *Bulletin of the Atomic Scientists*, September 1989.

65 Burrows, *Deep Black*, p. 306.

66 'The mind of a missile', *Newsweek*, 18 February 1991, pp. 22–25.

67 Neville Brown, *New Strategy Through Space*, Leicester, Leicester University Press, 1990, pp. 73, 78.

68 Edwards, *Artificial Intelligence*, 1986, p. 26.

69 Skirrow, 'Hellivision', p. 330.

70 James S. Grotstein, *Splitting and Projective Identification*, New York, Jason Aronson, 1981, pp. 138–141.

71 Hanna Segal, 'Silence is the real crime', *International Review of Psycho-Analysis*, 14 (2), 1987, pp. 9, 7.

72 Johann P. Arnason, 'Culture and imaginary significations', *Thesis Eleven*, 22, 1989, p. 34.

73 Georges Corm, *L'Europe et l'Orient*, Paris, La Découverte, 1989, pp. 372, 13.

74 Pierre Lévy, *La Machine Univers: Création, Cognition et Culture Informatique*, Paris, La Découverte, 1987, pp. 42–43; cf. Pierre Lévy, 'La machine universelle', *Terminal*, 27–28, April–May 1986.

75 See, for example, David Bate, 'Photography and the colonial vision', *Third Text*, 22, Spring 1993.

76 Lance Morrow, 'The fog of war', *Time*, 4 February 1991, p. 13. Cf. Foucault's comments on Enlightenment ('the dream of a transparent society' and 'the fear of darkened spaces'), in his essay, 'The eye of power', in Michel Foucault, *Power/Knowledge*, Brighton, Harvester, 1980.

77 Barlow, 'Being in nothingness', p. 37.

78 Primo Levi, *The Sixth Day*, London, Michael Joseph, 1990, p. 110.

3 SIGHTS OF WAR

1 Kenneth L. Adelman and Norman R. Augustine, *The Defence Revolution: Strategy for the Brave New World*, San Francisco, ICS Press, 1990, p. 53.

2 Cf. Les Levidow and Kevin Robins, 'Vision wars', *Race and Class*, 32 (4), 1991; Kevin Robins and Les Levidow, 'The eye of the storm', *Screen*, 32 (3), 1991; Kevin Robins and Les Levidow, 'Socialising the cyborg self: the Gulf War and beyond', in Chris Hables Gray, Heidi Figueroa-Sarriera and Steven Mentor (eds), *The Cyborg Handbook*, New York, Routledge, 1995.

3 David Whitehouse, 'Eyes of the world are on Saddam', *Guardian*, 18 September 1990; cf. Duncan Campbell, 'Under U.S. eyes', *Independent on Sunday*, 30 September 1990. On the role of surveillance satellites in the post-war period, see Bhupendra Jasani, 'Keeping the peace in orbit', *Guardian*, 8 March 1991.

4 Robert J. Lifton, 'Techno-bloodshed', *Guardian*, 14 February 1991; cf. Robert J. Lifton, 'Last refuge of a hi-tech nation', *Guardian*, 12 March 1991.

5 Paul Virilio, 'L'acquisition d'objectif', *Libération*, 30 January 1991.

6 Zygmunt Bauman, *Modernity and the Holocaust*, Cambridge, Polity, 1989, pp. 24–26.

7 James Adams, 'Pentagon bans video of doomed Iraqi driver', *Sunday Times*, 10 February 1991.

8 John Berger, 'In the land of the deaf', *Guardian*, 2 March 1991.

9 John Balzar, 'Video horror of Apache victims' deaths', *Guardian*, 25 February 1991.

10 Bob Dogrin, 'Desert claims death convoy', *Guardian*, 11 March 1991.

11 Harold Evans, 'Necessary shock to our image of war', *Observer*, 10 March 1991.

12 Berger, 'In the land of the deaf'.

13 David Morrison, *Television and the Gulf War*, London, John Libbey, 1992, pp. 5, 10, 33, 22.

14 Philip Taylor, *War and the Media: Propaganda and Persuasion in the Gulf War*, Manchester, Manchester University Press, 1992, pp. 11, 18, 9, 8.

15 *Ibid.*, pp. 14, 274.

16 *Ibid.*, pp. 274–275.

17 Christoper Norris, *Uncritical Theory: Postmodernism, Intellectuals and the Gulf War*, London, Lawrence and Wishart, 1992, pp. 25–26.

18 *Ibid.*, pp. 14–15.

19 *Ibid.*, pp. 122, 66.

20 W. R. Bion, *Bion in New York and São Paulo*, Perthshire, Clunie Press, 1980, p. 30.

21 Ernest Larsen 'Gulf War TV', *Jump Cut*, 36, 1991, p. 8.

22 Jean Baudrillard, *La Guerre du Golfe n'a pas eu Lieu*, Paris, Editions Galilée, 1991, p. 90.

23 *Ibid.*, p. 16.

24 Paul Hoggett, 'A place for experience: a psychoanalytic perspective on boundary, identity and culture', *Environment and Planning D: Society and Space*, 10 (3), 1992, pp. 345–346.

25 Kevin Robins, 'The mirror of unreason', *Marxism Today*, March 1991.

26 Hoggett, 'A place for experience', p. 345.

27 Didier Anzieu, *The Group and the Unconscious*, London, Routledge & Kegan Paul, 1984, ch. 7.

28 John Berger, 'The screen and *The Spike*', in *The White Bird*, London, Chatto & Windus, 1985, p. 260.

29 Yehoshua Roger Dufour and Nicole Dufour-Gompers, 'Journalists, anxiety and the media as an intra-psychic screen', *Israel Journal of Psychiatry and Related Sciences*, 22 (4), 1985, pp. 319–320.

30 Les Levidow, 'The Gulf War: castrating the "bugger"', *Magazine of Cultural Studies*, 5, 1992, p. 40. See also, Les Levidow, 'The Gulf massacre as paranoid rationality', in Gretchen Bender and Timothy Drukrey (eds), *Culture on the Brink: Ideologies of Technology*, Seattle, Bay Press, 1994, pp. 317–327.

31 W. R. Bion, *Learning from Experience*, London, Heinemann, 1962, p. 84.

32 Bion, *Bion in New York and São Paulo*, 1980, p. 87.

33 Cornelius Castoriadis, *Le Monde Morcelé*, Paris, Editions du Seuil, 1990, p. 144.

34 John Berger, 'Mauvaises nouvelles', *Le Monde Diplomatique*, March 1992, p. 32.

35 Tony Harrison, 'Initial illumination', in *The Gaze of the Gorgon*, Newcastle upon Tyne, Bloodaxe Books, 1992, p. 46.

36 John Balzar, 'Video horror of Apache victims' deaths', *Guardian*, 25 February 1991.

37 Lloyd deMause, 'The Gulf War as mental disorder', *The Nation*, 11 March 1991.
38 Ingrid Carlander, 'Essor de la violence "satanique" aux Etats-Unis', *Le Monde Diplomatique*, February 1991.
39 Balzar, 'Video horror of Apache victims' deaths'.
40 Susan Sontag, *On Photography*, Harmondsworth, Penguin, 1979, p. 20.
41 See Les Levidow and Kevin Robins (eds), *Cyborg Worlds: The Military Information Society*, London, Free Association Books, 1989.
42 Robert Jay Lifton and Eric Markusen, *The Genocidal Mentality*, London, Macmillan, 1990, pp. 106–107.
43 Ignacio Ramonet, 'Télévision nécrophile', *Le Monde Diplomatique*, March 1990.

4 CYBERSPACE AND THE WORLD WE LIVE IN

1 Nicole Stenger, 'Mind is a leaking rainbow', in Michael Benedikt (ed.), *Cyberspace: First Steps*, Cambridge, Mass., MIT Press, 1991, pp. 53, 58.
2 Barrie Sherman and Phil Judkins, *Glimpses of Heaven, Visions of Hell: Virtual Reality and Its Implications*, London, Hodder & Stoughton, 1992, pp. 126–127.
3 *Ibid.*, p. 134.
4 Krishan Kumar, *Utopianism*, Milton Keynes, Open University Press, 1991, p. 28.
5 Howard Rheingold, *The Virtual Community: Finding Connection in a Computerised World*, London, Secker & Warburg, 1994, pp. 12, 14.
6 *Ibid.*, p. 5.
7 Kumar, *Utopianism*, p. 29.
8 Larry McCaffery, 'Introduction: the desert of the real', in Larry McCaffery (ed.), *Storming the Reality Studio*, Durham, Duke University Press, 1991, p. 8.
9 Cornelius Castoriadis, 'Le délabrement de l'occident', *Esprit*, December 1991.
10 Myron W. Krueger, *Artificial Reality II*, Reading, Mass., Addison-Wesley, 1991, p. 256.
11 N. Katherine Hayles, 'Virtual bodies and flickering signifiers', *October*, 66, Fall 1993, p. 81.
12 *Ibid.*, p. 72.
13 Sherman and Judkins, *Glimpses of Heaven, Visions of Hell*, p. 126.
14 David Sheff, 'The virtual realities of Timothy Leary' (interview), in Gottfried Hattinger, Morgan Russel, Christine Schöpf and Peter Weibel (eds), *Ars Electronica 1990, vol. 2, Virtuelle Welten*, Linz, Veritas-Verlag, 1990, p. 250.
15 Rheingold, *Virtual Community*, p. 147.
16 *Ibid.*, p. 155.
17 Michael Benedikt, 'Introduction', in Benedikt, *Cyberspace*, p. 6.
18 Jaron Lanier, 'Riding the giant worm to Saturn: post-symbolic communication in virtual reality', in Hattinger *et al.*, *Ars Electronica 1990*, pp. 186–187.
19 *Ibid.*, p. 188.
20 Richard Kearney, *The Wake of Imagination*, London, Hutchinson, 1988, p. 169.
21 David Tomas, 'The technophilic body: on technicity in William Gibson's cyborg culture', *New Formations*, 8, Summer 1989, pp. 114–115.
22 *Ibid.*, pp. 124–125.
23 Nick Land, 'Machinic desire', *Textual Practice*, 7 (3), Winter 1993.
24 Donna Haraway, 'A manifesto for cyborgs: science, technology, and socialist feminism in the 1980s', *Socialist Review*, 80, 1985, pp. 66–67 (Haraway's emphasis).
25 Claudia Springer, 'The pleasure of the interface', *Screen*, 32 (3), Autumn 1991, p. 306.

26 Sadie Plant, 'Beyond the screens: film, cyberpunk and cyberfeminism', *Variant*, 14, 1993, p. 16.
27 *Ibid.*, p. 14.
28 Springer, 'Pleasure of the interface', p. 306.
29 Thomas H. Ogden, *The Matrix of the Mind: Object Relations and the Psychoanalytic Dialogue*, Northvale, NJ, Jason Aronson, 1986, pp. 179–180.
30 See, *inter alia*, Stephen Frosh, *Identity Crisis: Modernity, Psychoanalysis and the Self*, London, Macmillan, 1991; Anthony Giddens, *Modernity and Self-Identity: Self and Society in the Late Modern Age*, Cambridge, Polity Press, 1991; Barry Richards (ed.), *Crises of the Self*, London, Free Association Books, 1989.
31 Frosh, *Identity Crisis*, pp. 57–58.
32 Carlo Mongardini, 'The ideology of postmodernity', *Theory, Culture and Society*, 9 (2), May 1992, p. 62 (Mongardini's emphasis).
33 Christopher Lasch, *The Minimal Self: Psychic Survival in Troubled Times*, London, Pan, 1985, p. 32.
34 Mongardini, 'Ideology of postmodernity', p. 62.
35 *Ibid.*, pp. 56–57.
36 Mary Ann Doane, 'Technology's body: cinematic vision in modernity', *Differences: A Journal of Feminist Cultural Studies*, 5 (2), 1993, pp. 13–14.
37 Mongardini, 'Ideology of postmodernity', p. 61.
38 Brenda Laurel, 'On dramatic interaction', in Hattinger *et al.*, *Ars Electronica 1990*, pp. 262–263.
39 Joyce McDougall, *Theatres of the Mind: Illusion and Truth on the Psychoanalytic Stage*, London, Free Association Books, 1986.
40 Frosh, *Identity Crisis*, p. 93.
41 Peter Weibel, 'Virtual worlds: the emperor's new bodies', in Hattinger *et al.*, *Ars Electronica 1990*, p. 29.
42 Istvan Csicsery-Ronay, Jr, 'Cyberpunk and neuromanticism', in McCaffery, *Storming the Reality Studio*, pp. 192, 190.
43 Marike Finlay, 'Post-modernising psychoanalysis/psychoanalysing postmodernity', *Free Associations* 16, 1989, p. 59.
44 *Ibid.*
45 Gérard Raulet, 'The new utopia: communication technologies', *Telos*, 87, Spring 1991, p. 51.
46 Michael Heim, 'The erotic ontology of cyberspace', in Benedikt, *Cyberspace*, pp. 75–76.
47 D. W. Winnicott, *Playing and Reality*, London, Tavistock, 1971.
48 D. W. Winnicott, *Human Nature*, London, Free Association Books, 1988, p. 107.
49 Ogden, *Matrix of the Mind*, pp. 193–194.
50 *Ibid.*, p. 196.
51 Krishan Kumar, 'The end of socialism? The end of utopia? The end of history?', in Krishan Kumar and Stephen Bann (eds), *Utopias and the Millennium*, London, Reaktion Books, 1993, p. 76.
52 Benedikt, 'Introduction', p. 15.
53 Heim, 'Erotic ontology of cyberspace', p. 73.
54 Allucquere Rosanne Stone, 'Will the real body please stand up? Boundary stories about virtual cultures', in Benedikt, *Cyberspace*, p. 111.
55 *Ibid.*, p. 112.
56 Rheingold, *Virtual Community*, p. 6.
57 *Ibid.*, pp. 25–26.
58 *Ibid.*, p. 14.
59 *Ibid.*, p. 10.
60 *Ibid.*, p. 110.

61 *Ibid.*, pp. 115, 56.

62 *Ibid.*, pp. 245, 110.

63 Iris Marion Young, *Justice and the Politics of Difference*, Princeton, Princeton University Press, 1990, p. 229.

64 Joshua Meyrowitz, *No Sense of Place*, New York, Oxford University Press, 1985; 'The generalised elsewhere', *Critical Studies in Mass Communication*, 6 (3), September 1989.

65 Giddens, *Modernity and Self-Identity*, p. 187.

66 Edgar Morin, 'Les anti-peurs', *Communications*, 57, 1993, p. 138.

67 Michael Sorkin, 'See you in Disneyland', in Michael Sorkin (ed.), *Variations on a Theme Park*, New York, Farrar, Straus & Giroux, 1992, p. 231.

68 Jean Baudrillard, 'Hyperreal America', *Economy and Society*, 22 (2), May 1993, p. 246.

69 Young, *Justice and the Politics of Difference*, p. 229.

70 Raulet, 'New utopia', pp. 50–51.

71 Young, *Justice and the Politics of Difference*, p. 233.

72 Sherman and Judkins, *Glimpses of Heaven, Visions of Hell*, p. 134.

73 Timothy Druckrey, 'Revenge of the nerds: an interview with Jaron Lanier', *Afterimage*, May 1991, pp. 6–7.

74 Serge Moscovici, 'La crainte du contact', *Communications*, 57, 1993, p. 41.

75 Richard Sennett, *The Uses of Disorder: Personal Identity and City Life*, Harmondsworth, Penguin, 1973, p. 109.

76 Richard Sennett, *The Conscience of the Eye: The Design and Social Life of Cities*, New York, Alfred A. Knopf, 1990, p. 97.

77 *Ibid.*, p.xii.

78 Sorkin, 'See you in Disneyland', p. 208.

79 Chantal Mouffe, *The Return of the Political*, London, Verso, 1993, p. 6.

80 Julia Kristeva, *Nations Without Nationalism*, New York, Columbia University Press, 1993, pp. 40–43.

81 Dieter Lenzen, 'Disappearing adulthood: childhood as redemption', in Dieter Kamper and Christoph Wulf (eds), *Looking Back on the End of the World*, New York, Semiotext(e), 1989, p. 71.

82 Paul Virilio, 'Marginal groups', *Daidalos*, 50, December 1993, p. 75.

5 CONSUMING IMAGES: FROM THE SYMBOLIC TO THE PSYCHOTIC

1 Stuart Ewen, *Captains of Consciousness: Advertising and the Social Roots of the Consumer Culture*, New York, McGraw-Hill, 1976, p. 25.

2 *Ibid.*, p. 43.

3 *Ibid.*, pp. 44–45.

4 *Ibid.*, p. 200.

5 Alan Tomlinson, 'Introduction: consumer culture and the aura of the commodity', in Alan Tomlinson (ed.), *Consumption, Identity and Style*, London, Routledge, 1990, pp. 14, 17.

6 Martyn Lee, *Consumer Culture Reborn: The Cultural Politics of Consumption*, London, Routledge, 1993, p. 53.

7 David Morley, *Television, Audiences and Cultural Studies*, London, Routledge, 1993, p. 296.

8 *Ibid.*, pp. 272, 276.

9 Zygmunt Bauman, *Freedom*, Milton Keynes, Open University Press, 1988, pp. 76, 57.

10 Don DeLillo, *White Noise*, London, Picador, 1985, p. 289.

11 Elias Canetti, *Crowds and Power*, Harmondsworth, Penguin, 1973, pp. 266–267.

12 Sigmund Freud, *Civilisation and Its Discontents*, London, Hogarth Press, 1972, p. 15.

13 *Ibid.*, pp. 17, 18.

14 Susan Buck-Morss, 'Aesthetics and anaesthetics: Walter Benjamin's artwork essay reconsidered', *October*, 62, 1992, pp. 16–17.

15 *Ibid.*, p. 16.

16 *Ibid.*, p. 18.

17 *Ibid.*, pp. 22–23.

18 Quoted in Tom LeClair, *In the Loop: Don DeLillo and the Systems Novel*, Urbana, University of Illinois Press, 1987, p. 215.

19 Giorgio Agamben, *Infancy and History: The Destruction of Experience*, London, Verso, 1993, pp. 16, 15.

20 Catherine Bennett, 'Game boys (and girls)', *Guardian*, 2 December 1993; cf. Ingrid Carlander, 'La drogue des jeux vidéo', *Le Monde Diplomatique*, November 1993.

21 Freud, *Civilisation and its Discontents*, p. 15.

22 Jacques Derrida, 'The rhetoric of drugs: an interview', *Differences: A Journal of Feminist Cultural Studies*, 5 (1), 1993, p. 7.

23 Buck-Morss, 'Aesthetics and anaesthetics', p. 21.

24 Agamben, *Infancy and History*, p. 16.

25 Derrida, 'Rhetoric of drugs', pp. 17–18.

26 Slavenka Drakulić, 'Close-up of death', *Index on Censorship*, 22 (7), 1993, pp. 17–18.

27 *Ibid.*

28 Ignacio Ramonet, 'Télévision nécrophile', *Le Monde Diplomatique*, March 1990.

29 Régis Debray, *Vie et Mort de l'Image*, Paris, Gallimard, 1992, p. 366.

30 Zygmunt Bauman, *Mortality, Immortality and Other Life Strategies*, Cambridge, Polity Press, 1992, p. 34.

31 Canetti, *Crowds and Power*, p. 265.

32 Philip Mellor and Chris Shilling, 'Modernity, self-identity and the sequestration of death', *Sociology*, 27 (3), 1993, pp. 425–426.

33 Drakulić, 'Close-up of death', p. 18.

34 W. R. Bion, *Attention and Interpretation*, London, Tavistock, 1970, p. 3.

35 Christopher Bollas, *The Shadow of the Object: Psychoanalysis of the Unthought Known*, London, Free Association Books, 1987.

36 W. R. Bion, *Elements of Psycho-Analysis*, London, Heinemann, 1963, p. 35.

37 Buck-Morss, 'Aesthetics and anaesthetics', p. 16.

38 Siegfried Kracauer, 'Photography', *Critical Inquiry*, 19 (3), 1993, [1927], p. 432.

39 *Ibid.*

40 Debray, *Vie et Mort de l'Image*, p. 380.

41 *Ibid.*

42 Agamben, *Infancy and History*, p. 380.

43 Ben Bachmair, 'From the motor-car to television: cultural-historical arguments on the meaning of mobility for communication', *Media, Culture and Society*, 13 (4), 1991, p. 531.

44 François Brune, '*Les Médias Pensent Comme Moi!' Fragments du Discours Anonyme*, Paris, L'Harmattan, 1993, pp. 45, 51.

45 *Ibid.*, p. 80.

46   Bauman, *Freedom*, p. 80.
47   Christophe Gallaz, 'La "planète nomade", un désert de la pensée', *Libération*, 13 January 1994.
48   Don DeLillo, *Mao II*, London, Jonathan Cape, 1991, pp. 33–34.
49   E. Goodheart, 'Some speculations on Don DeLillo and the cinematic real', *South Atlantic Quarterly*, 89 (2), 1990, p. 360.
50   *Ibid.*
51   DeLillo, *White Noise*, p. 64.
52   *Ibid.*, p. 66.
53   LeClair, *In the Loop*, p. 217.
54   Kracauer, 'Photography', p. 433.
55   Buck-Morss, 'Aesthetics and anaesthetics', pp. 22–23.
56   *Ibid.*, p. 22.
57   *Ibid.*, p. 24.
58   *Ibid.*, pp. 22–23.
59   Zoë Heller, 'The electric kinesthetic innerquest', *Independent on Sunday*, 15 December 1991.
60   Lieven de Cauter, 'The panoramic ecstasy: on world exhibitions and the disintegration of experience', *Theory, Culture and Society*, 10 (4), 1993, pp. 18–20.
61   David Phillips, 'Modern vision', *Oxford Art Journal*, 16 (1), 1993, p. 133.
62   Gianni Vattimo, *The Transparent Society*, Baltimore, Johns Hopkins University Press, 1992, p. 8.
63   François Brune, 'Néfastes effets de l'idéologie politico-médiatique', *Le Monde Diplomatique*, May 1993, p. 4.
64   Alain Ehrenberg, 'La vie en direct ou les shows de l'authenticité', *Esprit*, January 1993, p. 34.
65   Quoted in Philip Hayward, 'Situating cyberspace: the popularisation of virtual reality', in Philip Hayward and Tana Wollen (eds), *Future Visions: New Technologies of the Screen*, London, British Film Institute, 1993, p. 196.
66   Vivian Sobchack, 'New age mutant ninja hackers', *Artforum*, April 1991, p. 25.
67   Chris Hables Gray and Mark Driscoll, 'What's real about virtual reality? Anthropology of, and in, cyberspace', *Visual Anthropology Review*, 8 (2), 1992, p. 39.
68   *Ibid.*
69   Elizabeth Wilson, 'The invisible *flâneur*', *New Left Review*, 191, 1992.
70   Gillian Skirrow, 'Hellivision: an analysis of video games', in Manuel Alvarado and John O. Thompson (eds), *The Media Reader*, London, British Film Institute, 1990.
71   Timothy Druckrey, 'Revenge of the nerds: an interview with Jaron Lanier', *Afterimage*, May 1991, p. 7.
72   *Ibid.*
73   John Steiner, 'Turning a blind eye: the cover up for Oedipus', *International Review of Psycho-Analysis*, 12, 1985, p. 161.
74   Carlo Mongardini, 'The ideology of postmodernity', *Theory, Culture and Society*, 9 (2), 1992, p. 62.
75   On this, see Kevin Robins and Frank Webster, 'The communications revolution: new media, old problems', *Communication*, 10, 1987.
76   Brune, '*Les Médias Pensent Comme Moi!*', p. 77.
77   For a different way of relating postmodern consumer culture to psychotic behaviour, see Stephen Frosh, *Identity Crisis: Modernity, Psychoanalysis and the Self*, London, Macmillan, 1991, pp. 181–184.
78   DeLillo, *White Noise*, p. 303.

6 THE CITY IN THE FIELD OF VISION

1 James Donald, 'The city, the cinema: modern spaces', in Chris Jenks (ed.), *Visual Culture*, London, Routledge, 1995, p. 92.
2 Murray Smith, 'Film spectatorship and the institution of fiction', *Journal of Aesthetics and Art Criticism*, 53 (2), 1995, p. 122.
3 Vincent Amiel, 'Le corps en images (de Buster Keaton à John Cassavetes)', *Esprit*, February 1994, p. 146.
4 Donald, 'The city, the cinema', p. 93.
5 *Ibid.*, p. 81.
6 Didier Anzieu, *The Group and the Unconscious*, London, Routledge & Kegan Paul, 1984, p. 129.
7 Lewis Mumford, *The City in History*, London, Secker & Warburg, 1961, pp. 50–53.
8 Andrew Thacker, 'Imagist travels in modernist space', *Textual Practice*, 7 (2), 1993, p. 225.
9 Vivian Sobchack, 'Towards a phenomenology of cinematic and electronic presence: the scene of the screen', *Post Script*, 10 (1), Fall 1990, pp. 54–55.
10 Adam Phillips, *On Kissing, Tickling and Being Bored*, London, Faber & Faber, 1993, p. 68. Phillips is quoting from Masud Khan.
11 Donald, 'The city, the cinema', p. 93.
12 Johannes Birringer, 'Invisible cities / transcultural images', *Performing Arts Journal*, 33–34, 1989, pp. 121–122.
13 Donatella Mazzoleni, 'The city and the imaginary', *New Formations*, 11, Summer 1990, p. 97.
14 *Ibid.*, p. 100.
15 *Ibid.*, p. 101.
16 Paul Virilio, 'Marginal groups', *Daidalos*, 50, December 1993, p. 72.
17 Paul Virilio, 'For a geography of trajectories', *Flux*, 5, July–September 1991, p. 50.
18 Louis A. Sass, 'The epic of disbelief: the postmodern turn in psychoanalysis', *Partisan Review*, 61 (1), 1994, p. 106.
19 Maurice Merleau-Ponty, 'Eye and mind', in John O'Neill (ed.), *Phenomenology, Language and Sociology: Selected Essays of Maurice Merleau-Ponty*, London, Heinemann, 1974, pp. 283–284.
20 *Ibid.*, p. 284.
21 Thomas H. Ogden, 'The dialectically constituted/decentred subject of psychoanalysis, II: the contributions of Klein and Winnicott', *International Journal of Psycho-Analysis*, 73 (4), 1992, p. 616.
22 Christopher Bollas, *Being a Character: Psychoanalysis and Self Experience*, London, Routledge, 1993, p. 13.
23 *Ibid.*, p. 15.
24 *Ibid.*, p. 14.
25 *Ibid.*, p. 15.
26 Ludwig Wittgenstein, *Culture and Value*, Oxford, Basil Blackwell, second edition, 1980, p. 69.
27 Bollas, *Being a Character*, p. 13.
28 Gernot Böhme, 'Atmosphere as the fundamental concept of a new aesthetics', *Thesis Eleven*, 36, 1993, p. 122, 119.
29 On Freudian psycho-archaeology (Rome was the city of Freud's dreams), see Carl E. Schorske, *Fin-de-Siècle Vienna*, Cambridge, Cambridge University Press, 1981, ch. 4; 'The psychoarcheology of civilisations', in Jerome Neu (ed.), *The Cambridge Companion to Freud*, Cambridge, Cambridge University Press, 1991; 'Freud's Egyptian dig', *New York Review of Books*, 27 May 1993.

30 Sigmund Freud, 'Five lectures on psycho-analysis', in *Two Short Accounts of Psycho-Analysis*, Harmondsworth, Penguin, 1962, p. 39.

31 See Pierre Nora, 'Between memory and history: *les lieux de mémoire*', *Representations*, 26, Spring 1989.

32 Böhme, 'Atmosphere', p. 121.

33 Thomas H. Ogden, *The Matrix of the Mind: Object Relations and the Psychoanalytic Dialogue*, Northvale, NJ, Jason Aronson, 1986, p. 213.

34 J.-B. Pontalis, 'Perdre de vue', *Nouvelle Revue de Psychanalyse*, 35, Spring 1987, p. 231.

35 Melanie Phillips and Martin Kettle, 'The murder of innocence', *Guardian*, 16 February 1993.

36 William Leith, 'Terrorism and the art of fiction', *Independent on Sunday*, 18 August 1991.

37 Melinda Beck, 'Video vigilantes', *Newsweek*, 22 July 1991, pp. 42–43.

38 Beatrix Campbell, *Goliath: Britain's Dangerous Places*, London, Methuen, 1993, p. 257.

39 Yves Eudes, 'Les vidéo-vautours de Los Angeles', *Le Monde Diplomatique*, October 1993, p. 27.

40 Alain Ehrenberg, 'La vie en direct ou les shows de l'authenticité', *Esprit*, January 1993, p. 25.

41 Michel Maffesoli, 'Une télévision de la post-modernité', *Dossiers de l'Audiovisuel*, 55, May–June 1994, p. 25.

42 Jean Louis Weissberg, 'Des "reality shows" aux réalités virtuelles', *Terminal* 61, Autumn 1993, pp. 79–80.

43 Don DeLillo, *Libra*, Harmondsworth, Penguin, 1989, pp. 439–440.

44 J. G. Ballard, 'Motel architecture', in *Myths of the Near Future*, London, Vintage, 1994, p. 194.

45 Sobchack, 'Towards a phenomenology', p. 54.

46 *Ibid.*, p. 58.

47 Pascal Bonitzer, 'Les images, le cinéma, l'audiovisuel', *Cahiers du Cinéma*, 404, February 1988, pp. 18–19.

48 Sobchack, 'Towards a phenomenology', p. 58.

49 Weissberg, 'Des "reality shows"', pp. 79–80.

50 Ehrenberg, 'La vie en direct ou les shows', pp. 34–35.

51 Lieven de Cauter, 'The panoramic ecstasy: on world exhibitions and the disintegration of experience', *Theory, Culture and Society*, 10 (4), 1993, p. 18.

52 *Ibid.*, p. 21.

53 Thomas H. Ogden, *The Primitive Edge of Experience*, Northvale, NJ, Jason Aronson, 1989, pp. 21–22, 29. Note also his description of the experience of dreaming as 'a reflection of the dialectical tension between the paranoid-schizoid and depressive positions', Ogden, 'Dialectically constituted/decentred', p. 616.

54 *Ibid.*, pp. 80–82.

55 Ogden, *Matrix of the Mind*, p. 226.

56 Krysztof Wodiczko, 'New digressions of the stranger', *Creative Camera*, 323, August–September 1993, p. 41.

57 Phillips, *On Kissing, Tickling and Being Bored*, p. 55.

58 For different perspectives on this, see Dominique Mehl, 'La parole thérapeutique et cathartique', and François Niney, 'L'alibi thérapeutique', *Dossiers de l'Audiovisuel*, 55, May–June 1994.

59 Pascal Bonitzer, 'L'image invisible', in *Passages de l'Image*, Paris, Centre Georges Pompidou, 1990, pp. 16, 12.

60 Gilles Deleuze, *Pourparlers, 1972–1990*, Paris, Editions de Minuit, 1990, p. 102; 'Le cerveau, c'est l'écran', *Cahiers du Cinéma*, 380, February 1986, p. 32.

61 Italo Calvino, 'A cinema-goer's autobiography', in *The Road to San Giovanni*, London, Jonathan Cape, 1993, pp. 38, 60.

62 Giuliana Bruno, 'Streetwalking around Plato's cave', *October*, 60, 1992, pp. 114, 123.

63 Quentin Curtis, 'A truth too naked for us to bear', *Independent on Sunday*, 11 September 1994.

64 Walter Benjamin, 'Theses on the philosophy of history', in *Illuminations*, London, Fontana, 1973, p. 257.

7 WILL IMAGES MOVE US STILL?

1 Philippe Quéau, 'La révolution des image virtuelles', *Le Monde Diplomatique*, August 1993, p. 16.

2 William Mitchell, *The Reconfigured Eye: Visual Truth in the Post-Photographic Era*, Cambridge, Mass., MIT Press, 1992, p. 225.

3 Jonathan Crary, *Techniques of the Observer: On Vision and Modernity in the Nineteenth Century*, Cambridge, Mass., MIT Press, 1990, p. 1.

4 *Ibid.*

5 Mitchell, *The Reconfigured Eye*, p. 8.

6 Gianni Vattimo, *The Transparent Society*, Baltimore, Johns Hopkins University Press, 1992, p. 8.

7 *Ibid.*, p. 117.

8 Mitchell, *The Reconfigured Eye*, p. 8.

9 *Ibid.*, p. 225.

10 Cornelius Castoriadis, 'The crisis of Marxism, the crisis of politics', *Dissent*, Spring 1992, p. 223.

11 John Berger, 'Another way of telling', *Journal of Social Reconstruction*, 1 (1), 1980, p. 73.

12 John Berger, 'Appearances', in John Berger and Jean Mohr, *Another Way of Telling*, London, Writers and Readers, 1982, p. 99.

13 Mitchell, *The Reconfigured Eye*, p. 28.

14 *Ibid.*

15 William Mitchell, 'When is seeing believing?', *Scientific American*, February 1994, p. 49.

16 Mitchell, *The Reconfigured Eye*, p. 223.

17 *Ibid.*, p. 31.

18 *Ibid.*, p. 223.

19 *Ibid.*, p. 57.

20 Fred Ritchin, *In Our Own Image: The Coming Revolution in Photography*, New York, Aperture, 1990, p. 132.

21 Mitchell, *The Reconfigured Eye*, p. 119.

22 Fred Ward, 'Images for the computer age', *National Geographic*, June 1989, pp. 720, 750.

23 Allan Sekula, 'The body and the archive', in Richard Bolton (ed.), *The Contest of Meaning: Critical Histories of Photography*, Cambridge, Mass., MIT Press, 1989, p. 353 (Sekula's emphasis).

24 Jean Louis Weissberg, 'Des "reality shows" aux réalités virtuelles', *Terminal*, 61, 1993, p. 76.

25 *Ibid.*, pp. 77–78.

26 Ernest Gellner, *Reason and Culture: The Historic Role of Rationality and*

Rationalism, Oxford, Blackwell, 1992, p. 166.

27 Max Horkheimer and Theodor W. Adorno, *Dialectic of Enlightenment*, London, Allen Lane, 1973, p. 26.

28 Gellner, *Reason and Culture*, p. 2.

29 *Ibid.*, pp. 3, 13.

30 Berger, 'Appearances', p. 115.

31 Crary, *Techniques of the Observer*, pp. 1–2.

32 Roland Barthes, *Camera Lucida: Reflections on Photography*, London, Jonathan Cape, 1982, p. 9.

33 *Ibid.*, p. 16.

34 *Ibid.*, p. 21.

35 Berger, 'Another way of telling', p. 61.

36 Berger, 'Appearances', pp. 115–118.

37 John Berger, 'In defence of art', *New Society*, 28 September 1978, p. 704.

38 Berger, 'Another way of telling', p. 68.

39 Walter Benjamin, 'A small history of photography', in *One Way Street and Other Writings*, London, New Left Books, 1979 [1931], pp. 242–243.

40 *Ibid.*, p. 243.

41 Thomas H. Ogden, *The Matrix of the Mind: Object Relations and Psychoanalytic Dialogue*, New York, Jason Aronson, 1986, p. 176.

42 Susan Sontag, *On Photography*, Harmondsworth, Penguin, 1979, p. 15.

43 Pierre MacOrlan, 'Elements of a social fantastic', in Christopher Phillips (ed.), *Photography in the Modern Era: European Documents and Critical Writings, 1913–1940*, New York, The Metropolitan Museum of Art/Aperture, 1989 [1929], p. 32.

44 Barthes, *Camera Lucida*, p. 92.

45 Horkheimer and Adorno, *Dialectic of Enlightenment*, pp. 3, 16.

46 Mitchell, 'When is seeing believing?', p. 49.

47 Ritchin, *In Our Own Image*, p. 64.

48 Régis Debray, *Vie et Mort de l'Image: Une Histoire du Regard en Occident*, Paris, Gallimard, 1992, p.33.

49 Barthes, *Camera Lucida*, p. 92.

50 W. R. Bion, *Second Thoughts: Selected Papers on Psycho-Analysis*, New York, Jason Aronson, 1967, p. 86.

51 Berger, 'Another way of telling', p. 73.

52 Barthes, *Camera Lucida*, p. 53.

53 Christopher Rocco, 'Between modernity and postmodernity: reading *Dialectic of Enlightenment* against the grain', *Political Theory*, 22 (1), 1994, p. 80.

54 Martin Jay, 'The Apocalyptic imagination and the inability to mourn', in Gillian Robinson and John Rundell (eds), *Rethinking Imagination: Culture and Creativity*, London, Routledge, 1994.

55 Mladen Dolar, '"I shall be with you on your wedding night": Lacan and the uncanny', *October*, 58, 1991, p. 23.

56 John Steiner, 'Turning a blind eye: the cover up for Oedipus', *International Review of Psycho-Analysis*, 12, 1985, pp. 161–72.

57 Johann Arnason, 'Reason, imagination, interpretation', in Robinson and Rundell, *Rethinking Imagination*, p. 156.

58 David Roberts, 'Sublime theories: reason and imagination in modernity', in Robinson and Rundell, *Rethinking Imagination*, p. 172.

59 Cornelius Castoriadis, *Le Monde Morcelé*, Paris, Seuil, 1990, p. 144.

60 *Ibid.*, p. 145.

61 *Ibid.*, p. 147.

62 Arnason, 'Reason, imagination, interpretation', pp. 167, 169.
63 Geoffrey Batchen, 'Burning with desire: the birth and death of photography', *Afterimage*, January 1990, p. 11.
64 *Ibid*. See also Crary, *Techniques of the Observer.*
65 David Phillips, 'Modern vision', *Oxford Art Journal*, 16 (1), 1993, p. 137.
66 Raymond Bellour, 'La double hélice', in *Passages de l'Image*, Paris, Centre Georges Pompidou, 1990, p. 37.
67 Raymond Bellour, 'The power of words, the power of images', *Camera Obscura*, 24, 1990, p. 7.
68 Mitchell, *The Reconfigured Eye*, p. 7.
69 Esther Parada, 'Taking liberties: digital revision as cultural dialogue', *Leonardo*, 26 (5), 1993, pp. 445–446.
70 Ingrid Schaffner, 'Skin on the screen', *Artscribe*, 89, 1991, p. 56. See also Chantal Pontbriand, 'Un corps à corps photographique', *Passages de l'Image*, Paris, Centre Georges Pompidou, 1990, pp. 146–148.
71 Régis Durand, 'La force de l'évidence', *La Recherche Photographique*, 7, 1989.
72 Adam Phillips, *On Kissing, Tickling and Being Bored: Psychoanalytic Essays on the Unexamined Life*, London, Faber & Faber, 1993, p. 119.
73 *Ibid.*, pp. 120, 118.
74 *Ibid.*, p. 119.
75 Glyn Daly, 'Post-metaphysical culture and politics: Richard Rorty and Laclau and Mouffe', *Economy and Society*, 23 (2), 1994, pp. 176–177.
76 Mitchell, *The Reconfigured Eye*, p. 225.

ILLUSTRATIONS

Every effort has been made to contact copyright holders for material reproduced in this volume. In some cases this has proved impossible, for which the publisher apologises.

INDEX